WHAT'S SPECIAL ABOUT JUDAISM?

WHAT'S SPECIAL ABOUT JUDAISM?

Henry Cohen

Library of Congress Number:		2001116509
ISBN #:	Hardcover	0-7388-6667-9
	Softcover	0-7388-6668-7

This book was printed in the United States of America.

To order additional copies of this book, contact:
Xlibris Corporation
1-888-7-XLIBRIS
www.Xlibris.com
Orders@Xlibris.com

CONTENTS

PART THREE

RABBINIC JUDAISM AND THE LIFE-CYCLE

PART FOUR

MEDIEVAL JUDAISM AND A CALENDAR OF TRADITIONS

PART FIVE

JUDAISM MEETS THE MODERN WORLD

PART SIX

WHAT'S SPECIAL

This book is dedicated to three very special women in my life: Edna, Shelley and Lisa.

PREFACE

In 1993, when I became "emeritized," I told friends and colleagues that I had completed the required courses. Now I could pursue the electives. What I chose to do was become involved in the Outreach program of the Union of American Hebrew Congregations. After teaching for a few years the Introduction to Judaism course attended mainly, but not exclusively, by mixed-married couples, I was criticized by some students for not leaving sufficient time for discussion. So I began writing my presentations for the first several classes, insisting that the students do the reading in advance. This enabled us to devote most of the two hours to discussion. Seven years later, I had written this book which, I believe, can be used not only by Outreach classes but also by "In-reach" courses aimed at adult Jews who are not satisfied with what they had learned or experienced in their synagogues or religious schools.

It is a cliche to say that American Jewry is in a state of crisis. About half of American Jews marry non-Jews, and most of their children are not given an adequate Jewish education. Jews stay away from the synagogue in droves. Little wonder that some Jewish communal leaders and rabbis may feel a sense of urgency bordering on desperation. What will be left of the American Jewish community 50, 100 years from today? A handful of zealots clinging to Orthodoxy or huddling in *havurot* while the rest fade away, blending into a largely secular American civilization?

I am not so pessimistic. I believe that Judaism contains the seeds not only for survival but for renaissance. I believe that there are special qualities of Judaism that do have meaning for those skeptical Jews who have turned away from synagogues, and for the sons and daughters of mixed-married couples. Boundaries between groups are falling whether we like it or not. The free market extends not only to goods but to ideas. Judaism must compete in the world of ideas and values, but we need not fear the competition. We Jews are not in the habit—nor should we be—of persuading people to leave a faith in which they find meaning, but secularism is increasing among Gentiles as well as Jews. This gives us the opportunity to present a Judaism that may respond to the skeptical questions raised by barely believing Jews and Gentiles.

The theme underlying this text is "what is special about Judaism?" By special is meant, on one level, characteristics of Judaism that have positive value. Some of these characteristics are found in other religions or cultures. However, what is special in the sense of unique is the combination of characteristics of positive value. In the last chapter, I suggest that there is a Jewish gestalt, a whole that is greater than the sum of its parts.

The following chapters have been presented in a way which, I hope, makes sociological, ideological, and historical sense. Part One (Some Basic Jewish Beliefs and Values) begins with asking,"Who Are We? Semantic Dilemmas" (Chapter 1) and explores the possible meanings of Jew, the Jews, and Judaism,and distinguishes between the religious and secular aspects of Jewish culture. Chapter 2, "Beyond Ethnicity: The Dual Roots of Jewish Values," discusses how the values of social justice, family, and education are rooted both in Jewish historic experience and in Jewish religious beliefs and traditions. Chapter 3, "In the Beginning: Ancient Insights," emphasizes the Biblical roots of these values and the still-relevant Biblical concepts of: God as Creator and Redeemer; Covenants and Land; the Bush and the Mountain; the Prophetic Imperative; The Messianic Dream; and the Chosen or the Choosing People. Having established the Biblical understanding of God, we turn in Chapter 4 to "Paths to God," the diversity of ways that modern Jewish theologians have come to believe in and experience God. This is followed, in Chapter 5, by "applied theology" in the "Synagogue and *Siddur*."

Part Two (Judaism and Christianity: Jesus and Paul, Guilt and Death) begins with Chapter 6, "The Parting of the Waves: Jesus, Paul, and the Rabbis." This chapter examines candidly but respectfully: Why do Jews not believe in Jesus as the Messiah. What some Jews do or can believe about Jesus. How Paul led to the parting of the ways. It even suggests that some "aesthetic" Christians may be closer to Judaism than they may realize. Chapter 7, "Coping with Guilt," deals with the implication of the doctrine of original sin, the sources of Jewish guilt, and the ways our rabbis would have us deal with our sins. Chapter 8, "Coping with Death," discusses how Jewish beliefs and values help us cope with the loss of loved ones and confront our own mortality.

Part Three (Rabbinic Judaism and the Life-Cycle) begins with Chapter 9, which presents an overview of rabbinic law and lore and indicates how Jewish law deals with abortion and euthanasia. Chapter 10, "From Womb to Tomb: The Jewish Life-Cycle," presents ways that Jewish tradition can help us celebrate birth, adolescence and marriage and deal with loss and mourning. There are excellent books that explain in more detail the specific customs: See Resources. In this chapter I attempt to avoid duplication and present a fresh perspective on the life-cycle.

Part Four (Medieval Judaism and a Calendar of Traditions) begins by providing historic context. Chapter 11, "Persecution, Persistence and Jewish Survival," turns to Jewish history in the Middle Ages and explores the causes of anti-Jewish persecution as well as the factors that made for Jewish survival. Chapter 12, "Kabbalah, Hasidism and Jewish Mysticism," presents the most creative Jewish response to persecution and invites the reader to search for insights that will enhance one's spiritual life. Chapters 13 ("The Celebration of Time: Shabbat Shalom, L'Shanah Tovah Tikotevu"), 14 (From Freedom to Covenant: Pesach, Shavuot, Sukkot, Simchat Torah, Tu B'Shevat) and 15 ("Hanukkah and Purim: Not for Children Only) present variations on the ideas and insights of Shabbat, the High Holy Days, the festivals, and holidays. Again, in the Resources I refer the reader to excellent books that deal specifically with these traditions, and I focus on their underlying themes.

Part Five (Judaism Meets the Modern World) first turns to modern movements in Jewish life and thought: Chapter 16 ("The Evolution of Reform Judaism"); 17 ("The Evolution of Conservative Judaism"); 18 ("Reconstructionism, Renewal and Feminism"). Because I was raised in a Reform rabbinic family and was ordained at the Hebrew Union College in Cincinnati, my personal experience is reflected in the sixteenth chapter. However, I have found my studies of the Conservative and Reconstructionist movements and Jewish Renewal to be most rewarding and I have tried to present them not only with objectivity but with genuine appreciation for their contributions to American Jewish life.

Chapter 19 wonders what we can learn from the Holocaust. Chapter 20 presents an overview of various forms of Zionism, the moral issues relating to the Israeli-Arab conflict, and the dilemmas that confront American Jews in their relations with Israel.

Part Six (What's Special?) begins with Chapter 21, "Choosing Judaism, Then and Now," which presents an historical view of the place of proselytism in Jewish life and explains the purposes of the contemporary effort at Outreach. Chapter 22 is the most subjective: my own view of "What's Is Special about Judaism?" This leads into my concept of "the Jewish gestalt." My purpose is not to preach. Rather do I hope to encourage you to be better able to discover your own responses to the question, "What's Special about Judaism?" There is an Appendix on the mysteries of the Jewish calendar.

Beginning with the section on Judaism and Christianity, the chapters follow roughly the historical sequence of Jewish experience. Interspersed between several chapters are chronological charts. These time-tables are presented before the chapters that deal with the particular chronological period. I strongly recommend that the reader choose a book on Jewish history, from among the Resources.

The Topics for Discussion at the end of each chapter are intended to raise issues that the reader may wish to explore. I do not have all the answers, but I hope that I have been able to raise some of the pertinent questions. Some of the books in the Resources contain material on which the chapter was based; others contain the quotations cited; still others are suggested as recommended supplementary reading. I hope that my occasional lapses into anecdotes based on my background as a Texas-bred rebbe will be considered not an indulgence but will be viewed as humanizing the text.

I am most grateful to those colleagues who have read all or parts of this text and have offered constructive comments, often providing information of which I had been unaware. They include Rabbis Eric Yoffie, Arthur Waskow, David Wolpe, Andrew Busch, Deborah Pine, Joseph Forman, Albert Friedlander, Roy Rosenberg, and Professors Michael Cook, Michael Meyer, and Ellis Rivkin, and UAHC Outreach Director Dru Greenwood. As I am technologically challenged, I greatly appreciated the assistance provided by computer mavens, Harry Phillips, Sarah Woods, and Moe Comeau. I am most grateful for the editorial eye of Janet Ruth

Falon. My deepest thanks go to my wife, Edna, for her common-sense counsel and her moral support.

Henry Cohen, Rabbi Emeritus, Beth David Reform Congregation, Gladwyne, Pennsylvania, May, 2001

PART ONE:

SOME BASIC JEWISH BELIEFS AND VALUES

1.

WHO ARE WE? SEMANTIC DILEMMAS

It has been facetiously suggested that a Jew is a person who is willing to argue about who is a Jew. How would you complete the sentence, "A Jew is . . ." Would your definition include persons whose father was a Jew but whose mother was not? Would your definition include"Messianic Jews" who believe that Jesus was the messiah? Would you include those people born Jewish but who do not believe in God?

How would you complete the sentence, "Judaism is . . ." Is it possible to define Judaism in a way that would be acceptable to Orthodox, Reform, Conservative, Reconstructionist, and Humanistic Jews? Before we can discuss the beliefs and values of Jews and Judaism, we had better understand how Jews have defined themselves, their faith, and their culture. We will search for a common denominator behind the different definitions. Then we will attempt to distinguish between the religious and secular aspects of the Jewish people.

WHO IS A JEW?

The traditional definition of a Jew, according to the Talmud (*Kiddushin* 70a, 75b) is one who is born of a Jewish mother or who converts to Judaism according to *halakhah* (Jewish law). This includes *mikveh* (a ritual bath), *bet din* (a "court" of three rabbis), and (for men) circumcision or *tipat dam* (drawing a drop of blood). Why a Jewish mother? Perhaps because one could always be sure who the mother was. This definition does imply a dual standard: Born Jews need not hold any particular belief to be considered Jews, while converts must affirm the Jewish religion. Once they do so, they become fully a part of the Jewish people. This is made clear in the Talmud when the question is posed, Should the *ger* (convert) at the Seder say, "*avadim hayinu,*" we were slaves in Egypt? The answer: Yes, the convert is now part of the people and his or her"ancestors" were slaves in Egypt.

How a Jew ceases to be a Jew is less clear. What if he or she converts to another religion, i.e., becomes a *m'shumad* (apostate)? Some would say: Once a Jew, always a Jew, citing the Talmudic passage, "A Jew who sins is still a Jew."(*Sanhedrin* 44a) Solomon Freehof, in *Recent Reform Responsa*, finds a more ambiguous response in Jewish law:

"With regard to his trustworthiness as a witness in the Jewish court or . . . his acceptability as a witness at a marriage ceremony, or . . . his being counted in a *minyan*—in all these *mitzvot* he has lost his Jewish rights. But with regard to marriage and divorce these family rights are his by birth . . . He can marry a Jew and . . . Orthodox law would not free her from him unless he gives her a *get*" (Jewish divorce certificate.)

This very issue was raised in Israel, in 1958, by Oswald Rufeisen, born to Jewish parents in Poland. When he was a young man in the Zionist youth movement, he rescued hundreds of fellow Jews from the Gestapo at great personal risk. While hiding from the Nazis in a Catholic convent, Rufeisen willingly became a Roman Catholic, later became a priest, and changed his name to Father Daniel. After the war he joined the Carmelite order, in the hope that he would be transferred to one of its monasteries in Palestine. When he was permitted by the order to come to Israel, he applied as a Jew for an immigrant's certificate. He cited the Law of Return which provides that any Jew may come to Israel as a Jew so long as he poses no danger to the public. The case was brought before the Israeli Supreme Court.

Citing *Sanhedrin,* Father Daniel's attorney argued that according to Jewish law, Daniel was still Jewish. However, the Supreme Court based its decision not on rabbinic law but on the common usage of the term, Jew, and ruled that one is Jewish if one "in good faith declares himself to be Jewish and has no other religion."

Justice Moshe Silberg, representing the majority, reasoned: "Whatever the theological outlook of a Jew in Israel may be—whether he be religious, irreligious or antireligious—he is inextricably bound by an umbilical cord to historical Jewry from which he draws his language and his festivals and whose spiritual and religious martyrs have nourished his national pride. An apostate cannot possibly identify himself completely with a people which has suffered so much from religious persecution, and his sincere affection for Israel and its people cannot possibly take the place of such identification." Father Daniel was admitted to Israel as a Polish Christian.

A decade after the Daniel case, Commander Benjamin Shalit of the Israeli Navy, a Jewish atheist married to a non-Jewish atheist from Scotland, wanted his children to be registered as Jews. They were being raised as secular Jews in a Jewish state and would fight in the army in defense of Israel. Following the precedent of the

Daniel case (rather than *halakhah*), the Court ruled (5 to 4) that the children could have a Jewish national identity but would be subject to the rabbinic courts regarding their marriages. This triggered an uproar among the religious parties. The K'nesset (Israel's parliament) then nullified the Supreme Court's decision by legislating that for purposes of identity, a Jew is one who is born of a Jewish mother or who converts to Judaism, though not necessarily in accordance with Jewish law. The Orthodox were not, and are not, happy with this departure from *halakhah*, but it was considered necessary because so many immigrants whose conversions, according to *halakhah*, were not valid had come (or might come) from America and the former Soviet Union.

In both Israel and the United States a challenge has been posed by the so-called "Messianic Jews," who were born of Jewish parents but believe in Jesus Christ as the son of God and the only way to salvation. They may argue, "If one can be an atheist and still be Jewish, why cannot one believe in Christ and be a Jew?" These Messianic Jews claim to practice Jewish holidays. However, they interpret them according to fundamentalist Christian teachings, e.g., the Paschal Lamb at the Seder represents the redemptive power of Christ (the *Agnus Dei*, Lamb of God).

One could argue that according to *Sanhedrin*, they are still Jewish. However, they are clearly apostates in that they are affirming a faith that contradicts Judaism. They may also pose a danger to the Jewish people by providing a guilt-free channel out of the Jewish people, and they are subsidized by Christian missionary organizations. If, when one accepts the Jewish religion, one becomes part of the people, then when one accepts an entirely different religion, one leaves the people.

Finally, there is the difference between Reform Judaism's definition of a Jew and that of Orthodox and Conservative rabbis. In the case of a mixed marriage, the Reform movement gives Jewish fatherhood as much validity as Jewish motherhood. This recognition of "patrilineal descent" has been been the view of Reform Judaism for many decades. It has been publicized recently because of a 1983 resolution of the Central Conference of American Rabbis (CCAR), intended as a response to the large number of children of Jewish fathers and non-Jewish mothers who are becoming part of Reform congregations.

According to the CCAR resolution, all children of mixed marriage are "under the presumption of Jewish descent . . . but Jewish status must be established through appropriate and timely public and formal acts of identification with the Jewish faith and people," for example, giving the child a Hebrew name or a Bar/Bat Mitzvah ceremony. This definition is consistent with the custom in Biblical times when descent was through the father. In inter-tribal marriages paternal descent was decisive while the line of the mother was not. (See Numbers 1:2 and *Contemporary American Reform Responsa* by Walter Jacobs.) The more traditional community argues that patrilineal descent will lead to a dangerous division within the Jewish people, disqualifying large numbers of "Jews," not considered Jewish by *halakhah,* from marrying other Jews according to Jewish law. The Reform response is that such divisions have long been part of Jewish life: for decades, Jews who converted through Reform auspices or were re-married without Jewish divorces were not considered qualified for Jewish marriages by the Orthodox, and this did not cause serious disruption.

One reason the Reform movement has re-affirmed the significance of patrilineal descent is the Reform commitment to gender equality. It may be overlooked that, in one sense, the Reform standard is more strict than the traditional view: in intermarriages, the child of a Jewish mother is not given automatic Jewish status, but that status is contingent on an affirmation of the child's Jewish identity.

WHO ARE THE JEWS?

We may well be so confused by the diversity of definitions that we despair of finding any common ground. However, when one poses the question in the plural, "Who are the Jews?," there is, at least, hope of consensus. There was a time when Jews debated whether they were a religion or a nation. (As there are Black, Hispanic and Oriental Jews, we are clearly not a race.) One noted scholar, I believe it was Hebrew Union College professor, Jacob Lauterbach, after listening to the arguments, concluded: "We are a *mishpachah* (a family)." Erich Kahler has offered an anthropological definition. Jews are, in a technical sense, a tribe, i.e., "an ethnic group that has evolved out of and with its proper religion and before the development of a world religion, or out of its reach." As Martin Buber pointed out, the Jewish people came into being at the Exodus, but this event was inextricably linked to the Israelites' acceptance of their religion at Sinai. He concluded: "Israel was and is a people and a religious community in one, and it is this unity which enabled it to survive."

Mordecai Kaplan, the founder of Reconstructionism (See Chapter 18), considered the Jews to be a people who created Judaism, a religious civilization that includes a sense of common language and literature, an ancestral land now reborn, and common folkways.

All these definitions have in common the concept of the Jews as a people historically traceable to the tribes of Israel, a people who developed their own religion that has evolved over the centuries and taken a variety of forms. The religion is the essence of the people's lives, influencing values as well as the way they celebrate joy and deal with sorrow.

WHAT IS JUDAISM?

As our purpose is to discover, "What's special about Judaism?"—we had better consider what is meant by Judaism. A very broad definition has been offered by Rabbi Louis Silverman: Judaism is "the religion, philosophy and way of life of the Jewish people." This raises more questions than it answers. What is religion? What is the Jewish religion? How broadly does one interpret "way of life?"

The usual Hebrew term for Judaism, *Yahadut*, is first found among the Greek-speaking Jews of the first century CE (*II Mac.* 2:21). However, *Yahadut* is rarely used during the rabbinic and medieval periods. For most rabbis, "Torah" in its broadest sense included what we today call Judaism. The problem faced by the rabbis was, what, if any, were the required, or essential beliefs of Judaism or Torah? Maimonides is well known for his 13 principles, which include: believing with perfect faith that "the Law we now possess is the same which has been given to Moses on Sinai, and that the messiah will come, and that the revival of the dead will take place at a time pleasing to God." Other rabbis objected to such a "creed" and were content to select Biblical passages that expressed the essence of Judaism: e.g., Micah's command that the Lord requires us to "do justice, love mercy and walk humbly before God," (6:8) or Habakkuk's counsel, "The righteous shall live by faith." (2:4) A frequent attempt to arrive at a consensus is to state that all who adhere to the Jewish religion affirm some belief in God, Torah, and Israel. The implication is that so long as one believes in one incorporeal and invisible God; and in the Teaching of Torah that God, in some sense, has revealed; and in the essential link between the Jewish people and God, then one is adhering to some form of Judaism. Admittedly this is vague, and in the last chapter we shall suggest ten ways that Judaism may be considered "special." The reader may accept Kaplan's definition of Judaism as a religious civilization or may choose to consider Judaism to be the religion (with its variations) of the Jewish people.

The question remains, "What is meant by religion?" According to Mordecai Kaplan, religion is "man's conscious quest for salvation or the achievement of human destiny." It includes the "institutions places, historic events, heroes and all other objects of popular reverence to which superlative importance or sanctity is ascribed. These *sancta*, the attitude toward life they imply, and the conduct they inspire are the religion of the people." A more individualistic definition of religion was expressed by Whitehead when he wrote, "Religion is what man does with his solitariness." Such a broad concept could include religiously watching Sunday afternoon football. A more helpful definition has been suggested by Professor Alvin Reines (founder of "polydoxy"—see Chapter 16) who has stated that "religion is the human person's response to the conflict of finitude." His assumption is that on some level, we yearn for the infinite: eternal life, moral perfection, all our dreams coming true. Then we recognize that life has its existential limits: we die; we sin and feel guilty; we are plagued by the lack of meaning in life. Religion enables us to deal with these limits, whether through theology, values, or traditions.

However unsatisfactory specific definitions might be, we do recognize that religion is a dimension of life that deals with issues of ultimate concern. For Judaism those issues relate to the search for God; the commitment to and application of Jewish moral values; ways of coping with sin and guilt; beliefs and attitudes about death and immortality; choosing traditions, customs, or laws that teach Jewish ideals and preserve the Jewish faith; studying a religious literature(Bible, writings of rabbis, Hasidim, philosophers) that provides guidance in a confused world.

There is surely an overlap between the Jewish religion and the broader Jewish culture, particularly in the areas of ethics and values. Judaism as a religion provides a foundation, motivation, and guidance for ethical behavior. Furthermore, the broader historic experience of the Jewish people has helped shape those values that are consistent with our ethical ideals. There are those ethical ethnics who negate or minimize the influence of the Jewish religion and assert that all they need, in Alan Dershowitz's term, is a "political Judaism," based on centuries of persecution that made them sensitive to human rights. There are others who denounce the strictly ethnic aspect of Jewish life for being excessively tribal and for setting up unnecessary barriers between people. The following chapter will attempt not only to reconcile the religious and the ethnic, as well as the tribal and the universal, but will maintain that these very dual roots of Jewish values (in historic experience and religion) are *most* characteristic of Judaism and give our heritage a rare opportunity to influence its adherents and have an impact on society.

TOPICS FOR DISCUSSION

1. Would you consider the following people to be Jewish: a) Father Daniel? b) The children of Commander Shalit? c) "Messianic Jews"?

Give your reasons.

2. How do you believe one joins or leaves the Jewish people? 37

3. For what reason, if any, can one person's definition of a Jew be considered more accurate than someone else's definition?

4. What do you mean by "being religious?" How has your _ 42 understanding of the term been shaped by your particular background?

5. Do you think that one can be religious without believing in God? What, if anything, must one believe and/or do to be considered religious?

RESOURCES

Abramov, S. Zalman. *Perpetual Dilemma: Jewish Religion in the Jewish State*. (Ch. 9: "Who Is a Jew?") New York, World Union for Progressive Judaism, 1976.

Freehof, Solomon. *Recent Reform Responsa* (Ch. 14) Cincinnati, Hebrew Union College Press, 1965.

Kahler, Erich. *The Jews among the Nations*. New York, Ungar, 1967.

Liebman, Charles S. "Reconstructionism in American Life," in *American Jewish Year Book*, Volume 71. Philadelphia, Jewish Publication Society,, 1970.

Silverman, Louis. "Judaism," in *Encyclopedia Judaica*, vol. 10. Jerusalem, Keter, 1971.

2.

BEYOND ETHNICITY:

THE DUAL ROOTS OF JEWISH VALUES

Some folks (both Jews and non-Jews) have a problem with Jewish ethnicity. My mother did. When I was a child growing up in Texas, my mother would say, "The only Jewish food is matzah balls; everything else is Russian." She would never buy bread labeled "Jewish rye," because "there's no such thing." Raised as a "Classical Reform" Jew (to be explained in Chapter 16), I associated Jewish ethnicity and Zionism with a parochial outlook that could or would one day stifle the universalist ethic of the prophets. If the moral perspective of the Jewish people became trapped in tribalism or buried in bagels, then what would be the point of Jewish continuity?

Fast forward to Camp Polk, Louisiana, 1953. That's when I experienced the positive values of Jewish ethnicity. As an Army chaplain, I had to meet the needs of Jewish soldiers from Brooklyn College and the City College of New York, who were traumatized by the culture shock of living five miles from Leesville and who were not at all committed to Jewish religious tradition. So what to do? I asked the Sisterhoods in Beaumont, Shreveport, and Alexan-

dria to send in deli food; our slogan was: "Far from home, miss
your Mommy; come to chapel and eat salami." It was then that I
realized the existential power of salami as symbol, but a symbol of
what? Perhaps a reminder of a nurturing family—but the ethnic
values of these young men went beyond mama's kitchen. They
eagerly organized a discussion group called Cogitators and found
stimulation in mental exercise and arguments about the issues of
the day.

Some years later secular ethnic Jews made up about one-third
of the young idealists who took great risks in the deep South in the
summer of 1964 to help Blacks achieve equal rights. While most
of these young Jews did not have a mature understanding of Judaism, they were demonstrating by their lives the rabbinic interpretation of Deuteronomy 16;20: "Justice, justice shall you pursue."
The word, justice, is repeated in order to teach that you shall
pursue justice for Jews and non-Jews alike. I came to realize that
Jewish ethnicity could lead to empathy with other oppressed
groups. I came to view Jewish values as rooted *both* in religion (in
the sense of faith, tradition, sacred texts) *and* in the secular history
of the Jewish people(especially the consequences of anti-Semitism).
Indeed, the dual roots of values(faith and folk) is something special about Judaism, whether one is considering social justice, family, or education.

RELIGION, HISTORY, AND SOCIAL JUSTICE

Many Jews have been moved by Jewish experience to feel empathy for all victims of injustice and oppression. How can we, who
are indignant at the indifference of the "civilized" world during
the Holocaust, be apathetic when other innocent humans are subjected to persecution because of their religion, race or ethnic background? Jews have been prominent among those Americans who

urged our government to do more to stop the slaughter of Bosnian Muslims. As has been well documented, American Jews have been in the forefront of those who struggled for the rights of working men and women and for civil rights of all minority groups. In the fall of 1994, when American voters turned to the political right, almost 80% of American Jews voted for Congressionl Democrats whom they perceived as being more responsive to the needs of the poor.

It is often claimed that the Jewish concern with social justice is based not only on empathy but on enlightened self-interest. This was the point made by Bernard Malamud in *The Fixer.* The character representing Mendel Beiliss, the Jew in Czarist Russia falsely accused of ritual murder, speaks:

"We're all in history, that's sure, but some are more than others, Jews more than some . . . One thing I've learned . . . there's no such thing as an unpolitical man, especially a Jew . . . You can't sit still and see yourself destroyed."

Malamud's point is that Jews are enormously affected by the political process, that for us government matters, so we had better get involved and do all in our power to shape that process to defend all human rights or else we will once again be victims. Jews also have a vested interest in working for a society in which there is equal and ample opportunity for all citizens. Our history has taught us well that the most severe kinds of persecution occur when there is widespread frustration among the masses who turn their anger against the most vulnerable scapegoat—too often, the Jew.

Some have suggested that anti-Semitism led many Jews to develop a sense of alienation that gave them a more critical view of the"in"group. This perspective was summarized by Irving Howe when he wrote about the families of Jewish immigrants who came to America from Russia:

" . . . their greatest contribution has been . . . such distinctive traits of the modern Jewish spirit at its best as an eager
restlessness, a moral anxiety, an openness to novelty, a hun-
ger for the dialectic, a refusal of contentment, *an ironic
criticism of all fixed opinions.*

Being in the "out" group produced a sense of apart-ness that
could be creative and innovative. Freud said that because he was
Jewish in anti-Semitic Vienna, he was better able to "renounce
agreement with the compact majority." So the Jewish ethnic experience has encouraged many American Jews to support others who
have been oppressed, alienated and may be nursing anger that
could explode into violence.

There are, of course, those who argue that Jews have gone too
far in their concern for other minorities—so far, in fact, that they
have been reluctant to stand up for Jewish interests. Jews, they
contend, should oppose the kind of affirmative action that leads to
set-asides that give preference to others because of their gender or
race. Some have warned that if Jews continue to go their liberal
way, they will lose their influence on the American political scene.
My own view is that most Jews are quite capable of joining with
other minorities in the very broad areas of mutual interest while at
the same time reserving the right to differ when there is a genuine
conflict. I would, however, suggest that the issue of affirmative
action is morally more complex than is often recognized. It is worth
noting that when the state of Israel gave preferential treatment to
Sephardic immigrants, this was accepted by the Israeli people as
being in the national interest.

I am more disturbed when some Jews use the experience of
anti-Semitism as a rationale for focusing so intently on Jewish interests that the needs of other victims are either minimized or
ignored. I can remember when rabbis who were vocal in support

of integration or who opposed the war in Vietnam were told by congregants: "Don't you know how many Blacks and anti-war protesters are anti-Semitic? We have enough problems being Jewish. Let the *goyim* take care of themselves." In *From Beirut to Jerusalem*, Tom Friedman coined the term "victimology" to connote the attitude that because we have been victims, our needs take precedence over the needs of others, even if they, too, have been victims.

It should not be surprising that there are such opposite responses to a history of suffering. Psychologist Gordon Allport quotes studies showing that members of victimized minority groups tend either to be more sympathetic *or* less sympathetic than the average toward other victimized minorities. Perhaps it was always so. Perhaps the Torah, itself, without the benefit of Allport's studies, recognized that the bondage in Egypt had the potential to make the Israelites more provincial and prejudiced toward strangers, *or* more empathetic. Perhaps that is why one reads three times in the Torah variations of, "You shall not oppress a stranger, for you know the feelings of the stranger, having yourselves been strangers in the land of Egypt."(Exodus 23:9) It follows that before making moral choices, a Jew who takes Judaism seriously should move beyond ethnicity to the religious roots of Jewish values, to which we now turn.

That human beings were created "in the image of God" was interpreted by the rabbis to mean that God cares for us; therefore, we should care for each other. Whether one accepts the theology of Martin Buber or Mordecai Kaplan, God assures us that we will find a deeper level of meaning in life when we are loving, truthful, and responsible. A Buberian response to those who claim to be content caring only about their immediate interest and that of their family might be: You have not yet discovered the I-Thou experience of empathetic love and responsibility that gives the deepest meaning to life. Once you have this experience, you will not want to return to your limited life. The ultimate source of this meaning is God, the Eternal Thou (See Chapter 4.)

It is in Buber's *Ten Rungs* that one finds this Hasidic dialogue: a student asked his rebbe(leader of a Hasidic community), "Why is the stork called *hasidah*(the loving one)?"

The rebbe answered: "Because it gives much love to its mate and young."

"Then why," asked the student, "is the stork considered *trafe*(unfit for eating)?"

The rebbe answered: "Because it gives love only to its own!"

One reason that some Jews, as well as non-Jews, have dropped out of the struggle for social justice is frustration. The issues have become too complex, the obstacles too formidable. Here, too, we need faith. Many Reform, Conservative, and Reconstructionist rabbis believe in God as a Power that makes for life and love and peace but is not all-powerful. Because God's will is not omnipotent, there is evil in the world, but humanity—with God's help—can overcome.

Jewish law and lore can be quoted by both liberals and conservatives to support their respective positions. This has been called "*posuk* hunting," a *posuk* being a verse of Torah. Actually, rabbinic opinions were greatly affected by the historic condition of the Jewish people. When Jews were the objects of discrimination and persecution, their law tended to discriminate against Gentiles and Jewish lore may have expressed suspicion and fear. As persecution diminished, Jewish law was more likely to express the ethic of equality. For example, when Jews were being harassed the law was according to Rabbi Ishmael, who ruled that a Jew was legally bound to return a lost article only if its owner was Jewish. In the early feudal period in Europe, when there was less discrimination, the law was according to Rabbi Akiba: Return the purse, whoever its owner. During the Crusades, Rav Judah wrote in *Sefer Chasidim* that a Jew could violate the Sabbath to save the life of a Jew, but not of a non-Jew. However, after the Crusades, Menahem Meiri of Provence ruled in the fourteenth century that a Jew was obligated to desecrate the Sabbath to save the life of a non-Jew, any law to the contrary having been intended only for ancient times when non-Jews were heathens and had no sense of duty to society. Those laws which recognize the dignity of all human beings are consistent with faith in one God for one humanity. The discriminatory laws, while inconsistent with such a faith, were understandable reactions to a hostile environment in which any progress by human means seemed impossible.

Consulting Jewish law regarding contemporary issues should help us realize that as Jews, we are part of both a religious and an historic process that will continue to deal with age-old problems until they are resolved. Some examples of the rabbinic perspectives on social and economic dilemmas are the following:

Tzedakah: This term, sometimes translated as "charity," actually means "righteousness" or "justice." Therefore, caring for the poor is not simply an act of love or compassion but an obligation required by law.

Maimonides wrote that there are eight degrees of *tzedakah:* The highest level is to prevent poverty by assisting one's needy neighbors by a gift or loan or by teaching them a trade or by setting them up in business so they may earn an honest livelihood and not be forced to hold out their hands for charity.

The poor were expected to accept any kind of job (even "skinning a carcass in the street") rather than accept charity. According to the Mishnah, one should not say: "I am a priest, a great scholar, provide for me."According to a Talmudic version of "workfare," the community was *not* required to support one who, while able, refused to work. However, in the Middle Ages, the professional *schnorrer* was given minimal subsistence (food and lodging.)

If a poor man says, "I am hungry," feed him immediately. If he says, "Clothe me," determine if he really needs clothing.

The rabbis could require the entire community to participate in fund-raising if it was for the security and well-being of all. However, rabbinic scholars did not have to support expenditures for public safety because (it was assumed) God would protect them.

Market forces could be regulated for the sake of justice and mercy. A shohet (butcher who operated according to Jewish law) could not stop slaughtering animals before the holiday so the prices would rise. Price controls for basic goods were set at one-sixth above the seller's cost. However, if shortages led to higher prices, so be it.

American Jews find themselves challenged by the Biblical imperative: "You shall be holy, for I, the Lord your God, am holy." The root of *kadosh* (holy) means "to be set apart for a higher spiritual purpose." The great nineteenth chapter of Leviticus ("love your neighbor as yourself" . . ."you shall love the stranger as yourself") is surrounded by laws that separate the Israelites from their neighbors so that the Israelites might maintain their own moral standards. There is no longer such a wide cultural and moral gulf between Jews and their neighbors. Still, the concept of *kadosh*, of developing and maintaining a "holy skepticism" toward the conventional wisdom, brings together Biblical tradition with the sense of alienation that still lingers in the minds and hearts of many otherwise assimilated American Jews.

Finally, there is our treasure house of traditions, especially those holidays that would have us participate in the Jewish people's struggle for freedom and justice. At the Seder we are to read, "It is the obligation of every human (*adam*) to view him/herself as going out from Egypt." Pesach, Hanukkah, and Purim can enable each generation to identify with the oppressed, to respect the right to be different and to recognize and ridicule authoritarian autocrats. (See Chapters 14, 15.)

The relation of Jewish ethnicity, ethics, and religion in Israel is beyond the scope of this chapter; however, a few comments are in order. The philosopher and advocate of "Cultural Zionism," Ahad Ha-Am, believed that each nation had a *volkgeist,* a unique spirit, and the uniqueness of the Jewish people was its capacity for morality, particularly social justice. He warned against establishing a Jewish state that would find "glory in attaining material power or political domination." Because for almost all the years since 1948, Israel has been surrounded by neighbors bent on its destruction, one can well understand that at times some Israelis have behaved in ways that fell short of the highest moral standards. Assuming an era of peace in which the Jews will be the secure majority in their own nation, one can only speculate on what values will emerge from Jewish ethnicity. Perhaps the cultural traditions of the Jewish people, together with the development of non-Orthodox forms of Judaism, will provide a foundation for at least a partial fulfillment of the vision of Ahad Ha-Am. (See Chapter 20.)

To sum up: Jewish perspectives on social justice are rooted *both* in the historic experience of the people as well as in the beliefs, literature and traditions of Judaism. An important aspect of Judaism that is "special" is that its moral perspectives are grounded both in history and religion, in people and faith. Jewish faith should prevent ethnicity from becoming ethnocentric. Jewish ethnicity has provided experiences that should strengthen and support the moral perspective of Jewish faith.

RELIGION, HISTORY, AND FAMILY

When non-Jews convert to Judaism, one reason they often give is their belief that Jewish families tend to be warm and close. The young Philip Roth had a rather different perspective on Jewish families which he portrayed as smothering their children with closeness. Before confronting the question."Is the *haymisha* (warm) Jewish family beneficial or stifling?" let us first focus on the relations between the generations as influenced by both religion and history.

The first parental responsibility regarding children was to have a lot of them. *Halakhah,* according to Hillel, prescribes a minimum of one boy and one girl, but in practice the Orthodox took the command, "be fertile and increase," to mean *really* increase. According to the strictest view in Jewish law, the use of contraceptives is not permitted unless there is a medical or psychiatric threat to mother or child.

In the Midrash (rabbinic interpretations of the Torah and other Biblical books), the role of the father is made clear: He is assigned the task of discipline and is advised not to spare the rod, otherwise, the son will become a delinquent, and the father will hate him. It is the father rather than the mother who demands achievement, as indicated by the question and answer: "When is a child especially dear to his father?" "When he learns to talk." In contrast, the mother loves the child from birth. In fact, *rahamim,* from the root *rehem* (womb), means unconditional love.

There is a large body of literature about the child's obligation to his/her parents. The Biblical basis, of course, is the fifth commandment: "honor your father and your mother." The rabbis elaborated, saying there are three partners in creation: father, mother, and God, so to honor parents, it is as though one is honoring God.

Why such deification? Joseph Albo, in the fifteenth century, explained that honoring parents means respecting their traditions. Such respect is essential if Judaism is to survive and thrive.

In Rabbinic Judaism children are portrayed as being very submissive:

"In what does reverence for a father consist? In not sitting in his presence, and in not speaking in his presence, and in not contradicting him."Rabbi Eliezer said: "Even if his father ordered him to throw a purse of gold into the sea, he would obey him." There are exceptions to such obedience. If parents transgress the Torah, the children may point out their error. The Midrash gives us an early expression of feminism: After Pharoah decreed death to the male Hebrew infants, Amram, father of Miriam, told all Israelites to divorce their wives so they would have no more children to be killed by the Egyptians. However, Miriam voiced a strong protest: "Why, *Abba*, should you penalize female infants by preventing them from being born?" God was pleased that Miriam so rebuked her father. The Talmud does caution, however, that any contradiction of a parent should be done tactfully and respectfully.

A major thrust of rabbinic literature is the responsibility of adult children toward their aging parents. This is a matter not necessarily of love but of fairness. In the Mishnah we read, "A parent endows children with the blessings of beauty, strength, riches, wisdom and length of years. Just as the parent endows the child with five things, so, too, is the child obliged in five things: to feed, to give drink, to clothe, to put on shoes, and to lead." Remember, there were no nursing homes or condos in Florida, but there were three-generation households.

In addition to those rabbinic laws and commentaries that laid the foundation for a close family life, there were, of course, the treasure house of traditions centered in the home and preserved by the parents. Sukkot, Pesach, Hannukah, and the weekly Sabbath—all involved family experiences that transmitted Jewish values.

The roots of Jewish family life were also profoundly affected by changing historic conditions. According to *Life is with People*, by Zborowski and Herzog, when Jews lived in Eastern Europe under the heel of the Czars in the eighteenth and nineteenth centuries, life in the *shtetl* (Jewish village) produced a shift in parental roles. The father often spent more time away from home, as a traveling peddler or studying in the synagogue, while mother was more dominant in the home. To compensate for the hostility her children would face when they were grown, Mama gave an extra measure of protection:

> "The mother's love was manifested in two ways, by constant and solicitous overfeeding and by unremitting concern about every aspect of her child's welfare, expressed for the most part in unceasing verbalization. 'What have you done? What are you going to do? Are you warm enough? Put on another muffler. Have you had enough to eat? Look take just a little of this soup?'"

Does this sound familiar? Did your mother rebel against this overprotection and swing to the other extreme of permissiveness, or did she find a happy medium? What about your role as a parent?

Philip Roth claims that "what's really happening in that warm and cozy Jewish home is that a hard-working, well-behaved kid is being quietly smothered by an overly-watchful, overprotective mother while his father (poor oaf) remains a virtual stranger to him—working away, sleeping away or sitting across the table and silently stowing it away." With such a negative image of male initiative the boy does not know how to explore his awakening sexual capabilities.

Zena Smith Blau replies, in effect, "Speak for yourself, Phil." She finds that the encouragement of intellectual development together with a longer period of emotional dependence makes it more likely that the children will accept parental values rather than being swayed by the often self-destructive values of the youth culture. Of course, this is a matter of balance. Today, as liberals and conservatives alike are concerned with children suffering from family instability and lack of standards, the best prescription seems to be love and limits.

RELIGION, HISTORY, AND EDUCATION

Jewish parents may joke about "my two-year old, the PhD," but education and intellectual achievement have usually been highly prized in Jewish life. There have been notable exceptions, however. The Hasidic movement in eighteenth and nineteenth century Russia and Poland considered sincerity (*kavanah*), not study, to be the way to God for many poorly educated and often illiterate Jews. In the twentieth century, most Jews of North Africa—the *Sephardim* who migrated to Israel—were not highly educated and despite preferential treatment are still underrepresented in the universities. Therefore, let us not be tempted to make the false claim that Jewish intelligence is genetically superior to that of Gentiles, as suggested by the terms, *yiddische-kopf* and *goyisha-kopf* (Jewish head and Gentile head).

Still, in twentieth-century America and Europe, Jewish intellectual achievements have been very significant, as evidenced by the over-representation of Jewish scientists who have won the Nobel prize, of Jewish students in graduate schools and of Jews in the professions. As with the values of social justice and family, the explanation lies in a confluence of religious and ethnic experience.

The religious belief at the root of Jewish learning is found in the theological assumption of the Pharisees: God so loved the Jews that God gave them the Torah that they might achieve "salvation" or "redemption"(*y'shuah* or *g'ulah*). This would include *Gan Eden* (paradise or garden of Eden), and the *Olam Haba* (the world to come). Study of Torah pointed the way to salvation.

In contrast, early and medieval Christianity was based on the belief that God so loved humanity that God gave them His son, so that by faith in Jesus as Christ one could achieve salvation. The Christian way to salvation did not involve study but was essentially a matter of faith. The experts in Church law were a small group centered in Rome. Contrast this with the flourishing of *yeshivot* (schools for the teaching of Jewish law) in the Diaspora, where thousands of Jewish boys learned to reason like lawyers. Of course, girls were not admitted except for the fictional Yentl. From the Orthodox perspective, the role of the Jewish woman was to be a good wife and mother. However, an untold chapter of Jewish history is that of many Jewish wives who learned *Yiddish* and ran the family business, loaned money, and collected interest, while the husband was praying or studying in the synagogue.

It should be noted that legal reasoning did not mean questioning the fundamental assumptions of Orthodoxy: that the Torah was a verbal revelation from God and that its rabbinic interpretations had divine sanction. However, in a scientific cultural milieu (from the eighteenth-century "age of reason" to the present), this "Talmudic" emphasis on intellectual analysis may have led some Jews to question not only the assumptions of Orthodoxy but the foundations of religion itself.

In the seventeenth century, the English diarist, Samuel Pepys, happened to visit a synagogue on the holiday of Simchat Torah (Joy of the Torah). This celebration, in the eleventh century, was appended

to the end of Sukkot and Sh'mini Atzeret. He was amazed at the
seeming lack of piety as the men carried the Torahs round about the
room while the congregants followed, singing and laughing. Pepys
thought "there had never been any religion in the world so absurdly
performed as this." He did not realize that the Jews were rejoicing
because of the opportunity to study Torah. He did not understand
that when they read from the last verses of Deuteronomy and then
the first verses of Genesis, they were saying, in effect: "Never close one
book without opening another. Learning never ceases." This is something special about Judaism: a religious holiday dedicated to the ideal
of learning! (See Chapter 14.)

There are many rabbinic sayings about learning: "An ignorant
man cannot be pious." "He who does not increase his knowledge
decreases it." "Who are the guardians of the state? The scribes and
the teachers?" "One should divide one's time equally between earn-
ing a livelihood, eating, sleeping, and studying Torah." "Do not
hit a child with a book!"

When one turns to those aspects of Jewish history that may
have influenced attitudes toward learning, the most frequently cited
factor is anti-Semitism, from discrimination to pogroms. Even after Jews were freed from the ghetto, they encountered high barriers in the universities and professions, from Europe to America, so
they had to try harder. Isaac Babel, a Jewish communist who served
after the Russian Revolution with the Red Cavalry, recalled his
grandmother admonishing him, "Study and you will have everything—wealth and fame! You must know everything."

Furthermore, the economic roles of Jews in Europe required a
certain educational level, including literacy and math. Medieval
Jews often served as middlemen between the segments of the population (e.g., the serfs and nobility). With family connections
throughout Europe and the Middle East, these Jewish traders could
become involved in international commercial enterprises. In the

later Middle Ages, restricted from participation in the guilds and unable to own land or till the soil, many Jews were forced into areas of finance, from court advisor to petty moneylender. (See Chapter 11.) These experiences made them particularly ready and able to enter the business community as capitalism developed. To succeed in such economic roles, a basic education was necessary, as were the habits of diligence and responsibility.

Finally, there was the relatively high status of learning in the Jewish community. In the rabbinic and medieval periods, a Jewish boy could not grow up to be a nobleman or to be enormously rich. The most one could hope for was to learn enough to become a highly respected rabbi. There was great dignity in learning. Today the status of the rabbi is somewhat less exalted. Could it be that the value placed on religious study has been secularized so that during the last two centuries, learning, itself, has become highly prized in the Jewish community?

There could be a negative side to this pride in intellectual achievement. What happens to the self-worth of average Jewish children who are not high achievers? What happens to Jewish attitudes toward young people with learning disabilities? Are the Jewish federations, with their many social agencies, doing enough to provide group homes and other support systems for the learning-disabled adult?

When a religion emphasizes learning and critical thought, it may pose a challenge to itself. One cannot teach children to think critically and then declare their own religion to be off-limits. Could this emphasis on "higher education" be related to the low level of regular attendance at synagogues? Or might this emphasis produce a new generation of seekers who have been turned off by simplistic formulas and are eager to learn, to find a religion that appeals both to their minds and their hearts?

The values of social justice, family, and education are obviously not uniquely Jewish. However, what is special about Judaism is that the roots, the rationales, and the motivations for these values can be found both in the Jewish religion and in the secular experience of the Jewish people. This linkage provides Jews with a firm foundation for values at a time when right and wrong may be viewed as mere matters of opinion.

TOPICS FOR DISCUSSION

1. How would you respond to this argument from a self-absorbed Jew?

> I do not believe it is in the "enlightened self-interest" of Jews to become bleeding-heart liberals, to be so concerned with the plight of the underclass. It is not in my self-interest to be taxed so money can be poured into government programs that are rarely effective. I find my fulfillment and meaning in life by taking care of myself and my family.

2. From your experience or from what you have learned, compare the methods of fund-raising (*tzedaka* or charity) for worthy causes as it is done in the Jewish communities and in Christian communities. If there are differences, can you explain why?

3. How would you compare Jewish families today with the traditional picture of a warm, close-knit Jewish family that shows great concern for the well-being of the children and may at times be over-protective?

4. Are there significant differences today in the attitudes, values, and relationships in Jewish families as compared with families of other ethnic or religious groups?

5. What is your opinion of Zena Smith Blau's thesis that the longer period of emotional dependence of Jewish children on their

parents has the advantage of encouraging the children to accept parental values that may well be more beneficial than the values of today's youth culture?

6. .Jewish religion and culture has usually placed a high value on study, learning, and critical thought. Is this value a challenge to religion itself? Can one place a high value on "higher education" without encouraging skepticism toward the foundation of religion?

RESOURCES

Blau, Zena Smith. "In Defense of the Jewish Mother," in Rose, P. (ed.), *The Ghetto and Beyond.* New York, Random House, 1969.

Cohn, Haim. *Human Rights in Jewish Law.* New York, Ktav, 1984.

Frisch, Ephraim. *An Historical Survey of Jewish Philanthropy.* New York, Macmillan, 1924.

Goldberg, Harold. "Understanding Jewish Learning." *Response,* Issue No. 6, Winter, 1969-70.

Tamari, Meir. *"With All Your Possessions:" Jewish Ethics and Economic Life.* New York, The Free Press (Macmillan), 1987.

Vorspan, Albert and David Saperstein. *Tough Choices: Jewish Perspectives on Social Justice.* New York, UAHC Press, 1992.

Zhborowski, Mark and Elizabeth Herzog. *Life Is with People* (Part Two.) New York, Schocken, 1952.

BIBLICAL CHRONOLOGY

JEWISH HISTORY	RELEVANT WORLD HISTORY
2100-1500 BCE Probable origin of patriarchal traditions.	2060-1950: Third Dynasty of Ur.
1700-1570: Israelites migrate to Egypt; probably welcomed by Hyksos.	1792-1750: Hammurabi of Babylon.
	1700-1570: Hyksos rule Egypt.
1570: Possible date of enslavement of Israelites.	1570: Ahmose frees Egypt from "foreign" Hyksos.
1275-1250: Possible date of Exodus.	1301-1224: Rameses II.
1250-1200: Conquest of Canaan.	1100: Philistine cities on coast, conflicts with Saul and David.
1020-1002: Saul, first King of Israel.	
1002-962: David (prophet *Nathan*).	
962-922: Solomon: First Temple.	
Kingdom divides: Israel and Judah.	
	900-842: Ben Hadad I, Aramean King of Damascus.
869-850: In Israel: Ahab vs *Elijah*.	
786-746: Israel under Jereboam II. Prophet Amos appears at Beth-El.	
783-715: Uzziah rules in Judah, followed by Jotham, Ahaz, and Hezekiah. Isaiah and Micah prophesy.	
	745-727: Tigleth Pilesar IV rules Assyrian Empire.
722: Northern kingdom of Israel (Samaria) falls to Assyria.	
	701: Sennacherib invades Judah, pulls back from the gates of Jerusalem.
640-608: Josiah's reforms in Judah. *Jeremiah* begins his prophesies.	
	625-605: Nabopolasser last Assyrian King. Rise of Babylonian Empire.
586: Fall of Jerusalem to King Nebuchadnesser. Destruction of Temple. Judeans forced to go to Babylon. Prophets Deutero-Isaiah and Ezekiel.	
	546: Persian King Cyrus overthrows Babylonian Empire.
	538: Cyrus allows Judeans, led by Zerubbabel, to return to Judah, now a province of Persia.
530: Second Temple is rebuilt.	480: Xerxes's navy defeated by Athenians at Salamis.
485-398: More Jews return to Judea. Reforms led by Nehemiah and Ezra.	479: Spartans defeat Xerxes's army, which retreats in disarray to Persisa.(See Purim, Chapter 15.)

3.

IN THE BEGINNING: ANCIENT INSIGHTS

In Chapter 1, we concluded that the Jews are a people, traceable to the tribes of Israel, who came into being with their own religion. In terms of the Biblical narrative, the Exodus was linked to the Covenant at Sinai. In Chapter 2, we considered how the dual roots of history and religion, of people and faith, influenced Jewish values toward social justice, family, and education.

We shall now flash back to the Biblical period to discover how this link between people and faith began, and to focus on the foundations of Judaism established by the Biblical concepts of God as creator and redeemer, of Covenant, of the Prophetic Imperative and of the Messianic Dream. These ancient insights are still relevant today for all who would appreciate what is so special about Judaism.

The Hebrew Bible is called the *Tanakh*. This is an acronym based on the three sections of the Bible: Torah, *N'vi-im* (prophets) and *Ketuvim* (writings). When I was a student at the Hebrew Union College, we spent much time trying to determine who wrote which Biblical passage, when it was written, and why. We more or less accepted the "Documentary Hypothesis," which held that the Torah was a blend of at least four documents: 1) J (850 BCE, by the Yahvist who used the term *Yahveh* for God); 2) E (750 BCE, by the Elohist who used the term *Elohim*); 3) D (621 BCE, by the Deuteronomist whose scroll was "discovered" in the Temple during Josiah's reformation); and 4) P (500 BCE, by priests who led the return after the Babylonian Exile, and who were concerned with making sure the people were *kadosh* (holy), set aside for a spiritual purpose.) Finally, there was the elusive R, the Redactor(s) who integrated the documents into the whole we call Torah.

The proponents of "Biblical criticism" point to contradictions within the Torah that indicate more than one author. For example, the first chapter of Genesis presents one myth in which the order of creation is vegetation, fish, animals, man and woman together and in which God is referred to as *"Elohim."* In contrast, the second chapter of Genesis presents an earlier, more primitive myth in which the order of creation is vegetation, man, animals, and woman, and in which the words, *"Yahveh Elohim"* are used to refer to God.

Orthodox scholars reject this approach. An imaginative attempt at reconciling the accounts in Genesis One and Two was made by the distinguished scholar, Rabbi Joseph Soloveitchek. He suggested that Genesis One describes the creation of one dimension of the human personality: the Amoral Adam who is told to fill the earth and master it, who strives for self-fulfillment and personal satisfaction. However, in Genesis Two, the second dimension of Adam is created: an Adam confronted with the limits of life, an Adam who learns that we cannot have whatever we want when we want it, an Adam who faces pain, guilt, and death. Genesis One and Two describe the creation of the whole Adam and challenge us to somehow find a harmony between our drive for self-fulfillment and our recognition of limits. This is a beautiful commentary, even if it does not refute the Documentary Hypothesis.

A more widely accepted reservation about this critical approach is that whatever the original strands that were woven into the Torah, it is the weaver (R, the Redactor) who is most responsible for a Torah which despite inconsistencies, preserves the legends, history, values, and basic beliefs of our spiritual ancestors. The power of the Torah derives from our awareness that emerging from the pagan world, these ancient Israelites created a revolution, a new way of viewing nature and humanity that provided a foundation not only for Judaism but for Christianity and Islam as well.

GOD AS CREATOR

Scholars have found reflections of the Babylonian creation myth in Genesis One. As the Biblical account begins, only water and God exist. For the Babylonians, in the beginning there was water personified by the gods Tiamat and Apsu. There was also, in the Babylonian myth (as in Genesis One), a primal light. However, the differences between the two myths are much more profound. For the Babylonians, the world was created as a result of a war between the gods: Marduk cut up Tiamat and made her the sky between the upper and lower waters. Reality was at root chaotic, the result of conflict, chance, and irrational powers that had to be placated by magic. In marked contrast, in Genesis One, there is but one God who imposes order on chaos, and establishes a rational process of creation, reflecting an evolution from the simple to the complex. Because God has established laws by which nature operates, this means there is an order not merely in our minds but in nature, itself, an order that gives us a greater sense of security.

Harvey Cox, a specialist in religious studies, has suggested that Genesis One makes science possible—because science is based on the assumption that one may make predictions based upon the laws of nature. Of course, in modern physics chance plays a significant role, but it may be no coincidence that Einstein, who looked for a unified field theory, was Jewish. It is the Biblical belief that order is more fundamental than accident, that Oneness is, in some sense, more basic than diversity. This insight has important implications for our moral values: What unites us as human beings is more fundamental than what divides us.

The second Creation story (Genesis Two) provides the Biblical explanation of how evil entered the world. The rabbinic interpretation of Adam and Eve in Eden is not that humans are born evil but that we have the capacity to choose between good and evil. Adam and Eve made the wrong choice and had to face the consequences. There are scholars who suggest that God knew Adam and Eve would rebel and actually wanted them to be expelled from the Garden. Only through this expulsion would they enter history and begin the long struggle to re-establish a harmony with nature and other humans; in other words, to re-create that other Eden envisioned by Isaiah and pictured in Rousseau's painting, "Peaceable Kingdom."

The rabbinic commentators found in the creation of Adam the Biblical basis for the concept of one human family. In a midrash the question is asked: "Why did God (at first) create only one man?" The answer: "So that no one can boast, "I am of nobler lineage than you." Then there was the comment on the phrase, "God formed man from the dust of the earth." (Genesis. 2:7) Our sages added: " . . . dust from all over the world: yellow clay and white sand, black loam and red soil, that the earth can declare to no race or color of man that you do not belong here; this soil is not your home." Finally, in the Mishnah we read:

"Only one single man was created in the world to teach that, if any man has caused a single soul to perish, Scripture imputes it to him as though he had caused a whole world to perish and, if any man saves alive a single soul, Scripture imputes it to him as though he had saved a whole world."

OF COVENANTS AND LAND

The first covenant in the Bible was established after the flood. God sent the flood because the world was so full of *hamas* (violence). Noah, being righteous despite his wicked generation, was spared along with his family and enough animals to preserve all species. Then God put a rainbow in the sky and promised never again to send a flood to destroy the earth. Humanity was obligated to follow certain fundamental moral principles.

After God told Abraham to leave his father's house and go to an unknown land, God made a covenant with Abraham and promised that his descendants would multiply and would settle on the land that became Israel. Abraham was singled out so that he might instruct his descendants to keep the way of the Lord by doing what is just and right, and all nations would be blessed by him. This passage (Genesis 18:19) probably reflects a later development in the concept of covenant and chosenness. The main purpose of the stories of the patriarchs was to explain how and why they and their descendants had a just claim to the land of Israel. There was no attempt to portray them as moral role models. These tales conclude with the Joseph story that explains how the Israelites came to Egypt. It is with the appearance of Moses at the burning bush what we are introduced to the concept of God as redeemer.

THE BUSH AND THE MOUNTAIN

The bush of revelation is *ha-s'neh*; the mountain of revelation is *Sinai*. When Moses, standing before the bush, asked God, "Who am I that I should go to Pharoah and free the Israelites from Egypt?", God assured him, "I will be with you"(*Ehyeh imach*). Is it a coincidence that when Moses asked what is the name of the God who sent me, God answered: "*Ehyeh-asher-Ehyeh*"? Buber suggests that the phrase means: "I will surely be with you (as your redeemer)." That is, the name of God indicates the nature or power of God as redeemer. Others have interpreted the ambiguous phrase to mean: I have no name; that is, no one can know My nature; I simply am. This suggests a more mystical interpretation of God as Being, itself. The literary context seems to favor the concept of God as redeemer, because in the next section the redemption does take place with the exodus from Egypt.

The moral implication of the Exodus is the obligation of future generations of Jews to identify with the slaves in Egypt and so develop empathy for all the oppressed: "You shall love (the stranger) as yourself, for you were strangers in the land of Egypt."(Leviticus 19:34)

However, freedom—contrary to the Passover song, *Dayenu*—was not enough. The purpose of the Exodus was stated in the Biblical text: "Let My people go, *that they may serve Me.*" It was at Sinai that the Israelites learned what God required of them. The form of the Covenant was similar to that between the Assyrian king and his vassals: a proclamation of the power of the king followed by the command, "You shall have no other liege." However, the Biblical commandments spelled out the moral imperatives the Israelites had to follow if they were to survive the wilderness and find their promised land.

According to Martin Buber, the first three commandments affirm the nature of God: that God is the redeemer, is only one, and is not visible. The third commandment could mean that God's name is not to be used for magical purposes (implying a pagan deity) or that one should not swear falsely using God's name. The fourth and fifth commandments make possible the continuity of the people by observing the Shabbat week after week, and by honoring the parents and, therefore, their traditions. The next four commandments are intended to protect life as well as the institutions needed for any secure society: the family, property, and a legal system. The tenth commandment, "You shall not covet," suggests that jealousy is the prime psychological reason why the previous four commandments are violated.

The Decalogue is not the first statement of moral principles. Standards of personal behavior had been prescribed in other civilizations. However, according to Mordecai Kaplan, the *hiddush*, what was new about Sinai was that *this was the first time an entire people had been told: You, as a community, must follow these moral principles if you are to survive and prosper.* It is worth noting that in Judaism the first motive for the moral imperative is not to assure the individual of salvation in the future world but to assure the community of security and stability in this world.

THE PROPHETIC IMPERATIVE

The nomadic Israelites lived in a classless society in which the herd belonged to the tribe, and the individual had little more than his tent and weapon. It was, therefore, possible to follow an ethic of equality within the community. However, once the Israelites moved into Canaan (1230-1190 BCE), many became farmers. Some farmers were more fortunate and wealthier than others. Thus, the institutions and class structure making for inequality emerged. Such inequality bred injustice, which violated the Mosaic Covenant. Then it was that prophets arose to protest the injustice and the violation of the Covenant.

The Hebrew term for prophet is *navi,* spokesperson for God. However, the first prophets in the Bible were called *ro-im,* seers who went about in groups or who were attached to the court, serving as oracles to the king, predicting the consequences of his proposed actions. The first prophet to protest a violation of the Covenant was Nathan, who spoke truth to the absolute power of King David. The King had committed adultery with Bath-sheba and had sent her husband, Uriah, to the front line of battle to be killed.

Nathan, using nomadic imagery (II Samuel 12:1-8) condemned the King. David, whose shepherd-conscience was stirred by Nathan's parable of the lamb, was moved to repentance.

David's son Solomon succeeded his father and built the first Temple. After Solomon's death, the nation was divided into the northern kingdom of Israel and the southern kingdom of Judah. The next "apostolic" prophet (messenger of God) was Elijah who protested the appearance in the court of the pagan prophets of Baal, who had been brought into Israel by Jezebel, the Tyrean wife of King Ahab. After announcing a drought and then demonstrating the power of *Yahveh* to bring rain ("*Yahveh* alone is God!"-I Kings 18:38), Elijah slew the prophets of Baal and was forced to flee from Jezebel's forces. He took refuge at Mt. Horeb (another name for Sinai), and there on the mountain of revelation he heard the Lord not in the storm, fire, or earthquake but in "a still small voice." God commanded him to return and pronounce doom on the dynasty of Ahab. Elijah found Ahab in the vineyard of Naboth, who, at Jezebel's urging, had been framed and executed so that the King could confiscate his property. Elijah fumed, "Have you killed and also taken possession!" (I Kings 21:19)

Of the literary prophets the first to "publish" was Amos. The first *navi* who was not a member of the prophetic guild, Amos was a simple sheepherder from Tekoa in the southern kingdom of Judah. He became incensed by the injustice and hypocrisy of the Israelites in the northern kingdom. So he barged into the Temple at Beth-el during a Fall festival and, to avoid being expelled, began condemning the enemies of Israel for their sins and proclaiming their destruction. The

Gazans, Ammonites, and Edomites had sinned by showing no pity and by breaking their oaths to other nations. Amos then turned against Judah and condemned the southern Jewish kingdom for spurning the teaching of the Lord. He was even more scathing in his denunciation of the northern kingdom of Israel for selling the just people for silver and those who were needy for a pair of sandals (a reference to the practice of enslaving debtors) and for trampling the heads of the poor into the dust of the ground (one interpretation: being homeless, the poor had to live on the ground). He also condemned fathers and sons for going to "sacred prostitutes," associated with the pagan fertility cult. While the Israelites, under the prosperous reign of Jereboam II, were looking forward to a "day of the Lord" on which their nation would triumph over others in the region, Amos warned that the day of the Lord would be one of darkness and not light, a day of utter destruction as punishment for the sins of the people. Amos was particularly scornful of rituals that were celebrated while injustice was being perpetrated: "I loathe, I spurn your festivals, I am not appeased by your solemn assemblies . . . Spare Me the sound of your hymns and let Me not hear the music of your lutes, but let justice well up like water, righteousness like a mighty stream" (Amos 5:21-5.)

The Israelites were infuriated with Amos, and the high priest, Amaziah, told him to go back to Judah and prophesy there. The people simply could not believe that the God of Israel would destroy God's own people. Because in their minds God was linked inextricably to the people, this would have meant the end of God! Perhaps that is why Amos concluded his message by raising the Israelite religion to a new level:

> To Me, O Israelites, you are just like the Ethiopians, declares
>   the Lord.
> True, I brought Israel up from the land of Egypt
> But also the Philistines from Caphtor and the Arameans
>   from Kir . . .
> (Amos 9:7)

In other words, God's existence does not depend on the Israelites, but *Yahveh* is the God of the universe and of all nations. Therefore, every people (Israel included) is required to follow certain moral laws or face the consequences.

After the reign of Jereboam II, when Isaiah was prophesying in the southern kingdom of Judah, Amos's predictions came true. In 721 BCE, the Assyrian forces under Sargon conquered the northern kingdom of Israel. Isaiah protested the efforts of the Judean kings to make alliances with other nations against Assyria and called on them to return to the Covenant. However, he believed his message was falling on deaf ears. He did say that after the destruction a "seed" would remain, but was this said in despair or with hope in the future? If the famous messianic passages were, indeed, written by Isaiah (rather than a later author), there are grounds for hope—but for hope in a rather distant future.

THE MESSIANIC DREAM

In the first messianic dream of Isaiah (2:3-4), there is no messiah! Note that these verses do not portray, as is sometimes alleged, Israelite domination of the world. On the contrary, the peoples of the world willingly choose to go up to the mountain of the Lord to learn the ways of the God of Jacob. It is God, not a messiah, who will judge among the nations until they beat swords into plowshares, spears into pruning hooks, refuse to take up sword against nations, and know war no more.

In Isaiah 11, we find the classic Biblical description of the messiah or *mashiach* ("anointed one"): a wise, courageous, and reverential human being, descended from the house of David ("stump of Jesse"), who will decide with justice for the lowly. After the destruction of the wicked, there will emerge a world of such peace that the natural enemies (wolf and lamb) shall lie down with each other; it will be safe for a small child to lead wild beasts. "Nothing evil or vile shall be done for the land shall be filled with devotion to the Lord as water covers the sea." It is now clear why almost all of the Jewish people did not consider Jesus to be the messiah: He did not accomplish what was expected of the messiah; he did not bring peace. Also, his followers considered him to be a divine being and the Biblical concept envisioned the messiah to be a wise human. Most non-Orthodox Jews look forward to a messianic age. (See Chapters 6, 16, 17, and 18.)

This faith may sound rather naive, given the events of the past century. How on earth is such a moral revolution possible? The prophet Jeremiah, who witnessed the fall of Jerusalem to the Babylonians, provided some grounds for hope. In the prophetic tradition, he had warned the Judeans that because they had violated the ten commandments (Jeremiah 7), the presence of the Temple would not spare them. However, just as the Babylonians were descending on the city, Jeremiah bought a field in the nearby town of Anathoth and, to signify his hope in a future return, put the deed in an earthen jar (32:9-15). Perhaps the Judeans would learn from the painful experience of the past not to repeat the grievous errors of their history. The challenge is still with us: can *we* learn from history, lest we be condemned to repeat it? A more particular challenge, what is the role of the Jews in bringing about the messianic age?

ARE JEWS THE CHOSEN, THE CHOOSING, OR BOTH?

The phrase, "God chose" is first found in Deuteronomy 7:7, a verse probably dating from about 621 BCE, when Jeremiah was prophesying. Two hundred years earlier, Amos, speaking for God, had warned the people: "You *only* have I singled out of all the families of the earth. That is why I will call you to account for all your iniquities."(3:2) This implies that Jews are judged by a higher standard than are other people, a controversial view and one that some Jews simultaneously take pride in and resent. We are proud of high ideals, but we complain when we are judged by a harsher double standard.

The experience that convinced Jews they were chosen was their encounter with God at Sinai. As Gunther Plaut, noted scholar of the Reform movement whose Torah commentary is widely used, has written, "For while everywhere else in the sacred history of God and man it was the individual soul which opened itself to the Presence, at Sinai it was the whole people. Therein lies the uniqueness of the moment." According to the rabbis, the Jews were chosen not because they were morally superior to other nations but because they were willing to be chosen. Hillaire Belloc quipped: "How odd of God to choose the Jews." He was answered anonymously, "It was not odd; the Jews chose God."

Chosenness did not bestow on the Jews any special privileges, rather, the Jews were given special responsibilities. These were spelled out during the Babylonian exile by the prophet known as Deutero-Isaiah. Because the exile brought Jews into contact with other nations, the prophet was persuaded that God's purpose in scattering the Jews was to make them "a servant of the Lord" who would:

" . . . bring forth the true way
He shall not grow dim or be bruised
Till he has established the true way on earth
And the coastlands shall await for his teachings"(Isaiah 42:
    3-4.)

The people would fulfill this mission by testifying that the
Lord is God and by living according to God's law. Persuaded by
Israel's example, the nations would turn to God voluntarily.
Chosenness is no justification for parochialism:

"It is too light a thing that you should be My servant
To raise up the tribes of Jacob and to restore the offspring of
    Israel
I will also give you for a light to the nations
That My salvation may be unto the ends of the earth" (Isaiah
    49: 6.)

In other words, it is not enough to ask: what is good for the
Jews? Israel must be concerned with what is good for humanity.

Some rabbis, particularly in the Reconstructionist movement,
have rejected the concept of chosenness as being too exclusive and
have substituted the belief that the Jewish people have *chosen* as
their vocation to bring nearer God's kingdom of justice and peace.
This should and could be the vocation of all peoples. Gunther
Plaut has responded by eliminating the claim to exclusivity from
chosenness: "If God willed Christianity, surely Christianity is part
of the ongoing process of revelation." How much of Christianity is
due to a direct apprehension of God, Plaut does not know, but
surely many Christians have been led to love by their covenant: we
need only recall Dr. King who found through his understanding
of Jesus the power to lead Blacks and Whites toward freedom and
equality. Plaut quotes the Jewish philosopher, Franz Rosenzweig,
who in his *Star of Redemption* viewed the Jewish people as the

center of the star keeping the fire of prophetic faith burning, while the Christians who have more influence in the world are the rays of the star bringing prophetic ideals into history. One need not accept Rosenzweig's delineation of roles, but it is significant that a major Jewish philosopher found that both Jews and Christians are "chosen" for essential roles in history. This recognition of two covenants has become the basis for much interfaith dialogue.

Rabbi Leo Baeck, a Holocaust survivor who refused to leave his people to their fate and who after the war came to the Hebrew Union College, wrote, "Every people can be chosen for a history, for a share in the history of humanity . . . But more history has been assigned to this (the Jewish) people than any other." Historian Ellis Rivkin has written that when we learn truths from history, we are discovering the ways of God. The Jewish people, through no fault or merit of their own, happen to have been a microcosm of human history that can provide lessons for all. For example, the Jews have persistently shown the triumph of the spirit over brute force. Many people have at times been scapegoats in disintegrating societies, but Jews, more than others, have endured such fate and should have learned from it. Our history should have taught us and others the necessity of interdependence, tolerance for diversity within unity, and the importance of economic opportunity and human rights for all.

Richard Rubenstein cannot understand how one can hold to the "chosen people" concept after Auschwitz. Rivkin's response is that God did not create the nation-state, chauvinism, or racism. These are human inventions. God's redeeming power was present at Auschwitz, but it was not in God's power to use it. This dilemma of theodicy, how could a good and powerful God allow absolute evil, is one of the issues to be examined in the next chapter as we explore the diverse paths to God that are possible within Judaism.

TOPICS FOR DISCUSSION

1. Some rabbis take stands, from the pulpit or in the community, on controversial political or economic issues. These rabbis may claim they are following in the tradition of Amos or Isaiah, who were quite specific in the policies they advocated for the sake of economic justice and peace among nations. However, congregants who strongly disagree with the rabbi's position may counter, "But you are not a prophet. Neither are you an expert in the economy or Middle East diplomacy. Please, Rabbi, preach on something spiritual." Is the congregant correct? If not, what might be the rabbi's response?

2. Do you believe that synagogues (or churches) should take stands on or advocate policies and programs when some (perhaps a sizable minority) of the congregants disagree?

3. Do you believe that the Jewish people are, in any sense, chosen by God? If so, what does such Chosenness mean? If not, are you still willing to read the prayer before the Torah reading that includes "*asher bachar banu*"—who has chosen us?

4. One function of the Covenant and Chosenness was to provide the Jewish people with a purpose for being. How would you state that purpose?

RESOURCES

Buber, Martin. *Moses.* New York, Harper & Row, 1958.

Heschel, Abraham Joshua. *The Prophets.* Philadelphia, Jewish Publication Society, 1962.

Kaufman, Yehezkel. *The Religion of Israel.* New York, Schocken, 1972.

Kaplan, Mordecai. "The Contribution of Judaism to World Ethics," in Louis Finkelstein (ed.), *The Jews, Their History, Culture and Religion*, Vol. II. Philadelphia, Jewish Publication Society, 1949.

Kaplan, Mordecai. *The Purpose and Meaning of Jewish Existence.* (Part Three) Philadelphia, Jewish Publication Society, 1964.

Plaut, Gunther. *The Case for the Chosen People.* New York, Doubleday, 1965.

Plaut, Gunther (ed,) with Bernard Bamberger. *The Torah: A Modern Commentary.* New York, UAHC Press, 1981.

Sandmel, Samuel. *The Hebrew Scriptures.* New York, Knopf, 1963.

Sarna, Nahum. *Understanding Genesis.* New York, Schocken, 1979.

4.

PATHS TO GOD

When someone says, "I believe in God," or "I don't believe in God," that tells me very little. One may mean, "I don't believe in a just and all-powerful Supreme Being who is watching over me." Neither do I, but in Judaism there are many ways of conceiving or experiencing God. In fact, this very wide spectrum of theological belief is a distinctive characteristic of Judaism. In this chapter we shall explore the major contemporary paths to God and will observe a trend from metaphysics to mysticism, from pondering what we mean by "God" to having a "spiritual experience."

When I was a rabbinic student in the 1950's, we explored four rather distinct paths to God within non-Orthodox Judaism: There was the "theistic absolutism" of Rabbinic Judaism and the contrasting theologies of Milton Steinberg, Mordecai Kaplan, and Martin Buber.

The most traditional view, "theistic absolutism," is the affirmation that there is a *Ribono shel olam*, a Master of the universe, Creator of all, who is aware of our innermost thoughts, all-powerful and perfectly righteous, and, of course, one and incorporeal(without body). For six centuries after the Bible was canonized, this belief was accepted on faith, based on the experience of the Jewish people at Sinai and on the personal encounter of prophets and psalmists. In Psalm 19, we read:

> The heavens declare the glory of God, the sky proclaims His
> handiwork
> Day to day makes utterance, night to night speaks out . . .
>
> The teaching of the Lord is perfect, renewing life
> The decrees of the Lord are enduring, making wise the
> simple
> The precepts of the Lord are just, rejoicing the heart;
> The instruction of the Lord is lucid, making the eyes light
> up.

The first major challenge to this faith came in the ninth century when Aristotle was translated into Arabic, and the better-educated Jews under Islam had to confront Aristotle's objections to traditional rabbinic belief. The Jewish response to the challenge of Aristotle produced the flourishing of Jewish philosophy best represented by Maimonides, known in Jewish tradition as Rambam (Rav Moshe ben Maimon). For Aristotle, God was impersonal, the Unmoved Mover needed to explain motion and co-eternal with matter. For Maimonides, God was also the Prime Mover, but since there is no way of knowing if God is the creator of all or is co-eternal with matter, Maimonides followed the rabbinic interpretation of Genesis One and affirmed that God created the world out of nothing. Maimonides's conception of God as the Force that makes for interdependence sounds quite contemporary:

"It is impossible for any organs of the human body to exist by themselves and yet be an organic part of the body. Similarly, it is impossible for one part of the universe to exist without the other parts, for all are interdependent. Now just as there is a force in man that unites the organs of his body, thus nourishing and sustaining and protecting them . . . so too, there is a *unifying force in the world that protects and preserves the components . . . I call this force God, blessed be His name."*

Maimonides referring to God as a "unifying force" may call to mind Einstein's intuiting Unity in the universal laws of causation. The Rambam's emphasis on interdependence provides a basis for viewing God as sanctioning cooperation and love. Maimonides did differ from the rabbis who believed that God was aware of the humblest, most ignorant individual. For the Rambam, God's providence extended only to those who had developed their rational souls. Consequently, the rabbis regarded Maimonides with ambivalence. They admired his collection of laws (*Mishneh Torah*), and included his Creed in the liturgy, even as they burned his greatest philosophic work (the *Guide to the Perplexed*).

Maimonides is known for his doctrine of negative attributes: We cannot ascribe any positive attribute to the essence of God, for this would imply that God is not one. If God is wise, then an aspect of God is other than wise. We may say that God is not ignorant. We may also state what God does, e.g., as creator. Before labeling this as medieval irrelevance, put it in your memory bank, for we shall return to these ideas when we discuss Kaplan and "predicate theology."

Fast forward to the twentieth century when we confront the most serious challenge to the traditional view: theodicy. This challenge is expressed in the dilemma: How could an all-powerful and perfectly just God allow so much evil in the world? For Rabbi Richard Rubenstein, one cannot possibly believe after Auschwitz in a perfectly righteous and all-powerful God. Elie Wiesel gave voice to his bitterness as he watched the emaciated inmates praising God on the eve of Rosh Hashanah:

"But why should I bless Him? In every fiber I rebelled.

Because He had thousands of children burned in His pits?
Because He kept six crematories working night and day, and
on Sundays and feast days? . . . How could I say to Him:
'Blessed art Thou, Eternal, Master of the universe, who
chose us from among the races to be tortured day and night,
to see our fathers, our mothers, our brothers, end in the
crematory? Praised be Thy Holy Name, Thou who hast
chosen us to be butchered on Thine altar?'"

To this angry outburst, Emil Fackenheim replied that we should
not blame God for what humans choose to do to each other:

" . . . free will was one of God's greatest gifts to man, and
God meant him to make good use of it. But God would not
force man to be good. If He did, then man's will would not
be free . . . There is nothing here that contradicts divine
omnipotence. God is able to prevent man from choosing
evil, but He does not do this . . . for a higher good. That
higher good . . . is human freedom."

This response is not adequate for those who wonder: Why
could God not have created the human species without the capacity for such horrific cruelty?

Even more difficult to explain is the dilemma of natural catas-
trophes, or physical evil. Fackenheim suggests that there is often a
hidden good in pain. If we cannot find such good, we must recognize, with Job, that our limited human minds are not capable of
understanding the mystery of God's ways. When Job demanded
that God justify the horrendous pain that he, a righteous man,
had suffered, "the Lord replied to Job out of the tempest" and
said:

"Who is this who darkens counsel, speaking without knowledge? . . .

Where were you when I laid the earth's foundations?
Speak if you have understanding
Do you know who fixed its dimensions
Or who measured it with a line?
Onto what were its bases sunk
Who set its cornerstone
When the morning stars sang together
And all the divine beings shouted for joy . . . (38:1-7)

"And Job said in reply to the Lord
I know that You can do everything
That nothing you propose is impossible for You
Who is this who obscures counsel without knowledge?
Indeed, I spoke without understanding
Of things beyond me, which I did not know . . .
Therefore, I recant and relent,
Being but dust and ashes." (42:1-6)

For Job this recognition of his limitations came only *after* God spoke to him out of the whirlwind. Therefore, our *experience* of God may convince us of God's reality more than does any philosophic reasoning.

Once Judaism became exposed to modern thought, some philosophers and rabbis could not accept the traditional concept of God with its unresolved paradoxes. Among the first of these rebels was Baruch Spinoza, who was excommunicated by the rabbis of Amsterdam in the seventeenth century. Spinoza did affirm the Unity of God and held that from that Oneness there emerges a natural order of causation that explains both physical and mental phenomena. God does not choose these laws of nature and human nature. God is the law. God's "power" is the causal connections within nature without which there would be no nature. God's "creativity" is the unfolding of reality in accordance with the natural law. To speak of God as good or evil is as inaccurate as speaking of God as circular or square. The good is that which will bring human beings maximum happiness. The most certain path to happiness is to understand the causes of our emotions so that they may cease to be passions and so become more within our control, so that our mind suffers less: "He who clearly and distinctly understands himself and his emotions loves God, and loves Him better the better he understands himself and his emotions." After we understand the links in the chain of causation, we may then gain an intuitive insight as to how all fits into one harmonious whole. This is the "intellectual love of God."

Because of Spinoza's apparent denial of free will in the usual sense, and because his God is limited both in power and in goodness, Spinoza has not had much direct influence on mainstream Jewish theology. However, Isaac Mayer Wise, architect of American Reform Judaism, shocked his colleagues when he stated that he believed in the God of Spinoza. Spinoza's emphasis on self-understanding may appeal to those who are psychologically oriented.

A more widely accepted understanding of God was that held by Milton Steinberg, Conservative rabbi of New York's Park Avenue Synagogue, who tragically died in 1950 at the age of 46. As was set forth in his posthumous volumes, *A Believing Jew* and *The Anatomy of Faith,* God is a Being who is aware of and cares about us, is responsible for the rationality of the universe, is the sanction for our moral sense, *but is limited in power.* God is the Power behind the evolutionary process but, being limited, is not able to move that process in the direction of reason and love as speedily as we might wish. If we view the human personality as evolving from lower to higher levels, then evil is the persistence of lower levels of being(e.g., narcissism) into higher levels. Because everything is not under God's control, human and natural tragedies occur. However, the evolutionary record is the saga of life's continuous victory over the earlier stages of restraints. On the personal level, this faith in a good God, limited in power, has been eloquently presented in Harold Kushner's widely read, *When Bad Things Happen to Good People.* Reform rabbis whose theological views are somewhat similar to that of Steinberg are Levi Olan, *olav hashalom*, and Jack Bemporad.

Steinberg insisted that while God is, in some sense, limited, God must, in another sense, be Absolute. He acknowledged the influence of theologian Charles Hartshorne who referred to God as both Supreme Being and Supreme Becoming. The Absolute aspect of God provides a ground for the cosmos and prevents total relativism. The Becoming aspect of God is God's power to make order out of the original chaos. Within the universe is chance and irrationality, but God is the Power that makes for order and reason. (Should you wish to learn how Steinberg was influenced by philosophers Alfred North Whitehead, C. S. Peirce, and Edgar Brightman, read *The Anatomy of Faith*.)

Steinberg wrote: "The concept of . . . the irrational . . . of the chance events that crop out of the normal stream of life, seems true to reality, acceptable to the afflicted, and consonant with the essential goodness of God. The concept of irrational evil prevents us from ascribing to God that which probably should not be ascribed to Him. God is exempted, not from the struggle, but from the responsiblity for the elements of chance in the universe . . . It must be admitted that if we deny to God responsiblity for *all* (author's emphasis*)*, we must at the same time admit that His power is limited and His perfection is not complete," but is becoming. Steinberg's theological perspective seems consistent with what has been called "process theology." This is the belief that reality is in a constant process of change. God is seen not as immutable, all-knowing, or all-powerful but rather as responding to all that is changing. God is manifest in the process of creation and the preservation of values. Should you wish to delve further into this theology, you may read *Jewish Theology and Process Thought,* edited by Sandra B. Lubarsky and David Ray Griffin. (See Resources.)

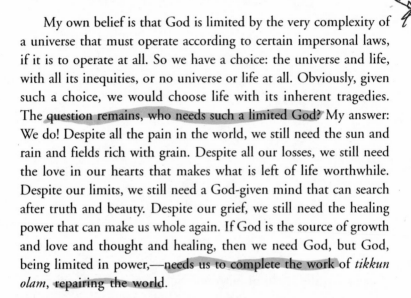

My own belief is that God is limited by the very complexity of a universe that must operate according to certain impersonal laws, if it is to operate at all. So we have a choice: the universe and life, with all its inequities, or no universe or life at all. Obviously, given such a choice, we would choose life with its inherent tragedies. The question remains, who needs such a limited God? My answer: We do! Despite all the pain in the world, we still need the sun and rain and fields rich with grain. Despite all our losses, we still need the love in our hearts that makes what is left of life worthwhile. Despite our limits, we still need a God-given mind that can search after truth and beauty. Despite our grief, we still need the healing power that can make us whole again. If God is the source of growth and love and thought and healing, then we need God, but God, being limited in power,—needs us to complete the work of *tikkun olam,* repairing the world.

A more radical reinterpretation of Jewish theology is that of the founder of Reconstructionism, Mordecai Kaplan. As a "transnaturalist," Kaplan believed that God is found *throughout* nature. God is the Power or Process that makes for "salvation" in this world. By "salvation," Kaplan meant "achieving an integrated personality" in which conflicting "impulses, appetites and desires" are harmonized. To achieve salvation, one found meaning, zest, and savor in life by using one's mind to achieve desirable ends. On the societal level, this implied a social order in which all will "collaborate in pursuit of common ends" that allow "the maximum opportunity for creative self-expression," in other words, self-actualization in a democracy.

Kaplan did not agree with Steinberg that God is a Being aware of us. For Kaplan, God is the Power that makes for salvation and is manifest in our tendencies toward authenticity (or truth), moral responsibility, love, and growth. These tendencies make up our soul. Had Kaplan stopped at this point, he would have been a religious humanist. However, he had the faith that our soul is linked to processes *throughout nature* that make for salvation. Because human nature is part of the cosmos, therefore, there must be something in the cosmos that is related to our deepest human needs. Obviously in nature there is growth, and there is interdependence, which in humans becomes moral responsibility. Also, Eros (the overcoming of separation) and natural law are related to love and truth.

So what? First, as individuals we are not alone in our efforts to achieve salvation. Kaplan compares humans to a magnetic needle: As the needle veers toward the north because of magnetism, so we veer in the direction of salvation because of the cosmic power throughout nature we call God. As Kaplan explained in *The Meaning of God in the Modern Jewish Religion,* to believe in God is to believe that reality, the world of inner and outer being . . . of society and nature, is so constructed as to enable us to achieve salvation. While God does give support, we have to do most of the work.

Kaplan's response to evil is similar to Steinberg's: "Nature is infinite chaos with all its evils forever being vanquished by creativity which is God as infinite goodness." God's power is inexhaustible but not infinite; therefore, the struggle continues.

Among the criticisms of Kaplan's theology is his lack of clarity regarding the Oneness of God. At times he writes of God as the "totality" of creative processes that make for salvation, but that is only a symbolic unity. However, Harold Schulweis maintains that Kaplan's God is *manifest* in the processes, which make up the *predicate* of God (what God does in contrast with who or what God is). We cannot know the subject or essence of the one God. This may remind us of Maimonides's willingness to write of what God does but not of what God is.

A more practical challenge that has been posed to followers of Kaplan is: How does one pray to a Process, or a Power not aware of us? Kaplan's response is: "When we address ourselves to God in prayers of petition, we raise to the level of consciousness those desires, the fulfillment of which we regard as a prerequisite to the fulfillment of our human destiny." His son-in-law, Ira Eisenstein, has responded, "We pray with our souls to our potentialities." In my view, for Kaplanites the petitionary prayer is less important than the faith that our striving for life and love and peace is not only dependent on our own efforts but is also supported by a Power throughout nature that is on our side.

The most radical reinterpretation of the God-concept is that of religious humanists, who unlike the transnaturalists, do not find God in fundamental processes of nature. For some humanists, God is a symbol of the best that human beings can become. When I was a rabbinical student, Rabbi Abraham Cronbach, through the inner glow of his personality, showed me that one can be a religious humanist and also have a very deep sense of spirituality. For Cronbach, God is not a discursive term but an emotive word, connoting the supreme importance we attach to the redemptive aspects of human experience, such as love, justice, beauty, and peace.

Humanistic Judaism, developed by Rabbi Sherwin Wine of the Birmingham Temple outside of Detroit, rejects the use of the term, "God," unless its meaning is a personal theism that affirms a God who is aware of us. Wine challenges Kaplan: "Why should perfectly rational human beings, who have at their disposal a host of English words more adequate than 'God' to describe the natural events they are interested in, feel emotionally compelled to rip a three-letter word out of its historic context in order to save it for their belief vocabulary?" Followers of Kaplan might respond first by noting that Rabbi Wine has ripped Judaism out of its historic context by affirming a Judaism without God. They might then go on to explain that for a pragmatist such as Kaplan, entities are defined either by what they do or by their functions. Therefore, in every age, God has always been whatever Power whose function is to make for salvation.

In 2000, the Society for Humanistic Judaism consisted of 20 congregations and 31 *havurot* (fellowships). Many communities develop their own services. Rabbi Wine's meditations use some Hebrew phrases (*e.g.,* *Baruch ha-or shel ha-olam,* Glorious is the light of the world; glorious is the light of humanity), and they include songs by secular Jews (e.g.,Tchernikowski's *Sachki,* which is paraphrased: "Rock, roar with laughter! I shall not change my faith in man . . ."). There are passages on such themes as beauty, happiness, honesty, love, peace, and reason. A Humanistic Congregation in Cincinnati applied to the Union of American Hebrew Congregations to be become part of the Reform movement, but was not accepted. Many of these humanists may agree with the ideas of Kaplan's transnaturalism or with Cronbach's religious humanism, but the services of Humanistic Judaism do not use theological terminology. They do not proclaim that God is one (*Shema*) or magnify and sanctify God's name (*kaddish*).

Perhaps the most influential non-Orthodox theologian of this century is Martin Buber. Born in Vienna in 1878, he was one of the existentialist philosophers who found truth not strictly through reason nor through the emotions but through the experience of dialogue, the encounter between one's entire self and the other. For Buber, there is no such thing as a totally independent entity, because each entity exists in relation to another. Therefore, fundamental to reality is relation.

The two primary relations are I-Thou (when the other is an end in him or her self) and I-It (when the other is regarded as an object to be used). I-It can be beneficial or harmful, as is obvious

when we meet each other's needs or use each other in family relations. However, if our existence is confined to I-It, we have missed
out on the real meaning of life: "all *real* living is meeting." The I-
Thou relation has certain characteristics:

1. Focusing on the other and not on the satisfaction we are
   receiving from the experience. As a child, Buber was in
   an I-Thou relation as he stroked his grandfather's mare,
   but when he became aware of the pleasure he was
   receiving, he was out of the relation. One knows one
   has been in the I-Thou experience by remembering it.

2. Being, in Buber's phrase, "fully present" before each other.
   This means not wearing invisible masks or being concerned with how we appear before others or even how
   we appear to ourselves. This does not mean always
   saying everything we feel but on not keeping up a
   pretense, on not being phony.

3. "Making present" for Buber enables us to imagine what
   the other is "wishing, feeling, perceiving, thinking,"
   and perhaps even experiencing the specific pain. Buber
   was engaged in a spiritual exercise when a young man
   called on him. Buber was so involved with own meditation that he did not fully focus nor was he totally
   present. When the man later committed suicide, Buber
   felt guilt over his failure to realize that the man had
   come not for a chat but for a decision. Soon Buber
   turned away from inner-personal spirituality and found
   God in the realm between I and Thou.

4. All this should lead to a "confirmation of being," the "yes
   which allows (us) to be and can only come from one
   human person to another." Once we are so open and
   empathetic, we are much less likely to be self-righteously

judgmental and much more likely to accept each other
as imperfect human beings.

One can understand why Buber is so appealing to modern
sensibilities that have been blunted by consumerism, the national
mall-aise, and both high and low tech. Still, it is legitimate to ask,
what has all this to do with God? If (as Buber believed) *relations*
(not independent entities) are fundamental to Being, then Being,
itself, may be considered the Eternal Thou that makes possible the
I-Thou relation. Further evidence for this faith is the fact that
millions of individuals have found life's deepest meaning in the I-
Thou relation. Many have had the sense that during those relations they were part of a cosmic Reality basic to Being. This can
occur not only through our encounters with people but also with
art and nature. One may now understand why Buber has been
labeled a "phenomenologist," i.e., his beliefs cannot be rationally
proved but depend upon others experiencing in the same way the
same phenomena.

Like all theologians, Buber faced the problem of radical evil.
His response was to speak of the "eclipse of God." Generally Buber
refused to write about the nature of God, because all images of
God are false. However, he did recognize that there are times when
God seems to be absent "because we do not let Him in." Could
not God enter the world without an invitation from us? Perhaps
that may have been Buber's meaning when he referred to a "cruel
and merciful" God: cruel, at times being only potentially present;
merciful, at times coming to us "through grace."

Buber had a special appreciation for eighteenth-century
Hasidism and the *kibbutzim*. (See Chapters 12, 20.) He saw both
movements as emphasizing the sense of community without losing the integrity of the individual. He promoted dialogue between
Arabs and Jews with faith that they could find a way of reconciling
two just claims. He did not accept the authority of Jewish law, as

he believed that once one was in the I-Thou relation, one would know what was required. He defined love as "responsibility in action."

In 1937, before Buber made *aliyah* to Palestine, he chose as his successor at the school for Jewish learning in Berlin, Abraham Joshua Heschel. Heschel found God in the relation between God and humans. He believed that the most fundamental religious attitude is wonder: "The most amazing fact is that there are facts." This sense of awe and radical amazement leads to the conviction that God, not humanity, is the subject of reality. We are creatures, and our purpose is to live in such as a way as to be worthy of being known by God.

Heschel is best known in this country, where in 1946 he began teaching at the Conservative movement's Jewish Theological Seminary as the mystically oriented rabbi who blended spirituality and social action. (See Chapter 17.) According to Heschel, the prophets identified with God's pathos, which "reveals the extreme pertinence of (humanity) to God. The prophet is keenly aware of this "divine attentiveness and concern . . . it is God's concern for (humanity) that is at the root of the prophet's work to save the people." For all of us, because God cares, so should we. When asked why he joined Martin Luther King on the March to Selma, Heschel replied, "I am praying with my feet."

Contemporary Jewish theology has moved from beliefs about God to the spiritual experience. Michael Lerner, editor of *Tikkun*, is the author of *Jewish Renewal*, an attempt to define the most recent movement that would rejuvenate Jewish life. Lerner, who considers Heschel his mentor, refers to God as "the Force that makes possible the transformation from what is to what ought to be." He believes that the universe pulsates with a spiritual energy of which most people throughout history have been aware and to which they have responded. He concludes that one is most authentically recognized by the other when one realizes what humans have in common, the pulsation through each self of God's Being and energy. In this sense God is a Force that is compassionate and caring and that points the way to a deeper level of meaning.

When Arthur Green was President of the Reconstructionist Rabbinical College, he wrote *Seek My Face, Speak My Name,* an attempt to go beyond Kaplan by way of Buber, Heschel, and the Lurianic Kabbalah. (See Chapter 12.) Green focused on the spiritual experience one could have in the midst of life, when confronting birth or death, or when feeling the wonder of nature, or in the midst of love. These experiences bring us closer to the hidden God, the source of all who is manifest in the flow of energy that makes life possible. As Schneur Zalman said, "The heaven and earth are garments of God." God is the cosmic oneness from which emerges diversity, but each distinct entity reflects the original oneness. Our attitudes and actions toward each other reflect our attitudes and actions toward God.

How does this latter-day Kabbalist deal with the dilemma of evil? The flow of life is morally blind, but God added compassion through the human spirit. We who reflect the primal oneness can help restore harmony to a broken universe through *tikkun olam,* repairing the world.

The most prolific and influential Jewish theologian affiliated with the Reform movement is Eugene Borowitz of the Hebrew Union College-Jewish Institute of Religion. In *Renewing the Covenant: A Theology for the Post-Modern Jew,* he indicates why he considers the philosophies of Kaplan, Buber, and Heschel to be incomplete. He does not believe that Kaplan can find a secure ground for moral values throughout nature, because cruelty is just as natural as love. He is more attracted to Buber and Heschel, who affirm the realm of the transcendent. However, he believes that Buber lacks a basis for commitment to the Jewish people, and he considers

Heschel's God to be so transcendent that the only law God prescribes is that of a strict Jewish tradition, without making sufficient allowance for individual choice.

Borowitz's own path is a "covenant theology" through which
the individual Jew interacts with God, the Jewish people, and all
of Jewish tradition. Once we have these encounters, we will "hear"
the *mitzvah* (commandment). If we are sufficiently attuned, we
will experience a God who creates the world, reveals Torah, chooses
Israel, rewards and punishes, and redeems us. Acccording to
Borowitz, modernist theologicans begin with the individual and
his/her reason and from there develop their concept of God. Post-
modernists consider the individual to be inseparable from God
and discover truth as that which emerges between God and people.
After the Holocaust, post-modernists became disillusioned with
the modernist's "belief that secular enlightenment would make
people ethically self-correcting." The post-modernist recognized
that inherent in the universe is "the value that makes a categorial
distinction between the S.S. death camp operators and their Jewish victims." (See Chapter 16.)

As a rabbi who has navigated these currents of theological
thought for half a century, I look back on the 1950's and 1960's as
having been more philosophically concerned with clearly contradictory views regarding responses to metaphysical and ethical issues. Within the past decade or two I sense a tendency to subsume
under the rubric of spirtual energy a large number of experiences
with varying degrees of emotional profundity. Still, I know of no
other religion that welcomes such a wide variety of theological
ideas and spiritual experiences. If one is searching for the security
of dogma, one will not find it in non-Orthodox Judaism. (For my
personal belief, see Chapter 22.)

Given such a wide range of paths to God, what, if anything,
do they all have in common? Each affirms the Oneness of God,

and Oneness implies God as pure spirit, being that any material form consists of parts. Each path rests on the faith that there is an objective basis for some moral standards. For Kaplan this faith is two-fold: that nature gives support to our highest values, and that humans (having tried other ways to satisfaction) conclude that life's deepest meaning is best achievable through love, truth, and moral responsibility. Borowitz affirms a transcendent realm of being from which issues a moral imperative. Borowitz also maintains that for the Jew the clearest direction will come only after he or she has become committed to an encounter with God, the Jewish people and Jewish law and lore.

Finally, whichever path one chooses, there is hope, based on the faith that deeper than our intellect and will there is a power that will help move us in the direction of life and love and peace. The words discovered on that cellar wall after World War II speak for most if not all of us at some time in our lives:

> "I believe in the sun, even when it is not shining.
> I believe in love, when feeling it not.
> I believe in God, even when God is silent."

TOPICS FOR DISCUSSION

1. Which of the following theological points of view has the most meaning for you? (You may choose more than one)

> 1) The belief in one incorporeal all-powerful and perfectly righteous God who is aware of us.
> 2) The belief in one incorporeal God who is perfectly good, aware of us, but limited in power.
> 3) God is the Power throughout nature that makes for our

this—worldly salvation of inner peace and creativity through love, truth, growth, and moral responsibility.

4) God is a symbol expressing the highest of human aspirations.

5) One experiences God through an I-Thou relation of openness, empathy, and love or through a sense of awe and wonder that there is anything at all.

6) When we encounter God and recognize God's covenant with the Jewish people, we realize what is morally required of us as Jews.

7) God is the Oneness behind all laws of nature and human nature. To understand these laws is to come closer to God and happiness.

8) God is experienced as the spiritual energy behind the surface of things, as the Oneness from which emerges our uniqueness which reflects that Oneness.

2. How would you respond to a parent whose child died at a young age and who asked, "How could God let this happen!" How would you respond to someone who asked: "How can one believe in God after Auschwitz?

3. Which of these experiences (if any) have enabled you to feel "closer to God" or have a spiritual experience:

1) Being aware of the wonder or beauty of nature

2) Being in an I-Thou relation with a loved one

3) Participating in a worship service

4) Joining with a group to protest moral evil or to advocate a just cause

(You may describe or elaborate.)

4. Which of the following needs (if any) does a belief in God fulfill for you?

1) Helps me make sense out of the universe

2) Gives me a foundation for moral values

3) Is a Power to whom I turn when my own powers are not enough

4) Gives me hope in the future

RESOURCES

Borowitz, Eugene. *Choices in Modern Jewish Thought.* New York, Behrman House, 1983.

Borowitz, Eugene. *Renewing the Covenant: A Theology for the Postmodern Jew.* Philadelphia, Jewish Publication Society, 1991.

Buber, Martin. *I and Thou.* New York, Scribner's, 1958.

Buber, Martin. *The Knowledge of Man.* New York, Harper & Row, 1965.

Fackenheim, Emil. *Paths to Jewish Belief.* New York, Behrman House, 1968.

Green, Arthur. *Seek My Face, Speak My Name.* Northvale, N.J., Jason Aronson Inc., 1992.

Hodes, Aubrey. *Encounter with Martin Buber.* New York, Penguin Books, 1975.

Heschel, Abraham J. *Man's Quest for God,* New York, Scribner's, 1956.

Hescchel, Abraham J. *The Prophets.* Philadelphia, Jewish Publication Society, 1962.

Kaufman, William E. *Contemporary Jewish Philosophies.* New York,

Reconstructionist Press, 1976.

Kaplan, Mordecai M. *The Meaning of God in Modern Jewish Religion.* New York, Behrman House, 1937.

Kushner, Harold. *When Bad Things Happen to Good People.* New York, Schocken, 1981.

Lerner, Michael. *Jewish Renewal.* New York, Grosset/Putnam, 1994.

Lubarsky, Sandra and David Ray Griffin (eds.). *Jewish Theology and Process Thought.* Albany, State University of New York Press, 1996.

Ochs, Peter. (ed.) *Reviewing the Covenant: Eugene B. Borowitz and the Postmodern Renewal of Jewish Theology.* Albany, State University of New York, 2000.

Soncino, Rifat and Daniel B. Syme. *Finding God: Ten Jewish Responses.* New York, UAHC Press, 1986.

Steinberg, Milton. *A Believing Jew.* New York, Harcourt Brace & Co., 1951.

Steinberg, Milton. *Anatomy of Faith.* New York, Harcourt Brace & Co., 1960.

Waskow, Arthur. *God-wrestling—Round 2.* Woodstock, Vermont, Jewish Lights, 1996.

Wine, Sherwin. *Humanistic Judaism.* Buffalo, Prometheus Books, 1978.

Yovel, Yirmiyahu. *Spinoza and Other Heretics: The Marrano of Reason.* Princeton, N.J., Princeton University Press, 1989.

5.

SYNAGOGUE AND *SIDDUR*:

THEN AND NOW

What's special about the synagogue and the *siddur* (the Jewish Sabbath and daily prayer book)? For openers, both are quite old. The earliest form of Jewish worship consisted of offering grain or animal sacrifices to God and the singing of psalms. This took place in the First Temple, from about 950 BCE until its destruction in 586 BCE. Among the earliest of these psalms were 92 ("It is good to give thanks to the Lord") and 93 ("The Lord is King, robed in grandeur"). They are still read or chanted to introduce Sabbath worship.

As a rabbinic student, I was taught that the first synagogues were probably in Babylonia. Did not Jeremiah say, "And seek the welfare of the city to which I have exiled you and pray to the Lord in its behalf; for in its prosperity shall you prosper."(29:7)? Today the scholarly consensus is that the first synagogues were established after the Jews had returned from Persia to Judea in 538 BCE. Once the second Temple was built (520 BCE), Ezra, in about 458 BCE, read to the people in Jerusalem from the Torah and explained its meaning. So for about 2500 years, study has not only been part of the service, but study was considered a form of prayer. As Louis Finkelstein, scholarly leader of Conservative Judaism(Chapter 16) was to say: "When I pray, I speak to God. When I study (Torah and its commentaries), God speaks to me."

In the second century BCE, the Pharisees wanted to make the Judean religion the concern of the entire people, not simply the priestly class in Jerusalem. So, while daily sacrifices were offered in the Temple, the Pharisees established the practice of Jews gathering in their own communities and reading portions from the Torah relating to animal sacrifices at the same time that those sacrifices were being offered in the Temple. From these communal gatherings, the synagogue developed. Eventually, psalms and prayers were chanted and the Torah was studied. Hence, the synagogue came to be known as a *Bet Ha-K'nesset*, *Bet Ha-Tefilla* and *Bet Ha-Midrash* (house of meeting, prayer, and study). Today's synagogues still fulfill those same functions.

By the first century CE, the prayers were arranged in a certain order (in Hebrew, *siddur*). The order, itself, expressed the theology of Rabbinic Judaism. After introductory psalms, public prayer began with the praise of God (the *Bar'chu*). Why? Because God is the source of the natural order in the universe ("who forms light and creates darkness . . . who brings on the evening twilight . . . changes times and seasons and arranges the stars in their watches in the sky"). One also praised God as the Source of the moral law ("Unending is Your love for Your people, the House of Israel. Torah, *mitzvot*, laws and precepts You have taught us").

These traditional prayers have been interpreted in a contemporary liturgy: "Let us imagine a world without order, where no one can predict the length of the day or the flow of the tide. Imagine a universe where planets leave their orbits and soar like meteors through the heavens and where the law of gravity is repealed at random. Praised be You O Lord, for the marvelous order of nature, from stars in the sky to particles in the atom. Let us imagine a world without love, a world in which the human spirit incapable of caring is locked in the prison of the self. Praised be You, O Lord, for the capacity to feel happiness in another's happiness and pain in another's pain. As the universe whispers of a Oneness behind all that is, so the love in our hearts calls on people everywhere to unite in pursuit of those ideals that make us human. As we sing of one God, we rejoice in the wonder of the universe, and we pray for that day when the human family will be one."

These prayers lead to the *Shema*, which I have understood as meaning: Hear, O Israel, the God of natural law and the God of moral law is one God. That flowers need sunshine and children need love are both principles of one Reality. These words of Malachi(2:10) have been interpreted by the rabbis to express the ethical implication of one God: "Have we not all one Father? Has not one God created us all? Why do we deal treacherously brother against brother?"

The "prayer-ology" continues, if we teach the commandments to our children and bring the commandments into our lives, then we will find *g'ulah*, redemption. As God did wonders for the Israelites by bringing them out of Egypt (when they sang, "*Mi-komocha*," who is like You, O Lord), so God will redeem Israel and humanity when the people learn to live according to the *mitzvot* of love and justice.

In the first-century CE, Simeon Ha-Pakuli set in order the *Tefilah*, on week days 19 blessings, which on the Sabbath are reduced to seven. The prayers of petition are omitted on Shabbat, so we should not nudge God too much. (Let the Almighty rest, too!) The first blessing (*Avot*) reminds us of the patriarchs, Abraham, Isaac, and Jacob. Some contemporary prayer books also recall the matriarchs, Sarah, Rebekah, Rachel, and Leah. In a broader sense, the *Avot* should help us recall and appreciate our entire Jewish heritage, which is the basis of all modern expressions of Judaism. The *Avot* has been interpreted as follows: "We are grateful for the heritage of Israel. In a world of warring gods, our people believed in one God whose law would unite all humanity in love. In a world of ignorance and superstition, they proclaimed learning to be worthy of sacred commitment. In a world of iniquity and injustice, they reminded the people never to oppress the stranger, for history had taught them how oppression feels. In a world that forced them behind ghetto walls, they found security in the warmth of family life. In a world where the sword was sovereign, they called on humanity to seek peace and pursue it. In a world where the masses often used them as scapegoats, they came to be skeptical of the popular platitudes of every generation . . . Let us affirm those values of the past, so sorely needed in every age."

The second blessing of the *Tefilah* praises God as the Power that can redeem us from suffering. According to Orthodox Judaism, this Power can "*m'hayay metim*," revive the righteous dead, body and soul. (See Chapter 8). The third blessing speaks of the holiness of God. *K'dushah* (holiness) conveys a sense of awe and mystery behind all that is. We are reminded that to be holy as God is holy requires us to bring into our lives love, justice, and truth. The fourth blessing would have us recognize the sanctity of Shabbat. (See Chapter 13.) The fifth and sixth blessings express the hope that our prayers are acceptable, and then give thanks to God for our many blessings. The seventh blessings, *Shalom Rav* in the evening and *Sim Shalom* in the morning, are prayers for a "great peace." In an interpretation taken from Reform Judaism's *Union Prayer Book* and included in *Gates of Prayer*, we read: "Grant us peace, Your most precious gift, O Eternal Source of Peace and give us the will to proclaim its message to all the peoples of the earth . . . Strengthen the bonds of friendship and fellowship among the inhabitants of all lands . . . Blessed is the Eternal God, the Source of peace."

The concluding portion of the service begins with the *Alenu:*
"We praise the Lord of all, the Maker of heaven and earth who has
set us apart from the other families of the earth giving us a destiny
unique among nations." In alternate versions of the *Alenu* in the
Gates of Prayer other, less particularistic wording is used. The *Alenu*
concludes with a prayer for universal peace: when humanity shall
be one family, "and then shall Your kingdom be established on
earth and the word of Your prophet fulfilled: 'The Lord will reign
for ever and ever' . . . On that day the Lord shall be One and
God's name shall be One."

The above overview of the *Siddur* should help the reader follow any Jewish service, although the English passages have been
taken from the *Gates of Prayer.* One reason for creating, in 1975,
the new Reform prayer book was implied in the previous chapter:
How can one have a prayer book which will enable Jews, who
differ in their theologies, to feel spiritually at home? The *Gates of
Prayer* attempts to resolve this problem by providing *ten* different
Sabbath-eve prayer services, some of which express theologies that
differ from traditional theism. There is even a service, called equivo-
cal, that uses the word, God, in Hebrew, but not in English. A
portion of that service, the *G'ulah* (redemption) reads as follows:

"We worship the power that unites all the universe into one
great harmony. That oneness, however, is not yet. We see imper-
fection, disorder and evil all about us. But before our eyes is a
vision of perfection, order and goodness: these too we have known
in some measure. There is evil enough to break the heart, good
enough to exalt the soul. Our people has experienced untold suffering and wondrous redemptions; we await a redemption more
lasting, and more splendid than any of the past . . . When will
redemption come? When we master the violence that fills our
world . . . when we grant to every person the rights we claim for
ourselves."

For worshippers who yearn for a more spiritual or mystical experience, there is another service in which the blessing of *kedushah*, holiness, is rendered in English: "A time can come to us when our hearts are filled with awe: suddenly the noise of life will be stilled, as our eyes open to a world just beyond the border of our minds. All at once there is a glory in our souls! *Ha-El Ha-Kadosh*—the Holy God! O majestic Presence! O World ablaze with splendor!"

Keriat Ha-Torah. Since the time when Ezra read the Torah to those Jews who had returned from exile, Torah reading and interpretation have been part of the Jewish service. "Without knowledge, how can one pray?" asked Judah HaNasi. If the purpose of prayer is to help bring God's law into our lives, then we must study to understand the meaning of that law for ourselves and the community.

The Torah has been read on those days when there was a large congregation: on Sabbath and festival mornings and also on Mondays and Thursdays, market days when farmers would come into town. Because in Reform synagogues the largest congregation usually gathers on Shabbat eve, the Torah may be read or chanted on Friday evening as well as on Saturday morning. There is a designated portion, or *parasha*, to be read or chanted each week. This is followed by the *haftarah*, a selection from the prophets in some way connected with the passage just read from the Torah. The term, *haftarah*, means "dismissal," and suggests that at one time the service concluded with the prophetic lesson.

Each worshipper has a prayer or prayers he or she considers most meaningful. For me, the *Hashkivenu* helps resolve whatever tensions I am feeling: "Cause us, O Lord, our God, to lie down in peace and raise us up, O Sovereign, to life renewed . . . Spread over us the shelter of Your peace . . . Blessed is the Lord, whose shelter of peace is spread over us, over all the people Israel and over Jerusalem."

TOPICS FOR DISCUSSION

1. Which kind of prayer do you find most meaningful: thanks-giving, praise of God, or petition?

2. Given the different ways that non-Orthodox Jews may be-lieve in or experience God, how do you think this theological di-versity can be respected in one prayer book?

3. Of the prayers in the *siddur* used by your congregation, which do you find most meaningful?

4. Of the three functions of the synagogue (house of meeting, study, prayer), which has the most significance for you?

5. When you pray, do you believe that God is aware of your thoughts? If you do not believe that God is aware of your thoughts, what meaning do you find in your prayers?

6. Do you believe it is important to include in the *siddur* prayers that Jews have said or sung for centuries, even if you do not accept their meanings?

RESOURCES

Bemporad, Jack(ed.). *The Theological Foundations of Prayer*. New York, UAHC Press, 1967.

Hoffman, Lawrence. *The Art of Public Prayer: Not for Clergy Only*. Washington, D.C., Pastoral Press, 1988.

Millgram, Abraham. *Jewish Worship*. Philadelphia, Jewish Publication Society, 1971.

Wigoder, Geoffrey. *The Story of the Synagogue: A Diaspora Museum Book*. San Francisco, Harper & Row, 1986.

Zeitlin, Solomon. *The Rise and Fall of the Judaean State*. Vol. I. Philadelphia, Jewish Publication Society, 1978.

HELLENISTIC PERIOD

JEWISH HISTORY	RELEVANT WORLD HISTORY
333: Alexander conquers Judea.	334-323: Alexander the Great, defeats Persia, rules Near East.
301: Judea under rule of Ptolemies, based in Egypt.	301: Empire divided between Ptolemies and Seleucids.
Jewish community in Alexandria.	Rise of the Roman Empire.
Parts of Bible translated into Greek.	223-187: Antiochus III leads Seleucids in war with Rome.
201: Judea under rule of Seleucids, based in Syria.	
	176-165: Antiochus IV.
171:Antiochus installs Hellenist Onias as high priest. Brother Lysimichas raids Temple treasury. Jews riot. Antiochus returns from Egypt to massacre Jews.	
169: Anti-Hellenists install Joshua as high priest.	169: Antiochus invades Egypt again and is captured by the Romans.
168: Antiochus desecrates Temple.	
167: Mattathias leads revolt. Judah takes command.	
165: Judah defeats Lysias. Temple is dedicated (*Hanukkah*).	165: Antiochus killed in Parthia.
163: Jews given religious freedom.	165-2: Antiochus V (Lysias guardian).
	162-150: Demetrius I.
161: Judah killed in battle for political independence.	
161-144: Jonathan, high priest.	146: Rome takes control of Greece.
143: Under Simon, Judea becomes an independent state.	
Pharisees challenge priest-party, Sadducees, for leadership.	
76-67: Rule of Salome Alexandra; Pharisees control Sanhedrin, which interprets religious law.	
	63: Roman General Pompey captures Jerusalem.

JEWS DURING THE ROMAN EMPIRE

JEWISH HISTORY	RELEVANT WORLD HISTORY
	48 BCE: Julius Caesar defeats Pompey.
37-4 BCE: Herod installed by Rome as king of Judea.	44: Julius Caesar assasinated.
32: Hillel, Pharisaic leader.	
	31 BCE: After civil war, Augustus becomes emperor.
6 CE: Roman government rules Judea.	
20 BCE-50 CE: Philosopher Philo in Alexandria.	14-37 CE: Tiberius, Roman Emperor.
26-36: Pilate is Procurator.	
30: Crucifixion of Jesus.	
40: Paul preaches salvation through Jesus Christ.	
66: Agrippa II, king of Judea.	
66-70: Revolt against Rome. Destruction of Second Temple.	
73: Fall of Masada.	69-79: Vespasian, Roman Emperor.
70's: Sanhedrin meets in Yavneh.	About 70: Gospel of Mark written.
	79-81: Titus, Roman Emperor.
90: Gamaliel II leads Sanhedrin; core of liturgy established.	117-138: Hadrian, Roman Emperor.
132-5: Revolt against Rome, led by Bar Kochba, fails.	
140: Jews flee destruction in Jerusalem for Galilee.	
170-217: Judah I is patriarch of Sanhedrin. Mishnah compiled.	
250-350: Rabbinic academies established in Babylonia at Sura (Rav) and Pumbeditha (Shmuel).	
	306-337: Constantine makes Christianity religion of Empire.
	344-407: St. John Chrysostum attacks Jews as Christ-killers.
350: Completion of Jerusalem Talmud.	

	400-470: Fall of Roman Empire.
500: Completion of Babylonian Talmud.	

PART TWO:

JUDAISM AND CHRISTIANITY: JESUS AND PAUL, GUILT AND DEATH

6.

THE PARTING OF THE WAYS: JESUS, PAUL

AND THE RABBIS

When I was a student in elementary school in Houston, I was told to play the part of a shepherd in the Christmas pageant. It was merely a supporting role, but I was willing. Our main musical number was "Away in a Manger." I told my mother that I sang the entire song with one exception: When I was to sing, "I love thee Lord Jesus," I just moved my lips. The point is that Jewish children, from a very young age, become aware that they are part of a minority religion. One may react to this realization with a sense of inferiority or with pride. I became a rabbi.

Both Jews and Christians should recognize and understand both the similarities and differences between their faiths. Discussion of Jesus, Paul, and the Rabbis can raise sensitive issues. Some may be reluctant to speak freely for fear of offending those who do not share their faith. With respect for religious differences, we will examine: 1) why most Jews in the first century CE did not believe in Jesus as Christ (Messiah); 2)what some rabbis believe about Jesus today; and 3) how Paul led to the parting of the ways. We will also suggest that some "aesthetic" Christians may be closer to Judaism than they realize.

JEWISH SECTS AT THE TIME OF JESUS

To understand how Jesus was similar to and different from the Jews of his time, we must first know something about the Jewish sects of the first century CE. The oldest sect was the Sadducees (*Zadukim*). They can be traced back to the priests who ruled Judea during the fifth-century BCE. After the Persians had defeated the Babylonians who had sent the Jews into exile, King Cyrus of Persia, in 538 BCE, allowed Jews, under the leadership of Zerubbabel, to return to Judea. The Temple was rebuilt and priests who claimed to be descended from Aaron established a theocracy. Some scholars credit the Sadducees with adding a priestly layer to the Torah and then compiling the first five books of the Bible. It was probably these priests(at times, called "Aaronides") who introduced Yom Kippur as a day of atonement. Because they believed that the reason the Jews had been forced into exile was that they had not followed the *mitzvot* (commandments), they wanted to establish a way that Jews could obtain forgiveness by atoning, and thus prevent any exile in the future. They believed that animal sacrifice was essential for atonement. The Sadducees accepted as literally true only the first five books of the Bible (the"Written Torah"). Therefore, they believed that God rewarded the righteous and punished the wicked in this world, but they did not have faith in the resurrection of the body after death or in the coming of a messiah. They were supported by large landowners and were concerned with the preservation of the Temple cult. So their leaders, at times, collaborated with the Roman authorities to protect their own interests.

Some time in the second-century BCE, there emerged a group

of scholars (often called "scribes") who believed that new conditions required new laws. When in the fourth-century BCE,
Alexander the Great defeated the Persian Empire, including Judea,
he brought with him Hellenistic civilization. The Greeks introduced commerce. This meant, for example, that if Jews were to
participate in the new economy, the Biblical law requiring the
cancellation of debts every seven years would have to be abrogated.
The legal scholars who justified such changes came to be called
"Pharisees" (*Perushim,* or Separatists). The basis for their right to
change, reinterpret, or add to the Written Torah they found in the
Written Torah, itself. Deuteronomy 17:8 states that if a case is
baffling, the Israelites should appear before the levitical priests, or
the magistrate (the legal authority) in charge at the time, and
accept his decision. The Pharisaic reinterpretations came to be called
Torah she-baal peh, or Oral Law.

In 63 BCE, Pompey led the Romans into Judea. By this time
the Pharisees had become the dominant party. Unlike the
Sadducees, the Pharisees believed in the resurrection of the dead
and in the coming of the *Mashiach* ("the anointed one" or messiah), a divinely sent human leader descended from the house of
David, who would free the Jews from the rule of Rome and usher
in an age of peace when all the Jews in exile would return to Jerusalem, and all people would recognize the sovereignty of God.

A smaller group, known as "apocalyptic Pharisees," expected
the messiah to be a divine-like being who would destroy all sin-
ners from the face of the earth. The judgment day would be followed by the resurrection of the dead, who would be part of a new
order of Being some called "the kingdom of God." One could be
assured of entering the kingdom by being a forgiving, compassionate, and selfless person. Also expressing this altruistic ethic
were individual pietists (*Hasidim Ha-rishonim,* "the first pious ones")
who considered the *thought* of sinning to be a sin, in itself.

Another sect was the Essenes (*Tzenuim*, humble or pious ones) who formed their own separate communities lest they become spiritually contaminated by the masses. Property belonged to the community and was shared in an equalitarian spirit. The Essenes believed that whatever happened was divinely ordained, and they considered it unjust to own slaves. The communes were often made up of older men who had already fulfilled the commandment of having two children. The Essenes believed that the souls of the righteous would enjoy eternal life but did not believe in the resurrection of the body. They were very strict in the observance of the Law and put great emphasis on ritual immersion. Possibly John the Baptist was an Essene who considered immersions or baptism to signify that one had, through righteous actions, been cleansed from sin.

Finally, there were the Zealots (*Kannaim*). Labeled by Josephus as the "fourth philosophy," they wanted to take up arms against the mighty Roman Empire. They could not imagine that a just God would allow such suffering and so, they reasoned, once the people began the rebellion, God would be on their side. After the Jews rebelled against Rome (64-70 CE), the Zealots at Masada were the last Jews to resist. They committed suicide rather than submit to slavery.

The Qumran community, described in the Dead Sea Scrolls, has been considered by some scholars to be an offshoot of the Essenes who shared the militarism of the Zealots. Like the Essenes, they strictly observed the Law, engaged in ritual immersion, and participated in solemn communal meals. They considered themselves to be the faithful remnant who would lead the sons of light against the sons of darkness as a prelude to the messianic age. This age, to be heralded by two messiahs, would begin forty years after the death of a "teacher of righteousness."

WHY WE CANNOT BELIEVE

As was stated in Chapter 3, almost all Jews at the time of Jesus could not accept him as the messiah, because he did not do what Jews expected of their messiah: to restore the Davidic monarchy and bring peace on earth. On the contrary, Jesus predicted that the "time is fulfilled and the kingdom of God is at hand." This Jews understood to mean the age-to-come that was being predicted by visionaries of the time, when the wicked (including the Roman Empire) would fall, and the righteous would be resurrected and live forever with God. As Morton Scott Enslin has expressed the message of Jesus, "In soberest verity, despite its strangeness to modern ears, the end of the world was at hand." Because this prediction did not come true, most Jews did not consider Jesus to be the messiah.

Christians have re-interpreted the phrase, "kingdom of God," to refer to an inner kingdom, or a state of being that would assure the believer of salvation, or a gradual amelioration of the world. Not only Jewish but non-Jewish scholars such as Enslin and Schweitzer do not accept such re-interpretations. The phrase in Luke (16:20) "the kingdom of God is within you," can as easily be translated "in your midst"—that is, imminent, about to happen. Another fundamental difference between Jewish and Christian understandings of Jesus is the Christian faith that the messiah would be God incarnate, the literal embodiment of God on earth, while for Jews the messiah was to be a human being sent by God.

Of course, Christians look to the Gospels as the foundation of their faith. However, Jews do not accept the Gospels as a reliable factual record of historic events. This is hardly surprising, since most modern Christian scholars recognize that the Synoptic Gospels (Mark, Matthew and Luke) were completed from 40 to 70 years after the death of Jesus by writers who were firmly convinced that Jesus was the messianic son of God. These writers presented accounts that were just as contradictory as were the first two chapters of Genesis. For example, in Matthew 1:1-17, the genealogy of Jesus is traced from David's son, Solomon, all the way to Jacob, father of Joseph. In contrast, in Luke the genealogy is traced from David's son, Nathan, all the way to Heli, father of Joseph. This hardly phases fundamentalists who may claim that Heli was Joseph's father-in-law. Because the Gospel authors knew that Jews expected their messiah to be in the wonder-working tradition of Elijah and Elisha, one may have expected the Gospels to include legends about Jesus that were reminiscent of the Elijah and Elisha stories.

WHAT WAS JESUS REALLY LIKE?

A reasonable conclusion might be that given the date of the documents, the social and political conditions, and the faith commitments of the authors, it is impossible to derive from the Gospels a clear picture of Jesus. Still given the enormous importance and impact of Jesus of Nazareth, both Christian and Jewish scholars have gone on the quest for the historical Jesus. Both Enslin and Albert Schweitzer portray Jesus as a charismatic visionary who predicted the end of the world but who agreed with the Pharisees that there are two laws, the Written (five books of Moses) and the "Oral" interpretations that should be followed by all Jews. As my teacher, Ellis Rivkin liked to explain: the priestly Sadducees (who understood the Torah literally) told the people what God *said,* while the Scribe/Pharisees told them what God *meant.*

If one considers the Sermon on the Mount to reflect the beliefs of Jesus, then he accepted the two levels of law and believed that if one did not change a "jot or tittle" of the law but followed it faithfully, then one would be assured of eternal life and eventual resurrection of the body together with the soul. What, then, of the changes in the law that Jesus seemed to advocate in the Sermon on the Mount? (Matthew 5) Both Enslin and Rivkin agree that Jesus was following the Pharisaic practice of interpreting the law to meet new conditions. In the Sermon, Jesus, in stating that divorce was possible only in the case of adultery, was following the stricter interpretation of rabbinic law as advocated by the "house (i.e., disciples) of Shammai."(See Chapter 10) In considering simply the *thought* of adultery to be a sin, Jesus was reflecting the early Hasidim's view that thinking about a sin is a sin. Perhaps he believed that such strictness was necessary if one was to prepare for the imminent coming of God's kingdom.

However, his major difference with the Pharisees (and the probable reason for their friction) was that Jesus was taking it on himself to make the interpretation ("You have heard it said . . . but I say unto you"). For the Pharisees this was spiritual hutzpa. Neither Jesus nor the Scribe/Pharisee was entitled to take it on himself to change the law or expound it in his own name. For any interpretation of the law to be valid, it was necessary to go through the appropriate legal procedures, specifically the Pharisaic *Bet Din Hagadol* (Great Court, later known by the Greek name, Sanhedrin).

The more specifically one delineates the portrait of Jesus based on Gospel stories, the shakier is one's historical ground. Rivkin tries to resolve the problem by relying primarily on the information the Jewish historian Josephus gives us about the Jewish setting at the time of Jesus, particularly regarding the various sects that were active and that he must have encountered. Almost a century before Jesus, the Pharisees believed that so long as Rome did not interfere with Jewish religious practices, Rome's political authority should be obeyed. That is, the Jews should, as Jesus was to say, "Render to Caesar what is Caesar and to God what is God's." There is no way the Pharisees would have brought Jesus to trial for claiming he was the messiah. There were others who made such claims and were allowed to preach their hearts out. The trial, as-

suming there was one, had to be held before an *ad hoc* Sanhedrin,
the type occasionally summoned by the priestly Sadducees whose
interests were linked to the Roman Empire. Not wanting to an-
tagonize Rome, the Gospel editors made sure that Pilate (the cruel
procurator and symbol of Rome) washed his hands of the whole
affair. Jesus was executed by the Romans for a political crime. The
Roman authorities made no distinction between charismatics who
preached that Rome would fall as a result of God's intervention
into history, and those Zealots who urged armed rebellion. These
rebels against the Empire were regularly executed by crucifixion.
The inscription, "king of the Jews," and the placing of the cross of
Jesus between two condemned revolutionaries is further evidence
that the Jew of Nazereth was considered a subversive political threat
to Rome.

It must be emphasized that any portrait of the historical Jesus
is speculative. Josephus does convince all but the utterly skeptical
that there was a Jesus, for he mentions, in passing, that James was
"the brother of Jesus, called the Christ." Josephus would surely
not have made such a reference unless his readers were well aware
that Jesus was a charismatic who claimed to be the messiah. Rivkin
adds that were it not for the messianic claim and the crucifixion,
there could have been no belief that Jesus was resurrected. This
belief was understandable: the authors of the Gospels were so committed to the faith that Jesus was the messiah that they could not
accept his death as final, especially because they were already convinced that resurrection would be the inevitable future of the righteous.

True, the more one attempts to "fill in the portrait," the more
problematic the conclusions. Still, given what the "intertestamental"
literature tells us about the smaller Jewish sects at the time of
Jesus, it is difficult not to continue "the search." The Sermon on
the Mount is well known for its advocacy of utter selflessness ("whoever smites you on your right cheek, turn to him the other also,

and if any man would go to law with you and take away your coat, let him have your cloak also." (Matthew 5: 38-45) This is quite consistent with the views of certain "apocalyptic Pharisees," as well as the *Hasidim Harishonim*. (See above) The Hasid is defined in *Pirke Avot* 5: 13, as one who says, "What is yours is yours and what is mine is yours." The apocalyptics in *The Testament of the Twelve Patriarchs* wrote:

> "Love you one another from the heart and if a man sin against you, speak peaceably to him . . . and if he be shameless and persists in his wrongdoing, even so, forgive him from the heart."

These Jesus-like sayings were spoken or written some decades before Jesus by those Jews who may well have believed that to have a share in the kingdom of God, one must be utterly selfless. As Jesus is quoted as saying, "If you would be perfect, go, sell what you have and give to the poor, that you shall have treasure in heaven, and come follow me . . . Verily I say to you . . . it is easier for a camel to go through the eye of a needle than for a rich man to enter into the kingdom of Heaven."(Matthew 19: 21-24)

The philospher of Cultural Zionism, Ahad Ha-Am, stated that a major difference between Judaism and Christianity is that Judaism advocates a literal interpretation of "Love your neighbor AS yourself," meaning that one's neighbor is of equal worth with oneself, and therefore has an equal right to self-fulfillment. In contrast, Christianity holds that one's neighbor's rights and needs are *more* important than your own, and you must place his needs over yours if you are to have a share in the Kingdom of Heaven. I would suggest this difference is overstated. Consider that the Roman Catholic doctrine of the just war is hardly a selfless ethic; rather, is it based on an ethic of equality as it implies that one's right to live and let live is more fundamental than the other's right to take one's life and liberty from you. Furthermore, Jewish Hasidic lit-

erature of the eighteenth and nineteenth centuries contains eloquent expressions of altruism (As we are all of one soul, if one
afflicts one's neighbor, one is punishing oneself. See Chapter 12).
Still, it may be accurate to state that the *emphasis* in Jewish ethics
is on equality while the emphasis in Christian ethics is on selflessness. However, both values are found in both traditions and each
of us must reconcile the two in our own lives.

Finally, our focus on the differences between the beliefs of Jesus
and the Pharisees may make us forget that their areas of agreement
are more far-reaching and fundamental. Not only did both Jesus
and the Pharisees hold to the belief in the two realms of law(written
and oral) and in a future of bodily resurrection, but their basic
ethical positions were remarkably or perhaps not so remarkably
similar. Jesus is known for warning, "Judge not that you be not
judged . . . why behold the mote in your brother's eye but consider not the beam in your own eye?" From 40 to 30 BCE, the
Pharisaic leader, Hillel, said, "Do not judge your fellow until you
have come into his place." When asked to summarize all of Judaism while standing on one foot, Hillel said, "What is displeasing
to you, do not do to your neighbor. That is the entire Torah. Now
go and study."(Compare the "golden rule" of Jesus) Also, Jesus
gave a Pharisaic response to the question, "Which is the greatest
commandment in the Law?" "Hear, O Israel, the Lord, your God,
the Lord is one, you shall love the Lord your God with all your
heart, with all your soul and with all your mind, and you shall
love your neighbor as yourself."

As for the personal qualities of Jesus, many of his words indicate a gentle and compassionate man. Again, remember, his biog-
raphers were devotees who lived forty to seventy years after his
death and had elevated him to a divine level. Surely, he must have
had enormous charisma and the words ascribed to him were eloquent. He did make one clearly false prediction, that the kingdom
of God was at hand, and he probably believed that he was either

the herald of that age or the messiah, himself. Perhaps just before his death he realized that he was not the messiah. Rivkin suggests that this realization gave special poignancy to his last words on the cross, "My God, My God, why have You forsaken me?"

HOW PAUL LED TO
THE PARTING OF THE WAYS

After the crucifixion, there was no rush to record the life of Jesus, because his followers expected him to return any day. Surely the Hellenistic Jew, Paul, had such an expectation, when, according to *Acts*, he believed he saw the resurrected Jesus on the road to Damascus. While Paul has been considered the first "Christian theologian," he viewed himself as Jewish. Still, his ideas made for an unbridgeable chasm between the two faiths.

According to Samuel Sandmel, it was the "genius of Paul" to blend his own personal needs with concepts from Greek, Jewish, and Persian thought until he arrived at a synthesis that not only satisfied him but appealed to millions in the Mediterranean world. Paul first turned to Jews in the Diaspora and preached that God's promise of a messiah had been fulfilled. For reasons stated above, almost all Jews rejected this message. So eventually Paul turned to the Gentiles and came to feel that the law that had guided his life was not a help but a hindrance. That's putting it mildly; listen to what he told the *Romans*:

7:7-18: "What shall we say then? Is the law sin? God forbid. Howbeit I had not known sin, except through the law: for I had not known coveting except the law had said, Thou shalt not covet . . . Sin dwelleth in me, for I know that in me, that is, in my flesh dwelleth no good thing: for to will is present with me, but to do that which is good is not."

According to Sandmel's interpretation, the law told Paul what he should not do, but did not give Paul the *power* to turn from his evil ways. Paul found the power to change his inner being through his faith that the redeemed Christ would cleanse his body from the stain of what came to be called original sin. Only then would he be assured of eternal life.

Given Paul's philosophic context, he could well have turned to the Hellenistic Jewish philosopher, Philo-Judeas, who also had a somewhat skeptical view of the law as not sufficient for salvation (even though he insisted on following it as the best human approximation to divine truth). Philo accepted the Greek notion of dualism between mind and body. The body was the source of evil, and the mind strove to free itself from the body and achieve communion with God. This was to be accomplished through the *Logos,* that aspect of God that could be apprehended by man. While Paul did not use the term, *logos,* he did believe that there was an aspect (or an off-shoot) of God that could be apprehended by humans. According to Sandmel, Paul took the decisive step of asserting that an aspect of God took the human form of Jesus, "and, in consequence, the Christ (Messiah) Jesus was really a divine being . . . Paul does not deify Jesus; rather he humanizes the divine Christ." One identified with Christ through baptism and the eucharist. This vicarious atonement was another departure from Judaism, which did not believe that through death and resurrection one person could achieve salvation for another.

This latter belief—so strange to modern ears—was not at all strange at the time of Paul, when millions of desperate people were joining mystery cults that promised salvation through the death and re-birth of gods. The cult from which Christianity seemed to borrow most freely was that of Mithras, the sun god who engaged in a struggle against a great and evil bull. By slaying the bull, Mithras made the earth fertile. Mithras was born of a virgin, a

birth witnessed by a few shepherds. Being a sun god, Mithras regarded Sunday as holy. December 25th, just after the winter solstice, was a time of elaborate rituals celebrating Mithras. After his death he was mourned in liturgy and placed in a sacred rock tomb called "Petra" from which he was removed after three days in a great festival of rejoicing. The appeal of Christianity may have been even more enhanced by its claim to be the *only* way to salvation, and to be based not on a myth but on a historic personage. Add to the Greek and Persian elements the powerful message of Jewish ethics transmitted through Jesus, and it is hardly surprising that Paul was preaching a message that had enormous appeal to millions in the Mediterranean world.

Some Christian theologians did not accept Paul's idea that "in (the) flesh dwelleth no good thing." In the sixteenth century, Arminius rejected the concept of original sin with its pessimistic view of human nature. In the late nineteenth century, liberal Protestant theologians saw Jesus as a progressive reformer dedicated to bringing a this-worldly kingdom of God, an age of social justice, and peace on earth. Von Harnack tried to separate this prophetic kernel of Jesus from dogmas like incarnation and resurrection which he viewed as pagan or Greek intrusions.

I detect a Jewish response to this liberal interpretation of Jesus in the writing of Joseph Klausner. In his work, *Jesus of Nazareth* (1922), Klausner presented Jesus as a progressive Pharisee concerned with moral principles rather than strict observance of the law. He praised Jesus for transmitting Jewish ethics to millions but insisted that Jesus departed from Judaism when he rejected Jewish peoplehood. Then, in 1935, Claude Montefiore went so far as to state that Jesus was totally Jewish. It was Paul who created Christianity by changing the function of the messiah from the herald of peace to the deliverer from the state of sin. While Jesus did not bring peace on earth, he did give eloquent expression to the prophetic dimension of Judaism and was worthy of admiration. However, added Montefiore, Jesus was not original. There was nothing in his message that had not been earlier stated, whether by the prophets who proclaimed a coming age of peace or by Hillel who stated the golden rule, or by the first century Hasidim who preached the ethic of selflessness.

However one evaluates these interpretations, it is striking that what seems to have happened is a hidden dialogue between Jewish and Christian scholars before the modern age of dialogue that began in the 1960's. This perhaps unintended exchange continued as Schweitzer in his *Quest for a Historical Jesus* insisted that Jesus was announcing that God was about to intervene into history to bring about the end of the world as we know it. Still, as part of this scenario, Jesus insisted, in Schweitzer's phrase, on an absolute "reverence for (all) life." The analog to Schweitzer is the scholarship of Solomon Zeitlin who first placed Jesus in the context of the apocaplyptic Pharisees predicting God's kingdom.

The German Protestant theologian, Rudolf Bultmann, asserted that it is both possible and necessary to interpret the New Testament *myths* in existential terms. A myth is a religious story which is in principle incapable of verification. Its truth can be found in certain insights that it embodies. For example, the historic Jesus has been transformed by faith into the mythological proclamation of a divine pre-existent being who became incarnate, died for the sins of men (and women), was raised from the dead, and whose return in triumph was shortly expected. While we can never know what really happened, still there has to be some continuity between the myth and the historical Jesus. This continuity does not require the Christian to accept as a matter of historical fact that Jesus was resurrected after he died.

So what *is* the truth embodied in the myth? Facing despair and death, we are all in need of divine intervention (Bultmann); the Fall of man is a symbol of our estrangement from authentic existence, but we are redeemed from estrangement through Love that is inherent in the Ground of Being, that is, in God. According to Paul Tillich, this unconditional love was expressed in the mythic portrait we find of Jesus in the Gospels. Tillich's assumption seems to be that some symbols are more adequate than others, and Christian symbols are the most adequate.

If these are the views of some Christian clergy and laypersons, then we are faced with a startling development in interfaith dialogue. Some of us may no longer be disagreeing over matters of substance. Do we not all want to overcome estrangement from authentic existence? Do we not all want to find the love that is at the Ground of Being? We Jews can look to Buber and the eighteenth-century Hasidim for more than ample resources to lead us in these directions. Could Jews differ from these unconventional Christian theologians not about contradictory facts or ideas but about which symbols to use?

Should this analysis be correct, if a significant portion of the scholarly and lay Christian community no longer believe in a literal sense that Jesus was God incarnate but that his divinity has certain symbolic meanings, then the ideological differences between Judaism and what I have called "aesthetic Christianity" become much reduced—a prospect that may not be welcomed by all Jewish or Christian clergy. Could it be that many of our non-Jewish neighbors do not accept the core theology of Christianity but, as Andrew Greely suggested in the *New York Times Magazine*, appreciate the Gospel's deeply human and humane stories? If that is the case, then they may be more Jewish than they imagine. Put differently: these "aesthetic Christians" may think Jewish while they still feel Christian. Still, let us not underestimate the power of symbols, even though their meanings might be universally embraced.

TOPICS FOR DISCUSSION

1. Which of the following beliefs about Jesus has meaning for you?

> 1) God came to earth as Jesus of Nazereth.
>
> 2) Jesus is the messiah.
>
> 3) Jesus was crucified and resurrected so that those who believed in him would be saved from sin and receive salvation.
>
> 4) Jesus, more than any other human, expressed and lived according to the highest ideal of love and, therefore, can be considered divine.
>
> 5) While the historic accounts in the Gospels cannot be verified, the truth of the Gospels is in their insights: facing despair and death we need the grace of God; the "fall of man" indicates our falling away from authentic existence; and we are redeemed through love that is fundamental to the Ground of Being.
>
> 6) God was manifest in Jesus just as God was present in the lives of other great moral leaders such as Gandhi and Martin Luther King, who lived according to the highest ideal of love.
>
> 7) Jesus was a visionary who predicted the end of the world yet who demonstrated a deep reverence for life.
>
> 8) Jesus was a charismatic human leader who preached the ethic of selflessness.

2. Rank the following kinds of behavior according to what you believe is the highest moral ideal. (1 for the highest; 4 for the lowest.) Give reasons for your responses.

1) To be totally selfless and always to place the well-being of others above one's own needs.( )   *4*

2) To fulfill one's own needs and aspirations while at the same time to do all in your power so that others will have the same opportunity for fulfillment as do you.( )   *1*

3) To be free to choose your own way to fulfillment so long as you do not interfere with the freedom of others to choose their way.( )   *2*

4) To act in accordance with one's own enlightened self-interest. ( )   *3*

RESOURCES

Cook, Michael. "The Start of the Rift," in *Keeping Posted*, New York, UAHC, December, 1973.

Enslin, Morton Scott. *The Prophet from Nazereth.* New York, McGraw-Hill, 1961.

Hook, Sidney(ed.). *Religious Experience and Truth.* New York, NYU Press, 1961.

Jacob, Walter. *Christianity through Jewish Eyes.* Cincinnati, Hebrew Union College Press, 1974.

McGrath, Alister. *The Making of Modern German Christology.* (Chapters 3 and 6: Harnack, Bultmann and Tillich.) New York, Basil, Blackwell, Inc., 1986.

Rivkin, Ellis. *What Crucified Jesus?* New York, UAHC Press, 1997.

Sandmel, Samuel. *Judaism and Christian Beginnings.* New York, Oxford University Press, 1978.

Sandmel, Samuel. *The Genius of Paul.* New York, Schocken, 1970.

Zeitlin, Solomon. *Who Crucified Jesus?* New York, Harper & Bros., 1947.

7.

COPING WITH GUILT

We have all heard the expression "Jewish guilt." Some may prefer the acronym, JAG, Jewish-American Guilt, which implies that Jewish Americans are more likely to carry around a guilt trip than are other Americans. Is this true or false? From a theological perspective, we must say, false. Judaism does not lay on us Paul's idea that our flesh is evil or the Augustinian sense of original sin. In contrast to Paul's warning to the Romans that "with the flesh is the law of sin," the rabbis said that when Hillel was taking a bath, he was performing a *mitzvah*, because the body is the temple of the soul. While medieval Christian tradition prohibited sexual intercourse Friday through Sunday (the days of the crucifixion and resurrection), the rabbis considered sexual union within marriage on Shabbat eve to be a double *mitzvah*. Of course, most mainstream Christian denominations today no longer accept this medieval attitude toward sexuality. Even the doctrine of original sin has been reinterpreted by some to mean alienation from our authentic being; modern Christians can also reinterpret.

Still it is worth noting that for centuries traditional Judaism has had comparatively healthy attitudes toward sexuality, e.g., it was the husband's obligation to satisfy the wife within a schedule

determined by his occupation and the number of days he would
be home. An anonymous Spanish Kabbalist of the 13th century
provided some remarkably specific sexual counsel in his *Iggeret
Hakodesh* (Letter of Holiness):

"Engage her first in conversation that puts her heart and mind
at ease and gladdens her. Speak words which arouse her to passion,
union, love, desire and Eros—and words which elicit attitudes of
reverence for God, piety and modesty. Tell her of pious and good
women who gave birth to fine and pure children. Speak with her
words, some of love, some of erotic passion, some of piety and
reverence. Never may you force her, for in such union the Divine
Presence cannot abide. You are not then in harmony and your
intent is different from hers. Quarrel not with her nor strike her in
connection with the act. Rather win her over with words of gra-
ciousness and seductiveness. Hurry not to arouse passion until her
mood is ready. Begin in love and let her semination take place
first."

There were exceptions to this welcoming of sexual union within
a loving marriage. Maimonides, perhaps influenced by Aristotle's
strict separation between body and soul, wrote, "We ought to limit
sexual intercourse altogether, hold it in contempt and desire it
only rarely . . . The act is too base to be performed except when
needed." The mainstream view is that of Nachmanides who rebut-
ted the *Rambam:* "The sexual union is holy and pure . . . whatever
(the Lord) created cannot possibly be shameful or ugly . . . When
a man is in union with his wife in a spirit of holiness and purity,
the Divine Presence is with them." David Biale, in his analytical
work, *Eros and the Jews*, perceives an ambivalence in Jewish literature toward sexuality, a tension between its affirmation and its
repression.

The larger point is that our rabbis did not believe that our
flesh was evil or that we were born in original sin. Some said we are
born essentially good (our soul comes "pure from Thee"), but be-

cause of the temptations of life, we make the wrong choices and so commit sins. Others implied that we are born neither good nor evil but with the capacity to choose. When we choose to go against the Moral Law, we have sinned, but that is no reason to despair being that we were not born "in sin." For the rabbis, sin was an act, not a state of being. Therefore, we do not have to be "re-born" in order to be cleansed from some primal evil.

For some rabbis, we sinned, because we did not channel the *yetzer hara,* the so-called "evil inclination" to constructive ends. I say "so-called" because the rabbis stated that the "evil inclination," having been created by God, is actually good, because without it no one would build a house, marry, or have children. In other words, this *yetzer* is made up of our sexual and aggressive impulses that are later channeled by the *yetzer hatov,* "the good inclination." Comparisons with Freud's id and super-ego may be overdrawn, but one wonders if Freud was familiar with this aspect of rabbinic literature.

Once we recognize where we have fallen short, we do not need some miraculous intervention through the grace of God, We *do* need to follow the process spelled out on Yom Kippur: *Teshuva,* repentance; *Tefila,* prayer; and *Tzedakah,* right action. (See Chapter 13.) God knows we will not become perfect, but if we go through this spiritual process to the best of our ability we will be forgiven, meaning, we need not go around with a guilt trip.

Given this rather down-to-earth approach, why do we hear so much about JAG? Perhaps this alleged Jewish guilt flows less from the theology of sin than from the psychology of some Jewish families. Contrast the film, "The Brothers McMullen," which deals with the guilt for violating the tenets of their Roman Catholic faith, with the works of Woody Allen, or Philip Roth, whose characters are struggling to become emancipated not from Jewish religious belief but from their stifling Jewish families. Some young

Jews (and, of course, non-Jews as well) may feel guilty for not
living up to the unrealistic expectations of their parents. One Jewish adolescent said to his highly successful father, who had grown
up poor: "You were lucky. You had nowhere to go but up."

Obviously, none of us is morally perfect. All of us have some
habits that are harmful to ourselves or to others. Maybe we are
addicted to smoking. Maybe we are so addicted to our work that
we do not have sufficient time for our family. You fill in the blanks.
For many of us these same problems hang on year after year. Some
may have become cynical about our capacity to affect any significant change. However, according to the *Unetaneh Tokef* prayer on
the High Holydays, we are able to relinquish harmful habits and
become more loving through repentance, prayer, and right action.
(See Chapter 13.)

Repentance begins by saying the most difficult sentence in
the English language, "I was wrong." We may have a tendency to
blame others, as Aaron did after the Israelites had worshipped the
Golden Calf. When Moses turned to his second-in-command and
asked, in effect, how could he have let this happen?, Aaron blamed
the people ("You know this people is bent on evil"). Then he blamed
the fire: "I hurled (the gold) into the fire and *out came* this calf"
(Exodus 32:21-4).

For Jews who have trouble recognizing their sins, our liturgy,
like Gilbert and Sullivan's Lord High Executioner, has "got a little
list"(the *Al Het*): two sins for each letter of the alphabet. Note that
the confessional reads "*hataNU*"—"for the sin that WE have sinned
against Thee." The traditional list reflects what medieval Jews considered the most serious sins. In some modern prayer books sins
committed against the earth, the poor, minorities, etc. are included.
Each of us is to search our souls and ask ourselves, which of these
sins have I committed? The pronoun, "We," also suggests that
even if *I* have not committed a particular sin, I do have an obliga-

tion to work toward the creation of a society where such sins as violence and prejudice will disappear. As Abraham Heschel wrote, "Some are guilty, all are responsible."

There are those who instead of denying their sins become obsessed by them. They face a different kind of challenge. When children develop emotional problems, how many parents have wondered, "Where did I go wrong?" Such questions often have no answer, as the factors that go into a child's personality are so many and varied, including psychological, physiological and cultural. The Hasidim said that the reason the *Al Het* is written in alphabetical order is that just as there is an end to reciting the alphabet, so there should be an end to dwelling on our sins. Within the *Al Het,* there is confession for the sin we commit *bli daat* and *bishgaga*, without knowledge and in error. This refers to acts that were harmful though at the time we had no knowledge that any harm would be caused. According to a strict interpretation of the Hebrew word, *het* ("missing the mark"), such an act is still a sin, but not one for which we should be blamed, particularly if we acted out of love and without understanding the consequences.

Some of our more rebellious rabbis held God partly responsible for our sins. Levi Yitzhak of Berditchev had the hutzpah to say to God, "We'll forgive you for this miserable world if You'll forgive us." The *Zedi (*Grandfather*)* of Shpole pleaded with God: "Don't think of man's sins, I beg of You. Think rather of his good deeds. They are fewer, I agree. But You must admit they are more precious. Believe me, it isn't easy to be good in this world. And, if I didn't see with my own two eyes that man, in spite of all obstacles, is capable of kindness, I would not believe it. And so I ask of you. Don't be harsh with Your children; rare as it may be, it is their kindness that should surprise You."

Repentance includes not only knowing and admitting where we went wrong, but understanding *why.* Once we understand the causes of our missing the mark, then *we do become morally responsible for what happens in the future.* We need not only insight but *Tefilah* (prayer) that will open us up to a Power deep within ourselves that makes for a fulfilling and loving life. In the previous chapter we noted that Paul did not believe that reason and willpower could turn us away from sin, so he looked for a supernatural act of grace. For the Hasidim, the response was not an either-or but a blending of enormous effort and what the Taoists called "creative quietude," trusting in help from God. This spiritual attitude was made clear in a Hasidic parable:

> "The souls descended from the realm of heaven to
> earth, on a long ladder. Then it was taken away. Now, up
> there, they are calling home the souls. Some do not budge
> from the spot, for how can one get to heaven without a
> ladder? Others leap and fall and leap again, and give up. But
> there are those who know very well that they cannot achieve
> it, but try and try over and over again until God catches
> hold of them and pulls them up."

The test of *complete* repentance is our capacity to be in the same situation as we were when we did wrong but this time to act in the *right* way. This turning from preoccupation with the sin to *tzedakah* (right or just acts) has been captured by the words of Isaac of Ger: Rather than brood over our wrongdoing, we should be "stringing pearls for the joy of Heaven." None of us will achieve perfection, but if we, to the best of our ability, engage in the process of repentance, prayer, and right action, then we may feel "forgiven."

What, then, of our ability to forgive others? Remember Hillel: "You shall not judge your fellow until you have come into his place." Because you can never be exactly in another's place, it is not for you to judge his or her moral worth. You cannot possibly know all the pressures he or she was under. Nor can you know what you would have done if you had the very same personal history. This does not mean condoning harmful or destructive behavior. Still, as for making a judgment on the moral worth of the perpetrator, let us leave the judging to God. It is God who knows the pressures we were under, how hard we struggled to overcome them, how free we were to rise above our pain.

There are extreme cases. Simon Wiesenthal lost 89 relatives in the Holocaust and saw his mother for the last time when she was crammed into a freight car with hundreds of other elderly Jewish women. Wiesenthal posed the issue of forgiveness through his story, *The Sunflower*. As a prisoner in a Polish ghetto near Lemberg, Simon was forced to do menial work in a nearby hospital. On the way to the hospital Simon would pass a cemetery where German soldiers were buried, and over each grave was a sunflower that seemed to link the dead to nature. Simon knew that for the murdered Jews there would be no sunflowers. At the Hospital a nurse asked him: "Are you Jewish?" When he said "yes," she took him to a dying SS soldier who had a guilty conscience because of the crimes he had committed against Jews and others. The soldier confessed to Simon how he had followed orders to facilitate the murder of 300 Jewish women and children in retaliation for the killing of 30 Germans. With almost his last breath, the officer pleaded with Wiesenthal for forgiveness. Wiesenthal responded with silence.

Years later, uneasy about his response, Wiesenthal invited both Jewish and Christian theologians to comment on the challenge posed by the story. Abraham Heschel pointed out that according to Jewish tradition one cannot forgive a criminal for what he did to someone else. The murdering officer would have to be forgiven by the dead, and that was impossible. According to Catholic theologian, Jacques Maritain, it would have been better if Wiesenthal had forgiven the SS soldier in the name of God. However, we Jews do not dispense God's forgiveness. In reality, most war criminals have remained defiant and unrepentant. In France, Klaus Barbie, who carried out the Nazi orders to deport Jews, tried to excuse himself by pointing to others who cooperated with ruling authorities. But some heinous crimes are beyond the power of human forgiveness. There are those of whom we may say, paraphrasing Shakespeare, Leave them to Heaven.

Meanwhile, let us not allow cases of extreme cruelty to make us unforgiving in our daily lives. The people who wronged us are not war criminals. They are probably ordinary folks like you and me who make mistakes, who at times crumble under pressure. There may have been reasons of which not only you but they were unaware. Let us give each other the benefit of the doubt. Maybe we should add to the *Al Het,* for the sin we have sinned against Thee by being overly critical and unforgiving.

TOPICS FOR DISCUSSION

1. Do you believe there is any difference between the sources or reasons for Jewish and Christian guilt? If so, what is that difference?

2. Which of the following do you believe? Give reasons for your belief. a.) Humans are born in a state of sin and need to be redeemed through the grace of God. b.) Humans are born morally neutral, and their ethical direction depends primarily on their experiences after birth. c.) Humans are born with certain innate tendencies (e.g., aggression and sexuality) that need to be channeled in a constructive, creative, and ethical direction. d.) Humans are born essentially good and, given sufficient security and love, will develop into moral persons.

3. How would you have answered the German soldier who pleaded with Wiesenthal for forgiveness?

4. What are some of the sins you commit against yourself?

5. When you do something you later realize was wrong, do you feel guilty? If so, how do you deal with your guilt?

RESOURCES

Biale, David. *Eros and the Jews.* New York, Basic Books, 1992.

Kook, Abraham. *The Lights of Penitence.* NewYork, Paulist Press, 1978.

Moore, George Foot. *Judaism in the First Centuries of the Christian Era.* Vol I , Part III (Man, Sin, Atonement). Cambridge, Harvard University Press, 1944.

Steinsaltz, Adin. *The Thirteen Petalled Rose.* (transl. by Yehuda Hanegbi.) New York, Basic Books, 1980.

Steinberg, Milton. *Basic Judaism.* New York, Harcourt, Brace & World, 1947.

Wiesenthal, Simon. *The Sunflower.* New York, Schocken, 1976.

8.

COPING WITH DEATH

There is a connection between coping with guilt and dealing with death. Religion has been defined as how one deals with one's finitude, with those existential limits all humans experience simply because they are human. As we all fall short of moral perfection, we can expect to feel some degree of guilt, a consequence of our finitude. Because we are all bound by our mortality, something in us would want to overcome that ultimate limitation, also a consequence of our finitude. It is only human to wonder: What will happen to me after I die? Will my loved ones go"to heaven?" If there is personal immortality, is it for everyone and, if not, who qualifies? How does one achieve "salvation?"

When the Hebrew Bible was written, *y'shuah* (salvation) was a this-worldly reward for righteous living. When David pleaded, "Save me, O Lord," he meant, Save me from the Philistines. After death, one went to Sheol, the netherworld. There one lived an ethereal shadowy existence. Psalm 88 poses the rhetorical question: "Are Your wonders made known in the netherworld, Your beneficent deeds in the land of *oblivion*?" (Another translation:"in the land of forgetfulness," i.e., where one forgets and is forgotten.) In his scholarly work, *Judaism and Immortality*, Levi Olan concludes that in Sheol all the faculties of the soul are suspended and there is no consciousness. Job (26:6) identified Sheol with Abaddon (destruction). He bemoaned his future fate:

> For there is hope of a tree,
> If it be cut down, that it will sprout again . . .
> But man dieth, and lieth low . . .
> Till the heavens be no more, they shall not awake,
> Nor be roused out of their sleep (Job 14:7, 10,12).

That this was not the only Biblical belief about Sheol is made clear by Daniel Syme and Rifat Soncino in *What Happens after I Die?* They point out that Isaiah (14: 9-11) predicts, when the wicked king of Babylon will die, Sheol will be astir, "the shades of all earth's chieftain . . . all the kings of nations. . . . *shall speak up* and say to you, You have become like us." (The Syme-Soncino text includes eight contemporary rabbis' personal beliefs about immortality).

In Biblical times, there was a belief in *communal* immortality, as the Israelite *people* would live on. Recall Ezekiel's vision of the Valley of the Dry Bones that represented the tribes of Israel who would come together again after the exile. (Ezekiel 37) There is one Biblical passage that expresses belief in resurrection for some. In Daniel, a book dated in the second century BCE, the author wrote: "Many of those that sleep in the dust of the earth will awake, some to eternal life, others to reproaches, to everlasting abhorrence." (12:2) Still, for almost all of the Biblical period, the Israelites found little or no solace in personal immortality. That is why the words of Psalm 90 are so powerful:

"We bring our years to an end as a tale that is told. The days of our years are three-score years and ten or even by reason of strength four score years; yet is their pride but travail and vanity; for it is speedily gone and we are in darkness (or, fly away). So teach us to

number our days, that we may get us a heart of wisdom." Because
life is so fleeting, we had better use our years wisely and make the
most of every moment allotted to us.

The Bible does assume that there is reward and punishment
in *this* life. However, we all know highly moral human beings who
have suffered greatly or who died prematurely. The deeper question is: Recognizing the inequities of life, does one who develops
the capacity to care and be fair find more satisfaction and meaning
in life than one who lives as a self-absorbed narcissist?

In the first century BCE, when the Pharisees became dominant in Judea, they no longer felt bound (as did the Sadducees) by
a literal understanding of the Torah and so could accept ideas not
found in the first five books of the *Tanakh*. Believing in God as an
all-powerful and perfectly righteous Being and having experienced
horrendous persecution, they could not imagine that this life was
all there was. They came to believe that the soul lived on after
death and would eventually be reunited with the body.

Among the rabbis there were widely differing views as to just
what happens to the body and soul after death. For some, when a
person dies, the soul retains a relationship with the body for one
year. After the body disintegrates, the soul (unless it is from a
totally righteous person) goes to Gehinnom (purgatory or hell)
and is purged of its sins. Then these souls go to Gan Eden ("garden of Eden," or paradise). When the messiah comes, the bodies
of the righteous will be re-united with their souls and will live
forever in the *olam haba* (world to come); that is, they will be in
paradise for all eternity. What will happen in paradise is a matter
of rabbinic fantasy. One rabbi's view of heaven is that the righteous would study Torah with God as the teacher. Another rabbi,
perhaps a gourmet, pictured paradise as a great feast, with food
provided by a mythical fish (Leviathan) and fine old wine, from
grapes preserved since the days of creation. The more "pure" pic-

ture of paradise was that of Rav who said, "There is neither eating nor drinking nor any sensual pleasure in the world to come, but the righteous with their crowns sit around the table of God, feasting upon the splendor of His majesty." Rav Johanan admits that we just don't know.

What of the wicked? Some imagined that God (like Gilbert and Sullivan's Mikado) would "let the punishment fit the crime." Those who had let their hair grow long to adorn themselves for sin would hang by their hair. Those who had perfumed themselves to sin would hang by their noses. Those who had stolen and robbed would hang by their hands. However, it was generally believed that *only the totally wicked would stay in Gehinnom forever.* On this both the house of Hillel and the house of Shammai agreed. They also agreed that the totally righteous would have life everlasting. As for those, practically the entire human family, who are both good and bad, Shammai believed that they would go to Gehinnom and then come up to be healed, while the more lenient Hillel believed that those who were both good and bad would go directly to paradise. There were even rabbis who said "there will be no Gehinnom in future times." The point is that we need not worry about eternal damnation. Perhaps that is why rabbis do not give "hellfire and damnation" sermons.

Without the threat of hell hanging over us, why be good? The Mishnah declared that "the reward of the good deed is the good deed and the punishment of evil is evil, itself" (*Avot*: 4:2). Even though resurrection was a tenet of rabbinic Judaism, the rabbis put their emphasis on life in this world. As a midrash tells us, "Whoever despises the good life in this world diminishes himself."

Who qualifies for eternal life? There is a passage in the Mishnah that holds that one who denies bodily resurrection, or the belief that the Torah is from God, or who is an *apikoros* (unbeliever) will be denied a place in the world to come. That is but one opinion.

Another holds that "all Israel has a portion in the world to come." The assumption seems to be that everyone will repent, and God will welcome all the penitent. Rabbi Joshua insisted that "the righteous of all nations have a share in the world to come." (You don't have to be Jewish to be "saved.")

The philosophers and the Kabbalists offered variations on the theme of resurrection. Maimonides, influenced by the Greeks who made a clear distinction between the lowly body and the exalted soul, held that when the messiah comes, all who had rational souls would be resurrected with their bodies, but their bodies would later die and only their souls would live on with God. Some Kabbalists believed in *gilgul* (transmigration) of souls. Those who were not sufficiently righteous in this life would be reincarnated in another body and then another, until they had become righteous enough to qualify for the world-to-come.

It is worth noting the similarities and differences between the Paulinian way to salvation and that of the rabbis. Both believed that purging of sin and atonement were prerequisites for salvation. However, for Paul and early Christianity, atonement could only be achieved through faith in Christ. He died on the cross to free humanity from their state of original sin. (Recall Chapter 6.) This redefinition of the function of the messiah was quite foreign to Judaism, which believed neither in original sin nor in vicarious atonement (i.e., one person atoning for another). For the rabbis the way to personal salvation was through the *mitzvot.* Jewish men were obligated to observe the 613 commandments in the Torah. Jewish women were not required to follow those positive commandments (you shall do . . .) that had to be done at a specific time. Non-Jews were obligated to follow the basic humanitarian laws based on the covenant made between God and Noah. The rabbinic consensus was, salvation is according to deed, not creed.

Today, while the ideas of *Gehinnom* and *Gan Eden* are considered folklorish speculation about an unknown world, Orthodox Judaism does hold firmly to the faith in *Tehiat Hametim*, the resurrection of the body after death. Many Jews are surprised at this traditional view, because from the modern pulpit they may have heard very little about consciousness surviving the grave, much less the soul being reunited with the body. The reason for such this-worldliness is that there has been a gradual humanizing trend in Jewish beliefs about immortality. It began with Moses Mendelssohn's best-seller, *Phaedon,* an eighteenth-century attempt to demonstrate by reason the immortality not of the body but of the soul. Mendelssohn used the traditional argument that a perfect God would not allow the soul to be destroyed. He added that the soul, by definition, is pure spirit, and because spirit cannot be divided into parts as can matter, it cannot be destroyed. This is another way of stating that the gap between mind and matter is fundamental, that pure mind cannot be reduced to or explained by even as complicated a mass of matter as the human brain. Therefore, while the belief that the body will be reconstituted does go against natural law, the belief that the soul will live on apart from the body is consistent with the view that mind cannot be reduced to matter. This hope in the immortality of the soul has been retained in the Reform Jewish liturgy.

Today, non-Orthodox rabbis may speak of the "immortality of the spirit." This may give rise to a naturalistic or humanistic view of immortality. For large numbers of Jews, faith in the immortality of the soul, aware of itself, is, shall we say, "iffy." What is not "iffy" is the effect we have on the life about us, for better and for worse. You may remember Frank Capra's classic film, "It's a Wonderful Life." In a somewhat sentimental way the movie dramatizes what an enormous difference it would have made to so many lives if the character portrayed by Jimmy Stewart had never lived. We need not be "heroic" to have impact on children, patients, customers, clients, friends . . . and how we affected them may well influence the way they affect others, and so on and on through time.

Not all effects are positive. In *Fathers,* a memoir in the form of a novel, Herbert Gold worked through his ambivalence toward his father, the grocer. Young Herb thought that he had successfully rebelled and separated himself from the compulsive bourgeois grocer, but eventually he realized how like his father he was. From his father and his Russian grandfather who lived through pogroms, Herb had absorbed the sense that the world is a scary place, and one must keep moving ahead to be safe. Herb found that to be a professional writer was just as scary and uncertain as being a struggling grocer. Herb's father felt he was only as good as his balance sheet while Herb felt he was only as good as his last book. How many of us have thought that we had, through rebellion, declared our psychic independence, only to find we were still more influenced by our parents than we had imagined! I would suggest that the most helpful resolution is to confront the past with total honesty, to remember both the good and the bad times, to understand what is behind our anger (if there is anger), to forgive our parents for what was beyond their control, to be grateful for the resources they have given us, and to go forward.

Jewish tradition gives us rather precise instructions as to how to go forward. The *Hilchot Avelut* (laws of mourning) are based on a wise insight: it is helpful for us fully to express our grief and then to turn gradually, step by step, back to life. (For the specific customs, see Chapter 10.) Of all the mourning customs none has more meaning than "saying *kaddish.*" This is a prayer in Aramaic that praises God and prays for the time when God's kingdom will be realized here on earth. There is no mention of death in the *kaddish,* but it does call on the mourner to return to life. The inner meaning of the *kaddish* has been eloquently expressed by Rabbi Soloveitchek: "Through the *kaddish* we hurl defiance at death and its fiendish conspiracy against man. (We) declare: No matter how powerful death is, notwithstanding the ugly end of man, however terrifying the grave is, however nonsensical and absurd everything appears . . . we declare and profess publicly that we are not giving up, that we are not surrendering, that we will carry on the work of our ancestors . . . that we will not be satisfied with less that the full realization of the ultimate goal: the establishment of God's kingdom . . ."

The overwhelming consensus in Judaism is that the way to whatever one means by heaven or salvation is a life of loving and righteous deeds. This is the underlying theme of "If Not Higher," a short story by the great Yiddish writer I. L. Peretz:

Every Friday morning before saying the *selichot* prayer (recited the month before Rosh Hashanah), the Rabbi of Nemirov would disappear. He was nowhere to be found. The people in his village would explain his mysterious absence by saying that the Rabbi had gone to heaven. A visiting Jew from Lithuania(a Litvak) was skeptical and ridiculed the gullibility of the townspeople. To prove how foolish they were, the Litvak hid beneath the bed of the rabbi all Thursday night. Early Friday morning, before the town was awake, the rabbi arose, disguised himself in the garb of a peasant and left his house. As the Litvak followed, the rabbi went to the forest on the outskirts of town and with an axe began chopping wood. He brought the wood to an ailing woman, too weak to fix her fire, too poor to pay for the wood. The rabbi kindled the fire and assured her that God would take care of any payment. So the rabbi went from house to house anonymously helping those in need. The Litvak followed the Rabbi of Nemirov, at first secretly. Then he became his disciple. Peretz concluded his story:

"And ever after, when another disciple tells how the Rabbi of Nemirov ascends to heaven at the time of the Penitential Prayers, the Litvak does not laugh. He only adds quietly: 'If not higher.'"

TOPICS FOR DISCUSSION

1. Which of the following beliefs about retribution, if any, do you accept? a. Those who live according to the principles of love and justice are more likely to find meaning and happiness in this world than are those who violate these principles. (b) Those who live good and loving lives on earth will be rewarded in their eternal life. (c) Those who live evil and selfish lives on earth will be punished in their eternal life. d. In order to find salvation in a life after death, one must accept Jesus as Christ (messiah)

2. Which of the following beliefs about immortality do you accept? Why? (a) I believe that my consciousness (awareness of myself) survives the grave. b) I believe that after I die, I will see my loved ones who have already died. c) I believe my body will at some time be re-united with my soul d) I believe I will live on in the effect I have on other lives.

3. Compare the English translation of the *kaddish* with "the Lord's prayer."

RESOURCES

Gillman, Neil. *The Death of Death: Resurrection and Immortality in Jewish Thought*. Woodstock, Vermont, Jewish Lights, 1997.

Gold, Herbert. *Fathers: A Novel in the Form of a Memoir*. New York, Random House, 1966.

Moore, George Foot. *Judaism in the First Centuries of the Christian Era*, Vol. II, Part VII (The Hereafter), Cambridge, Harvard University Press, 1944.

Peretz, I. L. "If Not Higher," in Irving Howe and Eliezer Greenberg's *A Treasury of Yiddish Stories.* New York, Schocken, 1973.

Olan, Levi. *Judaism and Immortality.* New York, UAHC Press, 1971.

Sonsino, Rifat and Daniel Syme. *What Happens after I Die?* New York, UAHC Press, 1990.

PART THREE:

RABBINIC JUDAISM AND THE LIFE-CYCLE

9.

RABBINIC LITERATURE: ABORTION AND

EUTHANASIA

Why is the Talmud like the Internet? Why are there one Mishnah and two Talmuds? What is the difference between *halakhah* and *aggadah?* What is a midrash? How does Jewish law view abortion and euthanasia?

One of the special characteristics of Judaism is the enormous body of Jewish law and lore that Jews, even today, are expected to consult when faced with ritual or moral decisions. You may recall that in the first century BCE, the Pharisees concluded that the laws in the Torah would have to be interpreted or re-interpreted to meet changing social and economic conditions. After the destruction of the Temple in 70 CE, the other sects (Saduccees, Essenes, Apocalyptics, and Zealots) were no longer relevant and disappeared, and so Pharisaic Judaism became Rabbinic Judaism.

The "Written Torah" that required interpretation or elaboration consists of the *Taryag* (613) *Mitzvot:* 365 negative and 248 positive. Among the negative commandments are laws against idolatry, tattooing oneself (as idolaters did), entering the sanctuary drunk before reading the Torah, not marrying a divorced woman if you are a *kohen*, and not boiling a kid in its mother's milk (interpreted to mean that one should not mix meat and milk at the same meal). Among the positive commandments are loving God, reciting the *Shema* each morning and evening, and loving your neighbor as yourself.

The rabbinic interpretations were called the "Oral Law," because for about three centuries they were not put in writing lest they become too rigid. After the defeat of a second revolt against Rome, led by Bar Kochba (133-135), Jerusalem lay in ruins. Then the center of rabbinic learning in Palestine shifted to the Galilee. In order to have a common set of laws for Jews in the Persian Empire and in Palestine, the interpretations of the Palestinian rabbis (the *Tannaim*) were put in writing in the Mishnah by Judah Ha-Nasi, patriarch of the Sanhedrin (170-217). The Mishna might clarify a Biblical law. For example, according to Leviticus 19:9, one must leave the corner of the field for the poor. However, the verse does not indicate how large a corner. The Mishnah states: a minimum of one-sixtieth of the field; how much more depends on the size of the field and the number of the poor(the concept of progressive taxation).The interpretations of the Mishnah by the Palestinian rabbis were called the Gemara. The Mishnah and the Palestinian Gemara were called the *Talmud Yerushalmi*(completed between 450 and 500 CE).

Meanwhile, the Jewish community in Persia was growing, its centers of learning in Sura and Pumbeditha becoming more important that those in the Galilee. The interpretations of the Mishnah by the rabbis in Persia (the *Amoraim*) became the "Babylonian Gemara" and together with the Mishnah were called the Babylonian Talmud, or *Talmud Bavli* (completed about 500 C.E.) A typical passage reads: In the Mishnah it is written, "Just as there is overreaching in buying and selling, so there is wrong done by words. Thus one may not ask, 'What is the price of this article,' if he has no intention of buying . . ."

The Gemara to that Mishnah reads, in part: "'You shall not therefore wrong one another' (Leviticus 25:17). This verse of Scripture refers to wrongs by words . . . Wronging by words is more wicked than monetary wrong . . . For monetary wrongs restitution is possible, but not for verbal wrongs . . . He who publicly shames his neighbor is as though he shed blood."(*Bava Metzia*, 58b-59b).

In the margins of a page of Talmud are commentaries by Rav Shlomo ben Yitzhak, known by his acronym as Rashi (an 11th century-scholar who made comments on the Talmud and the Written Torah) and by the *Tosafot* (additional commentaries by rabbis of the 12th century). So, on one page of Talmud, one can follow the development of Jewish law from the 1st century BCE to the 12th century CE.

A page of Talmud reminds an American Jewish writer, Jonathan Rosen, of a web page on the Internet. Just as rabbinic rulings "winged back and forth between scattered Jews," the Internet "is also a world of unbounded curiosity, of argument and information." On one page of the Talmud "a sage of one century can quarrel with a sage who died several centuries earlier as if he were standing in the same room with him." So, on the Internet, a web page can send us searching and finding different opinions on different issues from different times. Also, when studying the Talmud, one realizes that one is looking at but a fragment of a vast body of knowledge that no single individual will ever master. So when "surfing" the Internet, one realizes that one is looking at but a fragment of an enormous body of information that can never be completely absorbed. Also, because the Talmud is often referred to as a *yam*, a sea, then the yeshiva students become the "surfers." It is necessary, whether one is dealing with a fragment of the Talmud or a document on the Internet, to realize that it is okay not to know everything.

The Gerer Rebbe asked a student: "Have you learned Torah?"

The student answered, "Just a little."

The Rebbe responded, "That is all anyone has ever learned of Torah."

So it can be said of the worlds of knowledge available through the Talmud or the Internet. Still, as Rabbi Tarfon said, "It is not necessary to complete the task but neither are we free to desist from it altogether." Finally, the Aramaic term for "tractate" of the Talmud is *masechta*, which literally means "web" as in worldwide. (For more of such similarities, see Rosen's *The Talmud and the Internet*).

The evolution of Jewish law took various forms. Maimonides, in the twelfth century, wrote a monumental code of Jewish law, called the *Mishneh Torah,* a compilation of *halakhah.* In the sixteenth century Joseph Caro compiled the *Shulchan Arukh* ("Prepared Table") which summarized the laws considered binding by Sephardic authorities (rabbis whose ancestry is traceable to Spain, northern Africa or the Middle East.) Later that same century, Moses Isserles in Poland wrote the *Mapah* ("tablecloth" to the prepared table) so that the laws would be accepted as authoritative by Ashkenazic Jews (from central or eastern Europe). To this day the *Shulchan Aruch* with Isserles' commentary is viewed as an authoritative code for Orthodox Judaism. Another form of Jewish law one finds is the Responsa (*Teshuvot),* which are answers to questions posed to prominent rabbis from the seventh century to the present. For example, Elijah ben Shlomo (the Vilna Gaon) in the eighteenth century was asked, Is one required to cover one's head during prayer? He responded, "One is not required by Jewish law to cover one's head during prayer, but it is *derech eretz* (good manners) to do so."

The term used to indicate a specific Jewish law or the entire body of Jewish law is *halakhah* (from the root, to go; therefore, the way a Jew must go to comply with rabbinic law). However, there is another form of rabbinic literature called *aggadah* (from the root, to tell) which consists of moral maxims, parables with ethical lessons and, on occasion, theological speculation. An entire tractate of the Mishnah, *Avot*, contains sayings of the rabbis that teach moral behavior: For example, "Hillel said: 'If I am not for myself, who will be for me? If I am for myself, alone, what am I? If not now, when?'"

There are also aggadic passages in the Gemara. One of the most interesting is the telling of an argument among rabbis regarding a ruling about whether a particular oven was unclean. The overwhelming majority of sages concluded that it was unclean. Rabbi Eliezer, however, held that the oven was clean, but his arguments did not convince the sages. He then said, "If I am right this carob tree will prove it." Lo and behold, the carob tree moved one hundred cubits. The sages were not impressed. Eliezer then said, "If I am right, this stream of water will prove it." Suddenly, the stream of water flowed in the opposite direction.

The sages replied, "No proof can be brought from a stream of water."

Eliezer tried again, "If I am right, the walls of this house of study will prove it."

The walls began to cave in, but Rabbi Joshua shouted to the walls, "If scholars are arguing about a matter of law, why should you care!" Out of respect for both Eliezer and Joshua, the walls stayed in an inclined position.

Finally, Eliezer said, "If my decision is right, let this be proved by Heaven!"

Sure enough, a voice from Heaven(*bat kol*) proclaimed: "What do you want of Rabbi Eliezer? The ruling is always in accordance with his views."

Rabbi Joshua then arose and quoted from the Torah: "The commandment is not in Heaven . . . rather is it in your heart that you may do it" (Deuteronomy 11-14).

What did Rabbi Joshua mean? Rabbi Jeremiah said, "He meant that once the Torah has been given on Sinai, no notice should be taken even of a voice from Heaven in matters of Jewish law, as it is written in the Torah, 'After the majority one must incline' (a free translation of Exodus 23:2).

Rabbi Nathan met Elijah and asked him, "What did the Holy One, Blessed be He, do at that time?"

Elijah replied: "He laughed with joy and said, 'My children have won! My children have won!'" What an amazing tribute to human reason! Even God could be overruled by humans who were using God's gift of reason to discover moral truths. Erich Fromm, in *Psychoanalysis and Religion*, cited the above passage as a prime example of a humanistic trend one can find even in the most traditional sources of Judaism.

The overwhelming majority of aggadic literature is found in the Midrash (from the root, to search). The *Midrash Rabbah*, the "Great Midrash," consists of ethical commentaries on the Written Torah as well as on the five scrolls (Song of Songs, Ruth, Lamentations, Ecclesiastes, and Esther). These commentaries contain what were probably the notes for sermons preached by rabbis from about

200 CE to 400 CE. For example, in Genesis 6, we read that Noah was "righteous in his generation." There are two interpretations of this: 1) Noah was righteous *despite* his generation. Because his entire generation was wicked, Noah must have had exceptional strength of character to resist such wickedness. 2) Noah was considered righteous relative to all others in his generation; however, in any other generation, Noah would not have been considered exceptionally moral.

Just as there are aggadic passages in the Talmud, so there are halakhic books that are midrash. These are commentaries on the laws in Exodus *(Mechilta)*, Leviticus *(Sifra)*, Numbers, and Deuteronomy *(Sifrei)*. The rabbinic authors lived during the first and second centuries CE. For example, in Deuteronomy 22: 8, we read, "You shall make a parapet for your roof, so that you do not bring bloodguilt on your house if anyone should fall from it." According to *Sifre*, the rule also applies to a pit or a well in the yard or a cellar. Neither Biblical nor rabbinic law considered property rights to be absolute. One is restricted in the use of one's property should that use endanger the lives or well-being of others. How might rabbinic law respond to a person selling his or her house who claimed: "If I do not want to sell my house to an African-American, I do not have to. After all, it's my house." Recall the midrash on the creation of Adam from the different colored dusts of the earth (Chapter 3).

RABBINIC LAW AND ABORTION

It is quite clear that in Biblical times the fetus was not considered a human being because its destruction was not considered murder. According to Exodus 21:22-4, if two men fight in the presence of a pregnant woman and the woman is pushed so that a miscarriage results, the "pusher" is not condemned to die, as he would be if the fetus were considered a human being. Instead, he is expected to pay a fine. In 1990, Rabbi Loewy, president of the New Orleans Board of Rabbis, quoted this verse to show that the Hebrew Bible does not consider abortion to be murder. Senator Mike Cross retorted: "That's not in my Bible." (As reported in J. J. Goldberg's *Jewish Power*.)

Rabbis who wanted to find a Biblical basis for considering the fetus to be a human being and for abortion to be murder actually mis-translated Genesis 9:6 to read "Whoever sheds the blood of man in man, his blood shall be shed." (The correct translation: "Whoever sheds the blood of man, by man shall his blood be shed.") However, even those rabbis who considered the fetus to be a human being permitted abortion if the life of the mother was at stake. Why? Because the fetus that endangered the mother's life was viewed as a *rodef*, an aggressor, and therefore, must be killed to save the life of the mother (Mishnah *Ohalot* 7:6). Almost all rabbis held that the *nefesh* (soul, or in secular terms, the person) comes into being at birth, when the fetus is separated from the mother. In Talmudic law, the fetus is deemed "part of the mother."

The stricter rabbis held that abortion, according to Rabbi Issar Unterman, is "akin to murder" and so can only be performed if the life of the mother is at stake. A more liberal approach, based on the ruling of Rabbi Jacob Emden, held that abortion may be permitted to spare the mother "great pain." According to some rabbis, the pain must be physical. Other rabbis believe that the pain can be mental anguish. (Most Conservative and virtually all Reform and Reconstructionist rabbis hold to this view.) One should note that if there is a very good chance that the baby will be deformed or will be afflicted with the fatal Tay-Sachs disease, abortion is permitted not because of the pain to be experienced by the child but because of the mental anguish the mother will feel. The most liberal view was expressed by Professor Alvin Reines, of the Hebrew Union College, who held that every person has the moral right to exercise authority over him/herself so long as one does no harm to others. Since the fetus is part of the mother, she has the right to choose whether or not to have an abortion.

Many Jews simply do not want the government to interfere in a personal decision about which reasonable people from different religious backgrounds may, in good conscience, disagree.

RABBINIC LAW AND EUTHANASIA

In order to allow our loved ones, or ourselves, to have a "good death," is it permitted to put a terminally ill and suffering patient out of his or her misery? According to rabbinic law, one is not allowed to take any action in order to hasten death. Such an action is sometimes called, "positive euthanasia." However, one is allowed to *refrain* from actions that would prolong the life of a terminally ill and suffering patient. This is called, "passive euthanasia."

According to the Talmud, the slightest action that might hasten death (e.g., closing the eyes of a dying patient) is forbidden (*Semachot* 1:2-4). The rationale for this view is expressed in the Talmudic story of Rabbi Chanina ben Teradion. He was wrapped by the Romans in a Torah scroll, with bundles of straw around him that were set on fire. The Romans also put tufts of wool soaked in water over his heart so that he would not die quickly. His followers pleaded with him to open his mouth "so that the fire enter" and put an end to his agony. He replied: "Let Him who gave me (my soul) take it away"(*Avodah Zarah* 18a). It was Job who said, "The Lord giveth; the Lord taketh away. Blessed be the name of the Lord" (Job: 1:21}.

However, Moses Isserles, in his commentary on Joseph Caro's *Shulchan Aruch (Yoreh Deah* 339), stated: If there is anything which causes a hindrance to the departure of the soul, (e.g., the noise of wood chopping or salt on the patient's tongue), it is permissible to remove them because there is no act involved in this . . . but only the removal of the impediment. Also, Rabbi Solomon Eger quoted another rabbinic authority, who stated "it is forbidden to hinder the departure of the soul by the use of medicines." (This assumes that death is imminent.) Other rabbinic authorities disagreed. Rabbi Moshe Hershler stated that withholding food or medicine from a terminally ill patient would be murder and therefore, is prohibited. Also a respirator that is keeping a terminally ill patient alive may not be turned off, but a respirator that is automatically turned off by mechanical means is permitted.

According to Jewish law, the patient is dead when breathing ceases. What if the patient is "brain dead" but is kept breathing by a respirator? Surely a respirator that is keeping such a patient breathing can be turned off, concluded the Central Conference of Reform Rabbis' Responsa Committee (1980). There is some basis for this view in Rabbinic Law. Rabbi Moshe Feinstein held that one may turn off the respirator for one hour to see if there is independent breathing. If breathing ceases, the patient is dead. Feinstein quotes a Talmudic commentary: "The lungs are the servants of the brain."

A terminally ill patient need not be kept alive by heroic measures. Whether the use of a feeding tube is a heroic measure may be debated. Rabbis differ.

The most basic differences among rabbis today concerns the authority of Rabbinic Law. Orthodox rabbis believe that when Orthodox rabbis agree as to what the *halakhah*(Jewish law) is, then a Jew must accept their authority because they are articulating the will of God. The Conservative movement considers *halakhah* to be "the norms taught by Jewish tradition." Conservative rabbis accept the parameters set by their Committee on Law and Standards. When there are significant differences within the Committee, each rabbi may follow his or her own interpretation. Conservative congregants are expected to look to their rabbi to learn what *halakhah* requires.

Almost all Reform rabbis believe that the interpretations of their Responsa Committee should be consulted but should not be considered binding. According to Mark Washofsky, co-author of *T'shuvot for the Nineties,* while the Reform responsa are halakhic documents (because they draw their source material from the texts of the Jewish legal tradition), they "do not partake of anything resembling an authoritative halakhic process"; rather are they advisory opinions. In the words of Mordecai Kaplan, founder of the Reconstructionist movement, "the past has a voice but not a veto." A fuller explanation of the beliefs and practices of these "movements" within Judaism will be found in Chapters 16 and 17.

TOPICS FOR DISCUSSION

1. Develop a sermon that could be based on: the midrash about Noah or a saying by Hillel.

2. Do you believe that the story of Eliezer and the voice from Heaven has any relevance for religious leaders who quote Scriptures to advocate particular political or legal positions? If so, what is that relevance?

3. Do you believe that any restrictions at all should be placed on a woman's decision to have an abortion? Give reasons for your response.

4. When do you believe the fetus becomes a human being? Why?

5. If an elderly parent who has dementia but no other illness refuses to be fed in the usual manner, should the parent be given food through a tube?

RESOURCES

Dorff, Elliot and Louis Newman. *Contemporary Jewish Ethics and Morality: A Reader.* (Section D. Jewish Perspectives on Medical Ethics) New York, Oxford University Press, 1995.

Feldman, David. *Birth Control in Jewish Law.* Northvale, N.J., Jason Aaronson, 1998.

Gersh, Harry. *Talmud: Law and Commentary.* (Teacher's Edition) New York, Behrman House, 1980.

Jacobs, Louis. *Jewish Law.* New York, Behrman House, 1968.

Neusner, Jacob. *Invitation to the Talmud.* New York, Harper & Row, 1973.

Novak, David. "Be Fruitful and Multiply," in Rela Geffen's *Celebration and Renewal.* Philadelphia, Jewish Publicaion Society, 1993.

Rosen, Jonathan. *The Talmud and the Internet.* New York, Farrar, 2000.

10.

FROM WOMB TO TOMB:

THE JEWISH LIFE-CYCLE

For some Jews, the only times their extended family comes together are at "brises," "bar or bat mitzvahs," weddings and funerals. These may be times of anxiety and apprehension, of celebration and hope. The traditions of Judaism help us overcome our fears and celebrate life.

BRIT MILAH AND *BRIT HAYYIM*

So what's to fear about a *Bris* (to use the Sephardic pronunciation), *Brit Milah*, Covenant of Circumcision? At the very first *Brit Milah* I attended as a rabbinical student, the father fainted. When a father or any man identifies with the infant, the removal of the foreskin from the penis can be stressful. There are several excellent books that describe just how the ceremony is performed. (See Resources.) This chapter will approach *Brit Milah* from a historical perspective, in order to shed light on the present meanings.

Ritual circumcision was not invented by the Jews. The custom was widespread among ancient peoples, from the Egyptians to African tribes. It was usually performed when the child reached puberty. According to Theodore Gaster, who viewed Jewish customs from an anthropological perspective, the prime purpose of ritual circumcision was to protect the penis and so assure the perpetuation of the tribe. There was a common belief that if one takes a part of something and gives it to the gods or God, then the entire "thing" will be protected. Similarly, the first sheaves of the Spring harvest were offered to God as a way of assuring a bountiful harvest. A second purpose of the circumcision was to initiate the young adolescent into the tribe or community.

Fortunately, Judaism moved the time of circumcision from puberty to the eighth day after birth. Still, the Jewish people retained the two basic purposes of circumcision: the perpetuation of the tribe (i.e., the Israelites) and the initiation of the Jewish male into the tribe. But Judaism transformed the ritual in profound ways. *Brit* means covenant, and by becoming part of the tribe, the child becomes party to the covenant between God and the Jewish people, as first commanded to Abraham (Genesis: 17:10-14). The perpetuation of the tribe is a purpose also expressed in the *Brit Mila* ceremony when we pray that the child will grow to "Torah, *Huppah* (wedding canopy) and *Maasim Tovim*(good deeds)," and the infant is given a Hebrew name. Obviously, an eight-day-old infant cannot choose to accept Judaism, but as a member of the tribe he will learn about and participate in the beliefs, values, and traditions of the Jewish people and, once he has the knowledge, he will choose to accept or reject the covenant.

You may be thinking, what a sexist tradition! Jewish girls are often given their Hebrews names by the rabbi's offering of a brief prayer during a synagogue service; however, this is hardly the equivalent of the *brit milah* ritual accompanied by festivity in the home. The inequality may be rationalized by saying that only men are bound by all the 613 commandments in the Torah. Women are not obligated to follow those positive commandments that must be observed at a particular time. To eliminate this inequality, non-Orthodox Jews have developed a ceremony (e.g., a *Brit Hayyim*, "Covenant of Life") during which the girl becomes part of the covenant, and we pray that she will grow toward Torah, *Huppah* and *Maasim Tovim*. This ceremony may be conducted at home or in the synagogue at a time agreed upon by the parents and rabbi.

Questions are often raised about choosing a Hebrew name: Does the Hebrew name have to be similar to the English name? No. Can the child be given the Hebrew name of a living relative? Yes and No. It is the custom among Ashkenazic Jews not to name the child after a living family member. The origin of this custom may be the fear that when a child is given the name of a living person, that person's strength may be diminished and so he/she may be in danger of death. Others suggest that if a child is given the Hebrew name of an adult, when the *malach hamavet* (angel of death) comes to take the adult, he may by mistake take away the child. However, among Sephardic Jews , babies are often named after living relatives. It was once believed that when this occurs, the adult is born anew. How convenient: You may follow either the Ashkenazic or Sephardic tradition.

BAR AND *BAT MITZVAH*

After the "*Bris*" the next time all the relatives may come together is for the celebration of a *Bar* or *Bat Mitzvah*(son or daughter of the commandment). Rabbis warn congregants not to throw parties so lavish that the meaning of the service is lost. So what's the meaning? A *Bar Mitzvah* may be told by hovering relatives, "Today you are a man." You can't drive or vote, but you're a man. Sure! Actually according to Jewish law, a thirteen-year-old boy does assume the responsibilities of an adult Jew. He is expected to follow all 613 of the commandments in the Torah. He is also expected to have sufficient knowledge of Jewish law, so that he will know the *mitzvot* he is obligated to perform. The link between adulthood and the education required to be an adult is the essence of the meaning of *Bar Mitzvah.*

A more realistic interpretation might be that when a boy becomes a *Bar Mitzvah,* he is taking a major step toward adulthood (as he enters adolescence), and he is also taking a step toward an adequate knowledge of Judaism. Rabbis often bemoan the fact that so many thirteen-year-old boys drop out of Religious or Hebrew School after becoming a *Bar Mitzvah.* This could be called, "*Bar Mitzvah* Fixation": when a child continues to grow in knowledge of all the secular subjects, from science to literature, but Jewishly remains "fixated" at the level of a thirteen-year old.

The first time a *Bar Mitzvah* was called upon to chant from the Torah portion of the week, as well as the *haftarah* (concluding) reading from the Prophets, was probably about the thirteenth century CE. It was not until the twentieth century that a girl became a *Bat Mitzvah.* The very first "Daughter of the Commandment" was Judith Kaplan, the daughter of Mordecai Kaplan. In the mid-nineteenth century, Reform Judaism discouraged the *Bar Mitzvah* tradition, because from a rational perspective a thirteen-year old was neither an adult nor did he have adequate knowledge of Judaism. The Reform movement substituted Confirmation, a group ceremony for boys and girls that came to be celebrated at about the age of 15 or 16, by which time the adolescent had a somewhat more adequate knowledge of the Jewish heritage. This takes place on or near the festival of Shavuot, which commemorates the giving of the Ten Commandments (or, for the Orthodox, the Torah) on Mt. Sinai. (See Chapter 14.)

In the mid-twentieth century, within the Reform movement,

Jewish boys were becoming *B'nai* (sons of) *Mitzvah* and toward the end of that century almost all Jewish girls were becoming *B'not* (daughters of) *Mitzvah*. The ceremony has great emotional power, because the focus is on one child (in contrast to a group), and the family and friends have come together to give their support to the boy or girl as he or she symbolically enters adolescence on the way to maturity. The ceremony also dramatizes the Jewish link between generations, as the Torah is often handed from grandparent to parent to son/daughter. Each child has his/her own Torah portion and most *B'nai Mitzvah* give a *d'rasha,* a short speech that may demonstrate their understanding of the Torah portion.

Some rabbis deliver a "charge" to the *Bar* or *Bat Mitzvah*. I usually include a story that illustrates one of the ceremony's several meanings. Among my favorites is a Hasidic tale about Reb Susya. When he was near death, Susya called his students to his bedside. One student asked,"Are you afraid that after you die, God will ask, 'Why were you not like Moses?'"

"No," said Susya. "I am afraid that after I die, God will ask, 'Why were you not like Susya?'"

There are times when children are intimidated by very high-achieving parents. Judaism challenges the *Bar* or *Bat Mitzvah* to discover his or her own uniqueness. Be all that you can be. That is all God or anyone can ask.

The most moving *Bar* or *Bat Mitzvah* ceremony in which I have ever been involved was held in Moscow, in 1986, not in a synagogue but in the apartment of Viktor and Irina Brailovsky, who for fourteen years had been refused visas that would have enabled them and their daughter, Dalia, to leave the Soviet Union. Viktor was a mathematician who had lost his job as an engineer. In 1981, he had been sentenced to thirty months internal exile in a remote province on the false allegation that he possessed state secrets. He was one of about 30,000 Soviet Jews who had applied for visas in order to live in freedom. Applying could mean losing one's job and then being arrested for being what the Soviets called a "parasite."

My wife and I were visiting "refuseniks" in Moscow and Leningrad in November, 1986. It was a Thursday evening when we met the Brailovskys. They had one request: Dalia was approaching her thirteenth birthday; would I conduct a *Bat Mitzvah* service? It was my privilege. Dalia and I studied together the *parasha,* the weekly portion of the Torah, *Va-yaytzay,* Genesis 28:10ff., the story of Jacob's ladder. It would have been illegal to hold such a service in the Moscow synagogue, so the next evening, as the Sabbath began, the Brailovskys, their family, and several close friends gathered in their apartment. After a festive dinner, we sang *Hinay mah tov,* "How good and pleasant it is to sit as brothers (and sisters) together." Dalia said the *Shema,* not only an affirmation of the oneness of God but historically the Jew's way of defying those who would force him/her to forget the Jewish heritage. We read several of the *Shabbat* prayers. As we had no Torah scroll, Viktor handed to Dalia a Hebrew Bible to symbolize her commitment to carry on her tradition and bring its values into her life. After family members read or chanted the Torah blessings, Dalia and I read her portion, she translating into Russian the Hebrew verses.

I then discussed a paradox in the story of Jacob's dream. The angels of God are described as *olim v'yordim,* going up and coming down the ladder. One would expect that angels, residing in heaven, would first come down and then go up, but the text says the opposite. Why? A rabbinic response is that the angels going up were those of Jacob's childhood, and those coming down were angels of his maturity. After relating this commentary, I asked Dalia: "What angel of childhood do you think will be leaving you as you grow to maturity as an adult?" She thought a while and answered, "The angel of happiness."

It was a painful moment: a revelation of the world of Soviet Jewry as seen though the eyes of a refusenik child. We spoke quietly of other childhood angels that we would want to leave us: angels of impatience, self-centeredness, and irresponsibility. We hoped and prayed that something of childhood would remain, such as a sense of wonder and joy, of questioning and curiosity. Her brother, Leonid, spoke of trips to the countryside he had taken with his young wife, when they felt for the moment free and alive. Leonid insisted, "The most important thing is, no matter what is done to you, not to waste your life." I prayed that Dalia would grow in mind, heart, and spirit. I remembered the words of Jacob when he awoke from his dream: "Surely the Lord was in this place and I knew it not."

Fortunately as Dalia became a woman, the angel of happiness did not leave her. Within a few years, the family was able to go to Israel. They are now among the almost one million Jews from the former Soviet Union who make up Israel's largest community of recent immigrants.

KIDDUSHIN: A JEWISH MARRIAGE

The Hebrew word for marriage is "*kiddushin*," from the root, *kadosh*, meaning "holy." The "idea of the holy" for some theologians carries with it a sense of awe, mystery, perhaps apprehension, feelings that bride and groom may well experience before or during the wedding. However, Heschel asserted that Judaism insists on the "ethicization" of the holy. Holiness is linked to morality, both justice and love. Beneath the mystery and awe of the unknown future, bride and groom will find the love that will enable them to conquer fear and find joy.

The symbols of the ceremony lend themselves to a variety of interpretations. The *huppah*, a symbol of the home the couple will create, has no walls. This could suggest that between husband and wife there should be no walls. Rather should the couple be, in Buber's phrase, "fully present," one before the other. In that way they will find the empathy that will enable them to know what gives each other pleasure and pain. Then they may not step on each other's ego so much and may find a deeper happiness together. No walls may also signify that the couple will be open to the world about them, to family and friends, to the Jewish people and to people of every race and creed.

Sharing the wine may remind the couple that they will be drinking from the cup of life together. When joy is shared, it is a greater joy. When sorrow is shared, it is a lesser sorrow. The wine, itself, may represent the joy of creation. The bride and groom will be creating as surely as any artist creates. They may pray that the home which they are about to build will be their masterpiece.

The ring signifies unbroken love. Two Hebrew words express the ideal of love. *Rachamim* has been interpreted to mean: I love you, even though you are not absolutely perfect. I accept you as you are, and I will not try to make you over into some ideal to meet all of my needs. It is so important to be able to say: *Rachamim*, I love you even though you are only human. The more usual Hebrew word for love is *ahavah*. Love may be fun and frivolous. Love may be quiet, without need of words. Love may be mystical, when the world fades away and the bride and groom are one with each other and the God of love. At the moment when the groom puts the ring on the bride's finger and before two witnesses says the words in Hebrew which translated mean, "Be thou consecrated unto me with this ring according to the law of Moses and Israel," they are married.

The breaking of the glass by the groom may have originally been intended to scare away evil spirits which, according to Jewish folklore, are present at weddings and funerals. The broken glass reminded the rabbis of broken moments in Jewish experience, such as the destruction of the Temple in Jerusalem. In a broader sense, the broken glass may be a symbol of reality: Every life does have its sad and broken moments as well as its happy times. Whatever interpretation may be given by the rabbi, the family and friends may respond to the breaking of the glass by shouting, *mazol tov*, good luck, may those evil spirits be gone forever.

The *Ketubah*, the Jewish marriage contract, a medieval document written in Aramaic, states the economic commitments that the bride and groom have made to each other. This was interpreted as giving assurance to the bride that she would be cared for in case of divorce. In non-Orthodox movements of Judaism, there are variations of the text which express the couple's emotional and spiritual commitment to each other.

There are many Jewish sayings and stories about weddings. My favorite is a Hasidic tale told about Reb Nahman of Bratzlav. Once, after attending a wedding, Reb Nahman lingered as the guests were leaving. He heard three of the guests talking. One said: "What a fantastic wedding! The food was fabulous."

A second guest said, "What a marvelous wedding! The music was great."

A third guest said, "I had such a wonderful time. I saw all my old friends."

Nahman shook his head and sighed, "Those people were not at a wedding."

A fourth guest joined the group and exclaimed, "*Baruch*

Hashem, praised be to God that those two found each other."

Nahman said, "Now *he* was at a wedding."

GITTIN: DIVORCE LAW

In Deuteronomy 24:1, it is written that when a man's wife "fails to please him because he finds in her an *ervat davar*(something unseemly, obnoxious), and he writes her a bill of divorcement . . ." The Mishnah raises the question: Just what is an *ervat davar*? According to the house of Shammai (the school of rabbis who advocated, as did Shammai, stricter interpretations), the woman must have committed a sexual sin such as adultery. However, according to the more lenient interpretation of the house of Hillel, virtually anything could be a reason for divorce ("even if she burned his meat.") The Gemara debates the issue at some length. While the law is according to the house of Hillel, the tractate *Gittin* concludes with the sentiment, "When a man divorces the wife of his youth, the altar weeps."

In the eleventh century Rabbi Gershom of Mainz issued *takkanot* (special regulations) regarding marriage and divorce. He banned polygamy among Ashkenazic Jews. He also ruled that a wife could not be forced to accept a *get* (divorce certificate) unless she had committed adultery. Later rabbis ruled that a man may divorce his wife without her consent under certain circumstances, e.g., if she refused him sex, if she had no children after ten years of marriage, if she was lax in religious observance. A rabbinic court (*bet din*) could force the *husband* to give his wife a divorce under certain circumstances, e.g., if he refused her sex, if he was cruel to her, if he acted immorally. Thus, the law *seems* to treat husband and wife more or less equally. However, if a man who has *not* given his wife a *get* re-marries, he is "only" committing polygamy and may even receive a *heter* (permission) from a group of rabbis to marry again. However, if a woman re-marries without receiving a *get,* she will have committed adultery. A further difficulty for women is that Orthodox rabbis in Israel may refuse (or, in the U.S., may be unable) to compel the husband, who according to Jewish law should be forced to grant the *get.* Today, both in Israel and the United States, some men have been known to refuse giving a *get* unless the wife meets certain conditions (e.g., giving up custody of the children, or agreeing to a financial settlement beneficial to the husband).

The Conservative movement requires a *get* but includes in the *ketubah* (marriage contract) an agreement that recognizes the authority of the *Bet Din* (court) of the Conservative Rabbinical Assembly, which would not allow the husband unfairly to withhold a *get.* Reform and Reconstructionist rabbis do not require a *get.* They have reasoned that there are enough tensions relating to divorce without requiring a legal procedure in addition to civil law. The Orthodox respond: By refusing to issue *gittin,* these modern movements are creating divisions within the Jewish community regarding who is or who is not eligible for a Jewish marriage.

ON DEATH AND MOURNING

Just as every life is unique, so the way we die and the way we mourn is unique. The Psalmist wrote that "even by reason of strength" we may live four score years (Psalm 90). Today, due to advances in medical technology, more of our dear ones are living well beyond four score years. If a life has been long with years and deep with love, then when evening comes, we may look back with gratitude on a beautiful day. How different are our feelings when a loved one dies as a child, as a young adult, or as a parent with young children. We may then feel resentment and anger toward

God. How unfair! How could a good God have allowed such a tragedy?

In Chapter 4, we recognized that how one responds to such painful questions depends on what one believes or how one experiences God. The traditional theist, with Job, acknowledges that with our limited human minds, we cannot understand the ways of the God of the entire complex universe. Other theologians hold that even God is limited in power. As Harold Kushner has written (in *To Life!*), God is limited by the laws of nature and by the free will that God has given us. We still need God to help our hearts heal and then return to life. However brief our loved one's life, we are grateful for whatever years were allotted to him/her. We feel the spirit of God in the love and support given us by family and friends.

We are also given support by Jewish mourning customs (*hilkhot avelut*), the purpose of which is to help us express our grief and then turn back, step by step, to life. According to the *halakhah*, for the first three days after the funeral, the mourner is expected to weep and wail and should not greet his/her guests or eat meat. Then after three days the mourner should stop crying, greet the guests, and may eat meat but, he/she should not leave home for work and should sit on low stools for the rest of the *shivah* (seven) period. After a week, one returns to work but does not shave or wear new clothes or attend any festive occasion for a month. After a month one resumes normal activities but says *kaddish* for eleven months. (Reciting *kaddish* for the entire year suggested to some Jews that the departed needed the extra month of *kaddish* to be assured of paradise. See Chapter 8.)

Reform rabbis viewed these traditions not as law but as custom. For Reform Judaism, the mourner should be made aware of the traditional customs but should follow those that are most helpful in enabling him/her to express grief and turn gradually back to life. The ideas underlying the laws of mourning, i.e., free expression of grief and then return to life, are valid but neither rabbis nor well-intentioned friends know precisely when a particular person is ready to move from one step to another. We can point the direction, gently encourage and give support. However, let us not be judgmental toward those who grieve in their own way.

The setting of a tombstone after about a year, while not originally a Jewish custom, is widely practiced. One interpretation is that by this ceremony we take the stone of sadness that has been in our hearts and place it on the grave. There remain within our hearts memories that are precious and love that is living, but this custom reminds us that we should not live in memory. Rather should we live in the present and for the future.

Orthodox Judaism affirms that when the messiah comes, the bodies of the righteous will be resurrected. That is one reason why Jewish law does not allow autopsy, unless the autopsy could help save the life of a human being suffering from the same disease. Respect for the body led the rabbis not only to oppose autopsy but to prohibit cremation and embalming.

Biblical and Rabbinic Judaism reject the denial of death that prevents some from dealing with their own mortality. Both Joseph and David, when they were terminally ill, realized the inevitable and said to their sons, "Behold, I now am going to die." Their sons did not deceive them saying, "No you're not. You'll be your old self very soon." The *Shulchan Aruch* tells us that we should advise the seriously ill to look over their affairs to be sure they are in order. Because we are all vulnerable, we had better not wait until we are critically ill.

Furthermore, the rabbis also have encouraged us to leave to our children more than our material assets. In Judaism there is an impressive literary tradition of ethical wills: parents leaving to their children advice, the benefit of their experience. Given today's idealization of youth, it may be unrealistic to expect our children to accept our counsel. (I cannot even persuade my daughters to listen to Mozart.) Parental preaching is ineffective. We can only hope that our children will have found something positive in our better qualities and that they will learn from our faults. My ethical will is my life, for better or for worse.

TOPICS FOR DISCUSSION

1. What is your opinion about the affirmation that a Jewish infant is becoming part of a people who have a covenant with God?

2. If you have attended the ceremony of a *Bar/Bat Mitzvah*, what was the positive aspect of that experience? If there was a negative aspect, elaborate.

3. Write what you consider to be ten commandments for a good marriage. (Five will do.)

4. Which Jewish mourning customs do you find helpful? Which do you not find helpful?

5. Write your own ethical will.

RESOURCES

Barth, Lewis M. *Berit Mila in the Reform Context.* New York, Berit Mila Board of Reform Judaism, 1990.

Diamant, Anita with Harold Cooper. *Living a Jewish Life*. (The Life Cycle) New York, Perennial, 1991.

Gaster, Theodor H. *The Holy and the Profane: Evolution of Jewish Folkways, Newly Revised*. New York, William Morrow & Co., 1980.

Goodman, Philip and Hannah. *The Jewish Marriage Anthology*. Philadelphia, Jewish Publication Society, 1965.

Kolatch, Alfred J. *The Name Dictionary: Modern English and Hebrew Names*. Middle Village, N.Y., Jonathan David, 1967.

Kushner, Harold. *To Life! A Celebration of Jewish Being and Thinking*. Boston, Little, Brown & Co., 1993.

Meiselman, Moshe. *Jewish Woman in Jewish Law*. New York, Ktav Publishing House, 1978.

Riemer, Jack(ed.). *Jewish Reflections on Death*. New York, Schocken, 1975.

Salkin, Jeffrey. *Putting God on the Guest List: How to Reclaim the Spiritual Meaning of Your Child's Bar or Bat Mitzvah*. Woodstock, Vt., Jewish Lights, 1996.

Syme, Daniel. *The Jewish Home: A Guide for Jewish Living*. (Ch. 13-18) New York, UAHC Press, 1988.

JEWS IN THE MIDDLE AGES, 500 - 1492

JEWS IN NEAR EAST AND SPAIN

JEWS IN CENTRAL AND EASTERN EUROPE

533: Justinian Code discriminates against Jews.

540-604: Pope Gregory the Great treats Jews fairly.

622: Muhammad's flight from Mecca to Medina (The Hegira).

650: Geonim become religious authorities for Jews under Islam.

711: Islamic Arabs conquer Spain, bring Jews with them.

762-767: In Bagdhad, Gaon's authority resisted by Karaites.

882-941: Saadia, Gaon of Sura and Jewish philosopher.

912-1056: Chasdai ibn Shaprut, vizier in Cordoba, Samuel Hanagid, in Granada.

1055-1135: Moses ibn Ezra, poet.

1075-1141: Judah HaLevi, poet and philosopher.

1146: Almohades attack Jews and Christians.

1135-1204: Maimonides (Rambam) flees from Cordoba to Fostat in 1158.

1194-1270: Philosopher Talmudist Nachmanides.

1236: Christians invade Spain.

1286: Moses de Leon completes *Zohar.*

768-814: Charlemagne rules Holy Roman Empire.

814-840: Louis the Pious curbs anti-Jewish Agobard.

960-1028: Gershom's *takkanot.*

1040-1105: Rashi's commentaries.

1066: Jews settle in England.

1096: First Crusade (Jews slaughtered).

1140: Blood libel in England.

1215: 4th Lateran Council makes Jews wear special badge.

1240: Talmud burned in Paris.

1264: Jews welcomed into Poland by Boleslav the Pious.

1290: Jews expelled from England.

1306 and 1322: France expels Jews.

1348: Jews accused of poisoning wells and causing Black Death.

1334-1367: Jews flourish under Casimir the Great of Poland.

1391: Mobs attack Jews and synagogues in Seville, force conversions.

1449: Marranos accused of being secret Jews.

1483: Torquemada leads Inquisition.

1492: Expulsion of Jews from Spain.

PART FOUR:

MEDIEVAL JUDAISM AND A CALENDAR OF TRADITIONS

11.

PERSECUTION, PERSISTENCE,

AND JEWISH SURVIVAL

Of all the causes of persecution during the Middle Ages, how would you rank the following factors in order of importance: 1) The charge that Jews were "Christ-killers"; 2)economic decline in resident nations; 3) ignorance of the masses; 4)jealousy of Jewish achievements; 5) hatred of money-lenders? After reading this chapter, list the factors again and draw your own conclusions about how best to respond to anti-Semitism.

The Church Fathers preached that the dispersion of the Jews was a punishment for their refusal to accept Jesus as the messiah, and for their alleged responsibility for his crucifixion. In the second century, St. Justin claimed that Jewish misfortunes were due to the "murder of the Just One." In the fourth century, St. John Chrysostum raved that for the "odious assassination . . . no expiation (is) possible, no indulgence, no pardon . . . He who can never love Christ enough will never have done fighting against those (the Jews) who hate him."

However, this religious rationale for animosity against the Jews did not lead to systematic persecution in the early Middle Ages. The Theodosian Code(438) did ban conversions to Judaism, but it legalized Judaism and ruled that so long as Jews conducted themselves peacefully, they were not to be harassed. The Justinian Code (533) increased discrimination, prohibiting Jews from owning Christian slaves (although the reverse was legal), from practicing law, from testifying in court against Christians, and from observing Passover before Christians observed Easter. In contrast, Pope Gregory the Great was well known for his generally just treatment of the Jews.

THE RISE AND DECLINE
OF ASHKENAZIC JEWRY

("Ashkenaz" originally referred to Jews in Northern France and Western Germany but came to include Jews whose ancestors came from Central Europe and who spread to Poland, Russia, and other lands.)

During the early Middle Ages, the rise of the feudal system afforded ample economic opportunities for the still-small population of Europe. Perhaps because there was such opportunity, Jews fared well under Charlemagne and Louis the Pious (eighth and ninth centuries). Under this Carolignian dynasty, the bigoted Archbishop Agobard was prevented from enacting anti-Jewish restrictions. During these times, the Jews served important functions in the feudal world: first as sea traders in Italy and then as overland traders (called Radanites) to Russia. By the tenth century, some had become financial advisors and creditors to the nobility. A fictional portrayal is Isaac of York in Sir Walter Scott's *Ivanhoe*. When the Jews of Central Europe were well-treated, there arose rabbinic scholars who clarified (Rashi) or added to the evolving body of Jewish law (Gershom of Mayence).

Gradually, some cracks appeared in the feudal structure. The nobility consumed wealth without producing it. A class of angry poor blamed their poverty on the Jews. Many of these paupers joined the Crusades, and during the first Crusade (1096), they slaughtered about 10,000 Jews as they made their way to the Holy Land. To protect "their" Jews from such attacks, kings made Jews "serfs of the imperial chamber" and assumed total authority over them. At first, the Jews were relieved, but soon they discovered that with friends like these kings, they did not need enemies.

When the rulers were hard-pressed for funds, they simply canceled the debts owed to their Jewish creditors. In 1140, in Norwich, England, Jews were accused of killing Christian children and using their blood to make *matzot*. Some were executed for this "ritual murder." In 1215, the Fourth Lateran Council of the Church forced the Jews to wear a special badge to distinguish them from Christians. In 1240, in Paris, after a public disputation, Dominican priests persuaded the king to burn the Talmud, as it was considered one reason why Jews did not accept Jesus as Christ. In 1290, after most of their wealth was confiscated, all Jews were expelled from England. In 1306 and in 1322, Jews were expelled from France. Some fled to one of the duchies in Germany, but in 1348, these Jews were accused of poisoning wells and causing the Black Death, a plague that had struck Central Europe. Jews were not allowed to join guilds, so some became money-lenders who provided their services to the poor. When the poor could no longer repay the loans, they resented and attacked the Jews. Because there was no united German state, in 1348, Jews were expelled from several duchies (e.g., Cologne, Augsburg). Some would go from duchy to duchy while others migrated east into Poland.

As the persecution was becoming most severe in Central Europe, the feudal economy in Poland and Lithuania was just beginning to develop. Boleslav the Pious(1264) was the first of Polish rulers to welcome Jews into their land. These Jews became not money-lenders but tax collectors, managers of estates belonging to the nobility, merchants, craftsmen, even farmers. The Jews of Poland were granted a significant degree of communal autonomy. The Council of Four Lands was led by the most prominent rabbinic and lay leaders in all of Poland. Among the most influential was Moses Isserles (1525-1572) who, as was noted in Chapter 9, interpreted the *Shulchan Aruch* for Ashkenazic Jews. As Ellis Rivkin explained in his brilliant analysis, *The Shaping of Jewish History*, the flourishing of Jews and Judaism in Poland "had been possible only because (Ashkenazic Jews) had been transplanted from an area of stagnant feudalism to an area of developing feudalism."

The feudal economy in Eastern Europe began to decline in the mid-seventeenth century. Once again, the Jews were to become the scapegoats. The weakened central government of Poland was vulnerable to attacks by the Cossacks of the Ukraine, led by Bogdan Chmielnicki. The Cossacks vented their anger against the Jews, some of whom were managers of estates owned by the Polish nobility (*pans*). The slaughter of the Jews was particularly barbaric: infants killed in the laps of their mothers, children actually roasted over fire, adults skinned alive and their flesh thrown to the dogs. Chmielnicki has become a hero to the Ukrainians and the most venomous of villains to the Jews.

THE RISE, DECLINE AND RISE OF SEPHARDIC JEWRY

(*Sepharad* is the Hebrew word for Spain, and the Sephardim are Jews whose ancestors lived in Spain and who spread to North Africa, Palestine, and other lands)

When Muhammad traveled from Mecca to Yathrib (later, Medina) in 622 CE, Islam began to spread over the lands east and south of the Mediterranean (including Syria, Palestine, Egypt, Iraq, and Persia). The Jews at this time were led by a succession of *Geonim*(from *Gaon*, Excellency). They formed an elite hereditary hierarchy not dissimilar from the hierarchy of Caliphs who ruled Islam. Jews and Christians (called, "*dhimmi*," dependent people) were tolerated as minority religions. However, they were not allowed to proselytize, nor could they live in houses taller than those where Moslems dwelled. They also had to pay a special annual tax. As long as the economy flourished, Jews were able to participate in industry and commerce. Under these conditions, Judaism produced its first philosopher since Philo, Saadiah Gaon.

Meanwhile in Spain, Jews had been living under Christian rule and were persecuted between 612 and 620. In 711, the Islamic Arabs conquered Spain and thousands of Jews came with them. In 750, when the older dynasty of Caliphs (Ummayads) were overthrown by the Abbasids, the Arabs in Spain became independent of Baghdad, and the Jews in Spain became independent of the *Geonim*. Jewish culture flourished in Moslem Spain. Jews gained prominent positions as viziers to Moslem rulers: Chasdai ibn Shaprut (912-961) in Cordoba and Samuel Hanagid (1030-1056) in Granada. During this "Golden Age," Jewish philosophers found ways of reconciling revelation and reason. In the twelfth century, Judah HaLevi believed revelation was more reliable than reason. Moses Maimonides (See Chapter 4) in his *Moreh N'vuchim* (*Guide for the Perplexed*) used reason to find a middle ground between the philosophy of Aristotle and Rabbinic Judaism. In 1141, HaLevi followed his heart and moved to Palestine. Also in the twelfth century, Hebrew poetry was written by Moses and Abraham ibn Ezra. In 1146, the fanatic Almohades from North Africa took over Islamic Spain and persecuted Jews and Christians. So, in 1158 Maimonides fled to the court of Saladin in Fostat (later Cairo).

In 1236, the reconquest of Spain by the Christians began. The Jewish communities under Christian rule went into a gradual decline. In the thirteenth century, Moses de Leon of Guadalajara produced the *Zohar* (*Splendor*), commentaries that found mystical meaning in the Torah. (See Chapter 12.) In 1391, persecution of Jews was led by Christian clergy. Ferrand Martinez, a priest prominent in the court, let loose mobs who attacked the Jews of Seville and razed twenty-three synagogues. There were massacres in Toledo, Valencia, and Palma. It was in this atmosphere that many Jews became New Christians ("*anusim*," forced ones) in order to save their lives and possessions. Jews were compelled to live in separate neighborhoods. After 1449, these New Christians ("*conversos*") were suspected of secretly practicing Judaism and were called "*marranos*" (a derogatory term: swine). In 1480, the royal couple, Ferdinand and Isabella, established the Spanish Inquisition, and in 1483, the Pope appointed a Dominican priest, Torquemada, to be inqisitor-general. Thousands of *conversos* were accused of being secret Jews. If they "confessed," their property was confiscated and they had to do penance. If they refused to repent, they were burned at the stake (*auto da-fe*). After Christian soldiers captured the last Moslem stronghold, Granada, Ferdinand and Isabella made the practice of Judaism illegal in Spain. Some Jews converted rather than leave, but an estimated 100,000 to 150,000 fled Spain in the summer of 1492. Many went to Portugal, only to be forced to leave or be baptized in 1497. Others went to Amsterdam, North Africa, Italy, or the Ottoman Empire which then included Palestine.

Among the oldest Jewish communities in Europe were those found in southern Italy. Some Jews were traders in the port cities of Bari and Otronto. By the time of the Inquisition and Expulsion from Spain, Italian Jews, following commerce, had moved into such northern cities as Florence and Venice. The Sephardic Jews from Spain came to live alongside the Ashkenazim. From 1556 to 1576, Jews in Rome and Venice were forced to live in the ghettos (from the root meaning "foundries"; hence, the poorest section of town). Still, many Italian Jews had been influenced by the Renaissance. Azaria dei Rossi rediscovered Hellenistic Jewish writings(e.g., Philo and Josephus). Don Isaac Abarbanel, a prominent Spanish Jew in 1492, refused to convert and so moved to Italy. There he wrote philosophic commentaries, blending Judaism with the Renaissance. He wrote that the seven branches of the menorah represent the seven courses taught in the humanistic universities of the time. To me, Abarbanel suggests that the Torah in the ark, represents the light of spiritual and moral truths. One needs the lights of secular wisdom to shine on the Torah in order to bring its values to reality. One also needs the spiritual and moral teachings of the Torah to make sure that the knowledge of the universities was not misused to the detriment of humanity.

The Sephardim who settled in Palestine, particularly in the Galilee, developed a messianic mysticism (to be discussed in the next chapter). This was also the time of false messiahs: in Italy, Solomon Molcho and David Reubeni; in the Ottoman Empire, the more influential and charismatic Sabbatai Tzevi. Other Sephardim settled in the relatively tolerant Amsterdam, "the New Jerusalem." Still others became the first trickle of immigration from Europe to the New World.

Whenever the Jewish communities were well-treated, there emerged rabbinic commentators, philosophers, and poets. However, when the Jewish communities were poor and persecuted, the creative response to such persecution came to be variations on the theme of mysticism, such as the Kabbalah, Messianism, and Hasidism. Some of these responses are still relevant today as Jews of all ages seek renewal of the spirit in ways that go beyond reason.

TOPICS FOR DISCUSSION

1. What incidents or expressions of anti-Semitism have you encountered or observed?

2. What do you believe are the causes of anti-Semitism?

3. How would you rank these causes in order of their importance?

4. When demagogues make anti-Semitic statements, is it better publicly to engage them in debate in order to repudiate them, or to say nothing in public, lest publicity may help the demagogue?

5. Which of the following responses to anti-Semitism are most (and are least) helpful:

> 1) educating the public so as to show the fallacy of stereotypes.
> 2) working for a society in which there are respect for human rights and equal and ample opportunity for all.
> 3) modifying Jewish behavior so as not to give the bigot an excuse for bigotry.
> 4) letting the public know the identity of the anti-Semites.
> 5) Other_____.

6. How would you explain the ability of the Jewish people and Judaism to persist despite centuries of persecution?

RESOURCES

Baer, Yitzhak. *A History of the Jews in Christian Spain*, Vol Two. Philadelphia, Jewish Publication Society, 1961.

Flannery, Edward H. *The Anguish of the Jews: Twenty-Three Centu-*

ries of Antisemitism (Revised and Updated). New York, Paulist Press, 1985.

Rivkin, Ellis. *The Shaping of Jewish History*. ("Medieval Ways to Salvation") New York, Scribner's Sons, 1971.

Setltzer, Robert. *Jewish People, Jewish Thought*. (Chapter VII). New York, Macmillan, 1980.

FROM MYSTICISM TO *RATIONALISM*:
1500-1800

1516: Jews of Venice confined to ghetto.

1567: Joseph Caro's *Shulchan Arukh,* Code of Jewish Law in Palestine.

1570: In Poland, Moses Isserles' *Mapah*, commentary on Shulchan Aruch.

1572: Isaac Luria develops Messianic Kabbalah in Tzefat.

1590-1640: *Uriel Acosta excommunicated by rabbis in Amsterdam.*

1632-1677: *Baruch Spinoza excommunicated by rabbis in Amsterdam.*

1648: Chmielnicki leads Cossacks in massacre of Jews.

1665-6: Sabbatai Tzevi in Turkey claims to be the messiah, converts to Islam.

1700-1760: Israel ben Eliezer (Baal Shem Tov) and rise of Hasidism.

1727-1786: *Moses Mendelssohn, philosopher of the Enlightenment.*

1740-1809: Levi Yitzhak of Berditchef, the rebellious Hasid.

1772-1810: Nachman of Bratzlav, the "Tormented Master."

1797: *Izak Graanboom rabbi of Adath Jeshurun ("reformed Jews of Holland").*

12.

KABBALAH, HASIDISM,

AND JEWISH MYSTICISM

One summer in the 1970's, my wife and I were staying at a hotel in Tzefat, a town in the Galilee that had been a center of Jewish mysticism in the 16th century. Posted on a bulletin board in the lobby was a notice that invited guests to attend a class in Jewish meditation. Intrigued by what I assumed was a twentieth-century revival of Kabbalistic teachings, I found my way through narrow streets, came upon a hidden doorway, and entered a darkened room. There I found not a Hasidic rebbe but an American Jew named Chaim from California. There were two other "students," a professor from Bar Ilan University and his wife.

Chaim explained that after studying and practicing various methods of meditation, from TM to Zen, on the West Coast, he asked himself, "Could there be authentic forms of Jewish meditation that would enable today's Jews to achieve a mystical experience?" Where else to go but Tzefat, snuggled in the hills of the Galilee, which was becoming the center of a Hasidic revival. Chaim began his studies by reading the first book of Jewish mysticism, the *Sefer Yetsira,* the Book of Creation, written in Hebrew by a

Palestinian Jew sometime between the third and sixth centuries, CE. There he found a breathing exercise based upon Hebrew letters and words: arms held high toward the fire (*aish*) in the heavens and inhaling, you became the Hebrew letter, *shin;* crossing your arms over your chest (like an *aleph*) and holding your breath you became aware of the *avir,* the air in one's lungs; and exhaling to the sound of *mem,* making wave-like motions with the hands as they moved to the lower abdomen, as though *mayim*(water*)* was cleansing the system. The purpose of the meditation was to feel the link between what is most basic in oneself and the most fundamental elements of nature, between soul and Cosmic Soul. The meditation had but a minimal effect on me. It was not until I pursued my own studies of Jewish mysticism that I discovered insights that would help me find an inner self more fundamental than obsessive thoughts that disturbed my peace.

The first medieval forms of Jewish mysticism (called Kabbalah) emerged in thirteenth-century Spain, perhaps as a religious response to the increased persecution first by the Almohades and then by the new Christian rulers. Abraham Abulafia (1240-1292), by concentrating on Hebrew letters,"saw" the letters move and form combinations. His meditation led to an ecstatic experience that seemed to break through the knots that had tied up his being and that culminated in an immediate awareness of God.

Most Jewish mystics in Spain did not aim for such ecstasy but for *d'vekut,* a continual "cleaving" to God. These Kabbalists could achieve this experience by repentance, charity, and prayer, but most important, by studying the *Zohar,* a commentary that searched the Torah to discover the divine secrets of creation. The *Zohar* (*Splendor*) was ascribed to the second-century mystic, Simeon bar Yohai, but was actually written between 1280 and 1286 by Moses de Leon of Guadalajara. Unlike other forms of medieval mysticism, this "Practical" Kabbalah required much study and emphasized ritual practice.

These Kabbalists believed that God is hidden and unknowable (the *Ayn Sof,* without end). While one cannot know God directly, one can discover the divine emanations (*sephirot*), aspects of being that form the basis of the encountered world. At the top of the "tree of *sephirot")* is *keter* (crown of creation), which suggests that all other emanations flow from the hidden God. Beneath the *keter* is *hochmah* (wisdom, a male principle of penetrating insight) and *binah* (understanding, a female quality of contemplation, drawing conclusions from the original insight). *Din* (judgment) is balanced by *hesed* (lovingkindness). *Tiferet* (beauty) harmonizes both male and female qualities.

Hod (majesty) and *netzach (*permanence) are based on *y'sod* (foundation, the source of sexuality.) When a man and woman lovingly join together in sexual union, they give joy to the Divine Presence. At the base of the tree is *malchut* (kingdom), representing the Jewish people. By performing the *mitzvot* properly, the individual Jew was doing his/her part to keep the *sephirot* in harmony and to prevent the cosmos from collapsing. That is why, before performing a ritual, a Kabbalist would say, "It is with fear and trembling that I do this commandment." The Kabbalah gave the harried and harassed medieval Jew an exalted purpose in life: to preserve the world.

After the Inquisition and expulsion from Spain (1492), the Jewish people and their rabbis faced a terrible question. How could God have allowed such a tragedy to befall the Chosen People? The Kabbalistic response was ingenious and is still relevant today. It was developed by Rabbi Isaac Luria who lived in Tzefat, in the Galilee, where many Sephardic Jews found a home after their expulsion.

Luria wondered how God could have created the world out of nothing if before creation God was *Makom (*in every place, omnipresent) and there was no nothing. Therefore, God first had to create nothing. This God did by *tzimtzum* (contracting), thus creating space devoid of God. In that empty space God created the heaven and earth. Then God allowed divine light to enter the world. However, the divine light was so awesome, so intense, that it could have destroyed the world. So God created *kaylim,* containers to hold and restrain the light, but the *kaylim* could not hold back the light, and there was a cosmic explosion (*shevirat hakaylim).* This Kabbalistic "big bang" produced thousands of *k'lipot,* fragments of the containers, shards that still contained sparks of divine light.

This cosmology had both theological and moral significance. Not just the Jews but *even God is in exile!* God is not able to separate the sparks from the shards, the good from the evil, but *we humans can.* In fact, this is our task as human beings and as Jews: *to repair the world.* The Hebrew term is *tikkun.* We repair the world by freeing the sparks from the shards through prayer, meditation, charity, and *mitzvot,* especially those commandments that would have us pursue justice and peace. When enough Jews performed the *mitzvot,* the process of *tikkun* would be completed, the messiah would come and bring God's kingdom here on earth, hence the phrase, "Messianic Kabbalah." So, there *is* something special about Jewish mysticism: rather than being an escape from reality, it sends the Jew back into the world to repair it and so create a more just and peaceful place for us and future generations.

As noted in Chapter 11, the seventeenth century was extremely painful for Jews wherever they lived. In Poland, Jews were being butchered by Chmielniki. In Italy, the Counter-Reformation was hostile to the Jews. The exiles from the Spanish expulsion were trying to put their lives together from North Africa to the Ottoman Empire. Little wonder that thousands of Jews were praying for the messiah as never before.

Many believed that their prayers were answered by a Jew from

Smyrna named Shabbatai Tzevi, born in 1626, possibly on the ninth of Av, a midsummer fast commemorating the destruction of the Temple. He traveled from Greece to Jerusalem to Cairo. There he became part of a Kabbalistic circle. In 1665, in Gaza, he met a young man, Nathan, who convinced him that he, Shabbatai, was the messiah, that all the holy sparks had been freed from the *k'lipot*, and that he would soon lead the tribes of Israel back to Jerusalem. When Shabbatai proclaimed himself to be the messiah, thousands of Jews were swept up in the hysteria. Many sold their possessions and began to leave for Jerusalem. But there was a minor problem. The Sultan of Turkey was not about to allow his province of Palestine to be taken from him. The Sultan had Shabbatai brought before him and gave the so-called messiah a choice: He could convert to Islam, or he could be executed. Shabbatai converted.

This manic period in the lives of thousands of seventeenth-century Jews who believed in Shabbatai was followed by deep depression. There were some who refused to give up their illusion. Among these "Sabbateans" were those who emulated Shabbatai by publicly converting to Islam while, in private, practicing a perverted form of Judaism (e.g., flouting sexual laws). The Sabbatean heresy persisted as late as the eighteenth century, when a Polish Jew, Jacob Frank, proclaimed himself to be a reincarnation of Shabbatai and preached that disobedience to the Torah was holy. However, most Jews from Poland and the Ukraine remained in despair, desperately in need of a spiritual revival. This revival was called Hasidism.

THE HASIDIC MOVEMENT

Hasidism was initiated by Israel ben Eliezer, who came to be known as the Baal Shem Tov. Born in 1700 of poor parents in southern Poland, the Besht (as he was called) with his wife wandered in the Carpathian mountains, meditated on Kabbalah, and settled in the town of Medzibozh. There he became a healer, curing Jews of physical and mental illnesses, as did others called "Baal Shem"(Master of the Name). Israel was special in that he could help his followers have an intense spiritual experience, a *d'vekut*, a cleaving to God.

While for most earlier Kabbalists, *d'vekut* could be achieved only after studying the *Zohar*, the Besht believed that a mystical experience was available to any Jew who had sufficient *emunah*, faith. The Besht believed that God is everywhere, in nature, in human relations, in the everyday experiences of life. One could be with God at any time. Also, for the Besht, the mystical experience might begin with *d'vekut* but could lead to *hitlahavut*, a spiritual ecstasy.

Because most Jews did not normally have sufficient faith to induce a mystical experience, the Besht would encourage his followers to sing, dance, perhaps drink a bit of wine, and, above all, to love. The goal was *Yihud* (Oneness), when the core of one's being becomes one with the core of Being, itself. The *hiddush*, the innovation of Hasidism was that one can achieve *Yihud* in the here and now. According to Gershon Scholem, pre-eminent scholar of Jewish mysticism, "small talk with one's neighbor can be a vehicle for deep meditation." However, Scholem asserted that the true Hasid goes beneath the here-and-now and finds God behind appearances. Martin Buber, the existentialist so fond of Hasidic tales, believed that the Hasid finds God in the present reality.

The Hasidic movement took hold in southern Poland and the Ukraine, where the Jews were most impoverished and often illiterate. However, the Besht insisted that essential for prayer and a mystical experience was not learning but *kavanah* (sincerity, pure intention). He made this point at a Yom Kippur eve service. A deaf-and-mute child was standing in the midst of worshippers who were chanting the plaintive and beautiful *Kol Nidre* prayer, which according to custom, was sung three times. The Besht, who was leading the service, repeated the prayer more than the customary three times. The congregants was perplexed but went along with their esteemed leader. Meanwhile the child, who was fingering a wooden whistle he had made that day, was becoming increasingly frustrated because of his inability to join in the prayer. Suddenly he blew a shrill sound on his whistle. The worshippers were furious and wanted to expel the boy from the synagogue. The Besht calmed the people and explained: "After chanting the *Kol Nidre* three times, I did not sense that a single prayer had reached God, so I continued the chanting. It was not until this child who could not hear or speak blew on this whistle that the gates of heaven were opened." (See Chapter 13 for more on the *Kol Nidre*.)

For the Besht, happiness depended not on health or wealth but on one's capacity to appreciate whatever blessings one was granted. The Hasidic master once asked a water-carrier: "Yuchel, how are you today?"

"Oy, Rebbe," Yuchel sighed, "I am old and my shoulders are weak.

The children are busy studying Torah but not one thinks of me. My wife is old and sick. My sons-in-law spend so much time studying that I do all the work. I am depressed by all my woes."

The next day the Besht called to Yuchel: "How do you feel today?"

Yuchel chuckled and said: "Rebbe, you know, I'm a lucky man. I have five children and sons-in-law who study Torah. My wife, a darling, keeps the house clean even though she's old and sick. And I am able to bear all this on these old shoulders. Yes, rebbe, I'm a lucky man, thank God."

The Besht commented to his students who had heard both conversations: "Not a single thing had changed but today Yuchel received more of God's compassion."

With no books to study and with disciples who were uneducated, how could the wisdom of the Hasidic leaders be taught? By watching, observing, and listening to one's own rebbe, often called a "*tzaddik*" (righteous one). A disciple of the Maggid (preacher) of Mezeritch said of his teacher: "I went to the Maggid not to study Torah with him but to watch him tie his boot-straps."

Among the most intriguing Hasidic leaders was Nahman of Bratzlav (1772-1810), who lived and taught during the generation after the Besht. (Nahman is the subject of an insightful biography, *The Tormented Master*, by Arthur Green.) He taught his disciples the discipline of solitary prayer (*hidbodedut*), quite atypical of Jewish tradition. Nahman and his students would go outdoors, find an isolated spot, and offer this prayer: "Master of the universe, grant me the ability to be alone. May it be my custom to go outdoors each day among trees and grass, among all growing things. There may I be alone and talk to the One I belong to and express everything in my heart."

For Nahman, such catharsis was not enough. He believed that we have both sick thoughts (sometimes called "strange gods") and sane thoughts. Only after we pour them all out, the sick and the sane, can we know the difference. Nahman told the story of a king whose advisor informed him that the nation's crop had been poisoned and all who ate of it would go crazy. The king asked for advice and the advisor replied: "We could refuse to eat of the crop. Then at least *we* would be sane."

"No," said the king. "If we are the only ones who are sane, the people will think that *we* are crazy. Let us, instead, eat of the crop. True, we shall go crazy, but we will *know* that we are crazy."

Partaking of the crop of the human condition, confronting the conflicts and stresses of life—this makes us all, to one degree or another, "crazy." Nahman suggested that the first step to sanity is to know when you are being crazy. After we let our feelings flow freely, we may realize that some of them are absurd, a *mishagas*. When we envy others, when we are obsessed with worry (having done all we can), when we feel that we are failures because of not living up to someone's expectations, we may recognize that these thoughts are *mishagasim* (craziness). Then, we may be able to discover the oneness that is at the root of our being. In Nahman's words, "No matter how low you have fallen in your own esteem, bear in mind that if you delve deeply into yourself, you will discover holiness there."

The tale also has implications for our social attitudes. All of us eat of the harvest of our culture. We should ask ourselves: How am I affected by the bias and the bigotry, the delusions and illusions of society? Perhaps some of the pieties and platitudes we hear from politicians and pundits are also *mishagasim* that that we and our community should reject. Nahman's prayer concludes: "May all the foliage in the field awake at my coming, to send the powers of their life into the words of my prayer so that my prayer and speech are made whole through the life and spirit of all growing things, which are made as one by their transcendent Source."

Once we have returned to the holiness within, then we will be able to reach out to others in love—and by "others" the Hasidic leaders meant *all* others. When the wife of a *mitnaged* (a rabbinic opponent of Hasidism) threw garbage on the head of the saintly Levi Yitzhak of Berditchev (a contemporary of Nahman), the Rebbe pleaded with God: "Don't be angry with her. It's not her fault. She wishes only to please her husband." A more profound reason for loving the adversary was expressed in this passage quoted by Buber in his collection of Hasidic sayings, *Ten Rungs*:

"Love your neighbor as something which you yourself are. For all souls are one. Each is a spark from the original soul, and this soul is inherent in all souls just as your soul is inherent in all the members of your body. It may come to pass that your hand will make a mistake and strike you. But would you then take a stick and chastise your hand because it lacked understanding and so increase your pain? It is the same if your neighbor, who is of one soul with you, wrongs you because of his lack of understanding. If you punish him, you only hurt yourself."

Levi-Yitzhak was perhaps the most daring of the Hasidic masters. He went so far as to judge God. Once during a Rosh Hashanah service, Levi-Yitzhak cried out: "If You prefer the enemy who suffers less than we do, then let the enemy praise your glory! . . . *Zol Ivan blozen shofar* (Let Ivan blow the shofar)." On another occasion, the Rebbe of Berditchef was absent from services on *Kol Nidre* eve. His disciples wondered: How could the Rebbe miss the most important prayer of he year? A search party was sent to find him. They discovered their Rebbe sitting by the road, rocking a baby to sleep. He explained to them, "This infant was crying. If I could not stop to comfort a crying child, how can I expect the Almighty to listen to my cries?"

The Hasidim were known for their joyful spirit which they expressed through prayer, song and dance. However, they did not deny the suffering that was often their lot. Rebbe David Leikes summed up the essence of Hasidic wisdom when he said, "One must enjoy life in spite of life." In Hasidic song, the words are simple and repetitive. Some of their *nigunim* (chants) are simply sounds: ya, ba, bye. It was believed that the thought process may remove us from direct communion with God. Because words express concepts, the most spiritual experience is non-verbal. Reb

Leib, the Grandfather of Shpole, considered dancing to be a form of worship. He said, "Dancing is the purest form of worship, for when one dances, his entire being—body and soul—is at the service of his Creator."

The Hasidic movement was inevitably in tension with the rabbinic scholars who led the *yeshivot* (Talmudic academies) in northern Russia and Lithuania. After all, if one could have a mystical experience with God without studying Torah, by singing or dancing, then of what value is the elaborate system of rabbinic law that Jews are required to follow? These *mitnagdim* (opponents) were particularly concerned with leaders such as Levi-Yitzhak, who missed the Kol Nidre and argued with, even judged God.

To prevent Hasidism from becoming a sect separate from rabbinic Judaism, Schneur Zalman (1747-1812) founded "Habad" Hasidism. The Habadniks returned to *hochmah, binah,* and *daat* (wisdom, understanding, and knowledge). They attempted to combine study of Torah and Jewish law with the love and joy of the Besht. Their followers became known as Lubavitcher Hasidim. In the 1940's, some left the Soviet Union and eventually found themselves in Crown Heights, Brooklyn, where they established their headquarters. Their movement is led by the Lubavitcher Rebbe, who is a descendent of Schneur Zalman. They send their Hasidim throughout the United States and even into Russia to bring Jews back to the observance of Jewish law with joy. Their butchers sell only meat that is *Glatt Kosher* (more rigorously inspected.) They support those in Israel who would refuse to return any West Bank land to the Palestinians.

I have taken tenth-grade students to the Lubavitcher headquarters in Brooklyn. We were courteously treated and seated in the balcony overlooking the main hall where men were studying and praying. A young rabbi explained the history and ideology of their movement. He then invited the boys to go downstairs and learn to lay *tefillin* (phylacteries). When the girls asked why they could not go, he explained that boys are more aggressive than girls and need to channel that aggression by straps and boxes and prayers which restrain their anger. The girls in the class did not restrain their anger, which they freely expressed toward the young rabbi.

Bratzlaver Hasidim are today found in both Brooklyn and Jerusalem. Their leader is still Nahman of Bratzlav who died in 1810. So impressed were the Bratzlavers by his wisdom that they said, "Better a dead rabbi who is alive than a live rabbi who is dead."

The Hasidim themselves admit that they have lost some of the piety and spiritual power of the earlier masters. They expressed their sense of spiritual decline by, of course, telling a story:

"When the great Israel Baal Shem Tov saw misfortune threatening the Jews, it was his custom to go to a certain part of the forest to meditate. There he would light a fire, say a special prayer, and then the miracle would be accomplished and the misfortune averted.

"Later, when his disciple, the celebrated Maggid of Mezeritch, had occasion, for the same reason, to intercede with Heaven, he would go to the same place in the forest and say: "Master of the universe, listen! I do not know how to light the fire, but I am still able to say the prayer." And again the miracle would be accomplished.

"Still later, Moshe-Leib of Sassov, in order to save his people once more, would go into the forest and say, 'I do not know the prayer, but I know the place and this must be sufficient.' It was sufficient and the miracle was accomplished.

"Then it fell to Israel of Rizhin to overcome misfortune. Sitting in his armchair, his head in his hands, he spoke to God, 'I am unable to light the fire and I do not know the prayer; I cannot even find the place in the forest. All I can do is tell the story, and this must be sufficient.' And it was."

By telling the stories of those *earlier* Hasidic masters, we may remind ourselves of their respect for diversity and their capacity to love beyond their own community. The following stories express that respect:

Rebbe Baer of Radenitz once said to his teacher, the Seer of Lublin: "Show me one general way to the service of God." The Tzaddik replied: "It is impossible to tell others what way they should take. For one way to serve God is through learning, another through prayer, another through fasting and still another through eating. Everyone should carefully observe what way his heart draws him to and then choose this way with all his strength."

HASIDIC STORIES FOR DISCUSSION

Read these tales or sayings and then consider their meanings:

1. In a midrash, the world is compared to a castle and its owner with God. Based on this midrash, this Hasidic story was told by a rebbe:

> A traveler loses his way in the forest. He sees a castle in flames. It is an empty castle, thinks the traveler. Suddenly he hears a voice crying, "Help, help me, I am the owner of the castle!" The rebbe repeats, "The castle is ablaze, the forest is burning, and the owner cries for help; what does it mean? That the castle is not empty and that there is an owner."

2. There was once a man who was not very bright. When he arose in the morning it was difficult for him to find his clothes. One evening, as he undressed, he wrote on a piece of paper exactly where he put every item of his clothes. The next morning he read, "cap," there it was, he set it on his head; "pants," there they lay, he put them on, and so it went until he was fully dressed. "That's all very well, but now where am I, myself?" he asked with great concern. "Where in the world am I?" He looked and looked, but he could not find himself.

"And that is how it is with us," said the rebbe.

3. Rebbe Mendel said, "If I am I, because I am I, and you are you, because you are you, then I am I, and you are you. But if I am I, because you are you, and you are you, because I am I, then I am not I, and you are not you."

4. Rebbe Moshe Lieb of Sassov told this story: "I was sitting in an inn among peasants who were drinking heavily, and I heard this conversation between two of them:

"Do you love me?"

"Of course, I love you. You are dearer to me than my brother."

"Do you love me as you love yourself?"

"More."

"If you love me so much, why haven't you noticed that I've cut my hand and the blood is flowing?"

"From him," said Rebbe Moshe Leib, "I learned that to love means to feel the pain of another."

5. After the death of Rebbe Moshe, Rebbe Mendel of Kotzk asked one of his disciples, "What was most important to your teacher?"

The disciple thought and replied, "Whatever he happened to be doing at the moment."

6. When Rebbe Noah, Rebbe Mordecai's son, assumed the succession after his father's death, his disciples noticed that there were a number of ways he conducted himself differently from his father, and they asked him about this. He replied: "I do just as my father did. He did not imitate, and I do not imitate."

7. Susya was a very cheerful rebbe. His students asked: "Why are you always so happy? Don't you ever worry?"

Susya replied, "There is no reason to worry about the past. It is over. After I have prepared as best I can for the future, there is no point in worrying about what I cannot control. That leaves the present, which is over in a split second. Why worry about a split second?"

RESOURCES

Buber, Martin. *Tales of the Hasidim. Vol. I and II.* New York, Schocken, 1947.

Green, Arthur. *Tormented Master: A Life of Nahman of Bratzlav.* University of Alabama Press, 1979.

Green, Arthur(ed.) *Jewish Spirituality from the 16th Century Revival to the Present.* New York, Crossroad, 1987.

Hoffman, Edward. *The Way of Splendor: Jewish Mysticism and Modern Psychology.* Northvale, N. J., Jason Aronson, 1989.

Scholem, Gershom. *Modern Trends in Jewish Mysticism.* Jerusalem, Schocken, 1941.

Scholem, Gershom. *The Messianic Idea in Judaism.* New York, Schocken, 1971.

Seltzer, Robert. *Jewish People, Jewish Thought.* (Chapters IX and X) New York, Macmillan, 1980.

Weiner, Herbert. *9 1/2 Mystics: The Kabbalah Today.* New York, Holt Rinehart & Winston, 1969.

Wiesel, Elie. *Somewhere—A Master.* New York, Summit, 1982.

Wiesel, Elie. *Souls on Fire: Portraits and Legends of Hasidic Masters.* New York, Random House, 1972.

13.

THE CELEBRATION OF TIME: SHABBAT SHALOM, L'SHANAH TOVAH TIKOTEVU

There have been many excellent books written on the observance of the Sabbath, festivals and holidays. (See Resources.) Please choose at least one to read. I will try not to duplicate their content by focusing on the underlying themes of these sacred times.

SHABBAT SHALOM

It was Heschel's *The Sabbath* that helped me think of Shabbat in a luminous light. The eloquent theologian wrote:

> "The higher goal of spiritual living is not to amass a wealth of information, but to face sacred moments . . . Spiritual life begins to decay when we fail to sense the grandeur of what is eternal in time . . .

> "The Bible is more concerned with time than with space . . . There is no reference in the record of creation to

any object in space that would be endowed with the quality of holiness . . . The sanctity of time came first: "And God blessed the Sabbath day and declared it holy" (Genesis 2:3).

"The meaning of the Sabbath is to celebrate time rather than space."

"He who wants to enter the holiness of the day must first lay down the profanity of clattering commerce, of being yoked to toil. He must go away from the screech of dissonant days, from the nervousness and fury of acquisitiveness and the betrayal in embezzling his own life. He must say farewell to manual work and learn to understand that the world has already been created and will survive without the help of man . . . Six days a week we seek to dominate the world; on the seventh day we try to dominate the self . . . The day of the Lord is more important than the house of the Lord . . ." (According to Heschel, that is why synagogues could be built; one did not have to pray in the Temple)

In everyday language, Shabbat is the time to appreciate special moments with family, with friends, with ourselves, and with God. The Shabbat begins the evening after the sixth day of the week, for we read in Genesis 1:7, "and there was evening and there was morning a first day." Customs vary with time and place. When I was a child, we celebrated "Shabos" (the Ashkenazic pronunciation) at my grandparents' table. In Texas on Sabbath eve, the meal began not with gefilte fish and chicken soup but with avocado and grapefruit salad, followed by barley soup. Candles were lit. My grandfather chanted the *kiddush* over wine, said the *motzi* over the bread, and after the meal he sped through the *birkat hamzon* (blessing after the food). I did not understand what was being sung, but I did feel the warmth and joy of the family, a secure sense of belonging. When my own children were young, I developed a *Shabbat at Home* service in memory of my grandfather. It began: "We come together this evening as a family. During the week gone by, we have worked and we have played. We have fought and we've had fun. We have loved and we have hurt. We have laughed and we have cried, and now, as we welcome the Shabbat, we feel good, just being here together . . ."

Why do we say "Shabbat Shalom," a Sabbath of Peace? On Shabbat we try to achieve four kinds of peace:

1) Peace within ourselves. Buber wrote, "The man with the divided complicated contradictory soul is not helpless. The core of his soul, the divine force within its depths, is capable of . . . binding the conflicting forces together, amalgamating the diverging elements—is capable of unifying it." That is, the parts of our conflicted selves do fit together.

2) *Shalom bayit,* peace in the home. Whatever tensions there were between spouses or between the generations should be dissolved. A story is told about a husband who was quarreling with his wife, because she spent so much time listening to Rabbi Meir's lectures. The husband expelled her from the house and said, "Do not come back until you have spit seven times in the Rabbi's eyes." Rabbi Meir somehow learned what had happened. The next time the wife was in his class, he pretended to have an ailment which could be cured only by having someone spit in his eye seven times. He persuaded the woman to do so and sent her back to her husband. His students objected that by lying and suffering indignity the Rabbi and the Law had been dishonored.

Rabbi Meir replied, citing a saying of Rabbi Ishmael: "Great is peace for God has decreed that even His Holy Name may be blotted out in water to produce it."

"So," said Rabbi Meir, "if the Holy Name may be washed

away to make peace, how much more is this true of the honor of Rabbi Meir."

3) Peace within Israel. It was written in the Talmud: "The reason the Temple was destroyed (by the Romans) was that the children of Israel were divided by senseless hatred." On Shabbat we feel a link with Jews in every land. In the town of Santa Clara, Cuba, there are nine Jewish families numbering thirty people. Every Sabbath eve they hold services in someone's home. In February, 2000, I was one of fifteen Jewish tourists who joined them for worship. The Conservative *siddur* was written in both Spanish and Hebrew. A young man, Alberto, led the singing and reading. The service was abbreviated, but as we joined in singing *Hinay Mah Tov* ("How good it is . . . to sit together in unity"), some became teary. We American Jews were moved by the commitment of this tiny community, determined to keep the Jewish heritage alive. They were moved, because we represented to them a link to world Jewry.

4.) Peace throughout humanity. In Chapter 5, we quoted the beautiful prayer for peace that is an interpretation of the last blessing of the *Tefila, Shalom Rav*. The most recent frequently sung prayer for peace is taken from the last sentence of the *Kaddish*: *"Oseh shalom bimromav, hu yaaseh shalom aleynu v'al kol yisrael, v'imru imru amen. Yaaseh shalom . . ."* May the One who makes peace in the High Places make peace for us and all Israel and let us say, amen . . ." In Psalm *34:15*, we read: *Bakesh shalom v'radfayhu"* ("Seek peace and pursuit it.") According to the midrash, this means: "Seek peace in your own place and then pursue it elsewhere."

How is it possible for tensions to dissolve and for peace to be in our hearts simply because the sixth day has faded into twilight and Shabbat has begun? One response may be found in Heschel's *The Sabbath*. A rabbi who was a chain smoker was being pursued by anti-Semites. He hid in a cave that was totally dark. He lost all sense of time. He had two concerns: How could he endure the overwhelming need for a cigarette and how would he know when Shabbat had begun? After many many hours of extreme discomfort, his desire for tobacco suddenly left him. Then he knew that Shabbat had begun. (Once Shabbat becomes a habitual part of our lives, then not only will we remember Shabbat, but Shabbat may remember us.)

On Shabbat, according to tradition, we receive a *n'shama y'tera* (an additional soul). A secular understanding of a day of rest each week might suggest that the purpose of such a day would be to take it easy for one day so that we may be prepared to go back into the world of work and achievement. But the opposite is the case: The Shabbat does not exist for the days of the week; rather the days of the week exist for the Shabbat. The laws of Shabbat, which some see as restricting and demanding, are intended to free our spirits so that we may find the joy that comes from Sabbath peace. When Shabbat ends, there is the tradition of *Havdalah* (separation): We light a twisted candle, bless the wine, pass around the *b'somim,* spice box, dash the candle's flame in the wine and sing *Shavuah Tov* (good week) The smell of the spices are supposed to keep us going till next *Shabbat* when the extra soul returns.

L'SHANA TOVA TIKOTAVU
("May you be inscribed for a good year")

Several years ago, I took a survey of my congregation to discover the meanings that my congregants found in the High Holydays. Of the respondents, 92% viewed the Holydays as a time to reflect on their mortality; 68% found in the High Holydays a time to affirm their Jewish identity, to establish continuity with their Jewish roots, and to have a spiritual experience. For 64%, this was a time for self-examination. For 56% these days were considered a time to wake up their social conscience. For 52%, this was a time to pray for a good year, and only 28% believed these days were a time to seek forgiveness.

The High Holyday Prayers are found in the *Machzor* (literally, "cycle") or prayer book for the holydays and festivals. The main metaphor in our Rosh Hashanah prayers is that of God as *Melech* (King). We pray, "Remember us unto life, O King, who delights in life." Those of us who prefer a gender-sensitive prayer book have real problems with this Rosh Hashanah metaphor. We may substitute "ruler" for "king," but then comes the very traditional *Avinu Malkenu:* "Our Father, our King, hear our voice, we have sinned against you." "Our Parent, our Ruler" sounds awkward. So in many synagogues, *Avinu Malkenu* is said or sung in Hebrew, without translation: "Have compassion on us and on our children, Make an end to sickness, war and famine and to all oppression . . . let the new year be a good year for us." Perhaps for some, their minds may not believe that such prayers will be effective, but their hearts would have them hope. Rabbi Levi Olan preferred the metaphor of God as Father to that of God as King. A King suggests absolute power. For Olan, God's power is limited by the very laws of the universe that God created. When we are young, we believe our fathers are all-powerful, but as we mature, we realize that our fathers cannot know or do everything. Still we believe our fathers love us and want what is best for us. So does God.

The Torah portion that is read on the first day of Rosh Hashanah for Reform Jews and on the second day for Orthodox and Conservative Jews is the disturbing story of the *Akeda,* the binding of Isaac. Abraham was tested by God to see if his obedience was absolute, if he would bind and sacrifice his son, Isaac, simply because God said so. This raises troubling questions: How could a loving God have commanded the killing of an innocent? How could God have wanted Abraham to act contrary to his reason and conscience? How could Abraham have been willing to do so? The traditional response is that God knew all along that God would not let Abraham do the deed but would provide a ram as the offering. Many scholars maintain that the basic purpose of the story was to make clear to the Israelites that God does *not* want child sacrifice, a custom that was practiced among some pagan tribes. This, then, is a powerful denunciation of the taking of innocent life. The Torah is consistent with our Rosh Hashanah prayer, "Remember us unto life, O Sovereign, who delights in life."

The most compelling custom of Rosh Hashanah is the sounding of the shofar (ram's horn, or the horn of any animal except a bull, as a reminder of the Israelites' idolatry at Sinai). Many explanations have been given: for instance, as human rulers have horns blown at the time of their coronations, so the Sovereign of the universe wants the shofar to be blown, on the anniversary of the world's creation, for Rosh Hashanah is considered the birthday of the world. However, the reason most consistent with the theme of the Holyday was expressed by Maimonides: "Awake, you sleepers, from your sleep! Rouse yourselves, you slumberers, out of your slumber! Examine your deeds and turn to God in repentance. Remember your Creator, you who are caught up in the daily round, losing sight of eternal truth; you who are wasting your years in vain pursuits that neither profit nor save. Look closely at yourselves; improve your ways and your deeds. Abandon your evil ways, your unworthy schemes, every one of you!" So, the sound of the shofar should wake up our consciences, which at times doze or go into a deep sleep.

The sounds of the shofar have been interpreted to indicate how one might bring universal moral values down to earth. The *tekiah* is the long, straight, unwavering blast. It suggests that on some issues (e.g., respect for human rights) the moral imperative is clear and unwavering. The *shevarim* (three separate or broken notes) and *teruah* (a tremulo of nine consecutive notes) express humility. This suggests that that there are times when good people may differ over their fundamental moral assumptions (e.g., on abortion or euthanasia). So when we debate these issues with well-meaning opponents, we should approach the subject and each other with humility. There are times when we cannot be absolutely certain, so we study and pray and express our opinion without being dogmatic. Abe Lincoln once said, "I pray not that God will be on my side but that I will be on God's side."

Finally, there is the *tekiah g'dolah,* the great or prolonged *tekiah,* which according to tradition is to be sounded when the messiah comes, or the messianic age arrives. This is the sound that gives us hope that redemption will come. When the optimistic philosopher Hermann Cohen, in his seventies, said to his student Franz Rosenzweig, destined to become a great theologian, "I still hope to see the messianic age," Rosenzweig replied, "I must frankly say that I do not expect to live that long." Cohen then asked, "When do you believe a lasting peace will come?" Rosenzweig did not want to answer but said vaguely, "Maybe in a hundred years." Cohen grabbed his hand and cried, "Please, make it fifty."

The prayer that links Rosh Hashanah and Yom Kippur is the *Unetaneh Tokef,* which "proclaims the sacred power of the day." Ascribed to Rabbi Amnon of Mayence, this prayer is a medieval affirmation of the awesome God who has determined the future but still allows humans a way to alter what has been ordained. On Rosh Hashanah it is written, and on Yom Kippur it is sealed, "who (in the year to come) shall live and who shall die . . . who shall be tranquil and who shall be troubled, who shall be poor and who shall be rich." During those eight days between Rosh Hashanah and Yom Kippur, one may change the decree through "repentance, prayer and righteous deeds."(See Chapter 4) Today we do not take literally this medieval metaphor. After all, in the *Amida* or *Sh'moneh Esray* of the daily service, one prays for repentance each day throughout the year (except on Shabbat). Some interpret the *Unetaneh Tokef* prayer to mean, so much that will happen to us has been greatly influenced by factors (genetic, psychological, physiological, environmental) beyond our control. However, we are not simply puppets of the past. Through the self-searching of repentance, the spiritual effort of prayer and the deeds that we choose, we can change for the better.

Such change is not easy. That is the implication of the *Kol Nidre* chant that begins our worship on the eve of Yom Kippur. The literal meaning may startle us: "All vows . . . and promises . . . which we may vow, swear, promise from this day of Atonement to the next day of Atonement . . . may such vows be considered by God not as vows, nor such oaths as oaths . . . May they be null and void!" How strange, to say the least! Why would Jews, at the beginning of Yom Kippur, tell God not to hold them to their vows? Some have explained that the people were so afraid of the consequence, the punishment that would come should they break the vows, that they wanted to protect themselves from divine retribution. The rabbis added a postscript that amended the abjuration of vows: Pardon would be granted those Jews who transgressed *bishgaga*, in error or because one had forgotten the vow. In the *Gates of Repentance* used by Reform Jews, the interpretation is even more lenient: May the vows "be null and void should we, *after honest effort*, find ourselves unable to fulfill them." Whatever interpretation one may offer, the power of Kol Nidre comes more from the melody than from the words. Both words and melody express the awareness of human frailty.

In the *Viddui* (Confession) on Yom Kippur, we recite, "*Al het shehatanu l'faneicha*, for the sin that we have sinned before You." This confession has been discussed in Chapter 7. We would add only an observation by Rabbi Leo Baeck: Of all the sins in the *al het*, none pertain to the failure to perform rituals. Could this be a reflection of the prophetic view that morality takes precedence over ritual, or that ritual without morality is meaningless?

Yom Kippur is a fast day. Why? To set the day apart from

worldly concerns, to show that we do have the power to curb our appetites, to remind us of the hungry, to move us to help the poor and oppressed. In the words of the morning *haftarah* portion (Isaiah 58:1-14): "Is this the fast I look for? A day of self-affliction? . . . Is not this the fast I look for: to unlock the shackles of injustice, to let the oppressed go free, and to break every cruel chain? Is it not to share your bread with the hungry, and to bring the homeless poor into your house? When you are naked, to clothe them, and never to hide yourself from your own kin?"

On Yom Kippur afternoon the *haftarah* is the book of Jonah, the reluctant prophet who tried to flee from God's command that he should warn the people of Nineveh (enemies of Israel) to repent lest they be destroyed. After Jonah was swallowed by a great fish, he promised God he would do as ordered. Jonah did warn the people of Nineveh. They did put on sackloth and ashes and fasted, but it was not until they "turned from their evil ways," that God renounced the punishment. This underscores the rabbinic concept that redemption ultimately depends not on prayers or good intentions but on our deeds. After the Ninevites were saved, Jonah pouted in anger, because the Ninevites were Israel's adversaries. God rebuked him: Jews should care about all people, even the enemy.

The awesome mood of Yom Kippur, from the minor key of *Kol Nidre* to the catharsis of confession to the promise of the *Neilah* service when the gates of atonement and compassion are open, helps us follow Hosea's call (read on *Shabbat Shuvah,* between Rosh Hashanah and Yom Kippur): "Return, O Israel, to the Lord, your God."

I. J. Singer, Yiddish writer and author of *The Brothers Ashkenazi,* was concerned, lest some might insist that their way to atonement or personal redemption is the only way. He expressed this concern in his short story, "Repentance."

In this story, Reb Ezekiel of Kozmir believed that the only way to turn to God was through joy. A giant of a man, he loved nothing better than to dance and sing, eat and drink with his Hasidim. One afternoon before Yom Kippur, who should come to Kozmir but Reb Naphtali, his great adversary, who sternly preached that indulging the appetites (as Reb Ezekiel did) would surely lead to sin. So Reb Naphtali would fast daily, having only one bowl of soup each evening. He slept only two hours a night, and he would not let his students chant, lest the melody distract them from the meaning of the sacred words. So why should Reb Naphtali come to visit his rival before *Kol Nidre?*

It seems that Reb Naphtali was having recurring sexual fantasies, erotic thoughts that he could not get out of his mind. He concluded that his self-punitive practices were not helping him return to God. So, in desperation he turned to the proponent of joy, Reb Ezekiel. Perhaps his rival really did know "the way" to repentance.

The robust Reb Ezekiel explained to the frail Reb Naftali: "Repentance means turning and when a Jew takes a glass of brandy and turns it upside down, he is repenting." Then the happy Hasid initiated Reb Naftali into the pleasures of eating and drinking, singing and dancing. Reb Naftali did find that his fantasies were not so frequent. Then came Yom Kippur when, in Kozmir, all the prayers were set to joyful melodies. Reb Naftali became so caught up in the mood that he could not shed a single tear during the *Al Het.* After the *Neilah* (closing) service, as the Hasidim danced into the yard of the synagogue, Reb Ezekiel opened his arms to his new disciple: "Welcome to the way of joy!" he thundered. Just as he was about to draw the little rebbe into the dance, a violent trembling seized Reb Naftali, and he died. Reb Ezekiel would allow no mourning. He merely announced: "He had sunk too far into the habits of gloom and there was no saving him."

There are those who are absolutely convinced that they know just what others should do or believe in order to be "saved." How difficult it is for some to realize that what might be just fine for certain personalities might be of no help and even harmful to others. For many, the most helpful path might be found somewhere between Reb Ezekiel and Reb Naftali. The High Holydays offer us guidance. Ultimately, it is for each of us to discover—based on knowledge, understanding and soul-searching—which path can best help us discover "the way of pleasantness and the path of peace." So may we, with respect for differences and recognition of our common humanity, greet each other on the Awesome Days: "L'shana tova tikotevu b'sefer hayyim," may you be inscribed for a good year in the book of life."

TOPICS FOR DISCUSSION:

1. What are the ways that you have found helpful in discovering Shabbat Shalom, Sabbath peace?

2. How important—very, somewhat, little, or none—do you consider the following meanings that one might find in the High Holydays? a) a spiritual experience. b) pray for a good year. c) self-examination. d) seek forgiveness. e) wake up your social conscience. f) reflect your mortality. e) listening to the shofar sound or *Kol Nidre*. f) affirm your Jewish identity. g) establish continuity with your roots. h) express a commitment to the Jewish people.

3. Why do you think that in the *Al Het* confessional we never confess the failure to perform a ritual or ceremonial law?

4. How would you interpret the story, "Repentance," by I.J. Singer?

RESOURCES

Gaster, Theodor H. *Festivals of the Jewish Year*. New York, Morrow Quill Paperback, 1978.

Heschel, Abraham Joshua. *The Sabbath*. New York, Farrar, Strauss & Giroux, 1951.

Singer, I. J. "Repentance," in editors Irving Howe and Eliezer Greenberg's *A Treasury of Yiddish Stories*. New York, Schocken, 1973.

Syme, Daniel. *The Jewish Home: A Guide for Jewish Living*. New York, UAHC Press, 1988.

Waskow, Arthur. *Seasons of Our Joy*. New York, Bantam, 1982.

14.

FROM FREEDOM TO COVENANT:

PESACH, SHAVUOT, SUKKOT, SIMCHAT

TORAH, TU B'SHEVAT.

In or about 621 BCE, King Josiah of Judah ruled that the three major festivals celebrating nature and history—Pesach, Shavuot, and Sukkot—should be observed in Jerusalem. So, three (*shalosh*) times a year (at the beginning and the end of the Spring harvest and during the Fall harvest), the Israelites would make pilgrimages (*regalim*) to the Temple. These festivals were, therefore, called, *Shalosh Regalim.*

PESACH

In Biblical times, Nisan was considered the first month. The full moon of Nisan (the 15th) signaled the beginning of the Spring harvest. Even before there was a Passover, Israelite farmers would celebrate the *Hag Hamatzot* (the feast of unleavened bread) by disposing of the sour dough (*hametz*) of the previous year and eating only unleavened bread(*matzot*), perhaps as an expression of the hope for a bountiful crop. In even earlier times some scholars speculate that there was a *Hag Hapesach*, a feast of the paschal lamb, during which the pastoral Israelites would sacrifice the first lamb of the flock, perhaps as a gift to God, who in turn would bless them with many sheep.

However, once the Israelites were settled in their own land, the symbols of nature were transformed in order to celebrate the beginning of their national saga, from the time that Abraham was a "wandering Aramean" to the migration to and bondage in Egypt to their emancipation from slavery led by Moses through the redemptive power of God. The paschal lamb was a reminder of the blood placed on the doorposts of the Israelite homes so that the angel of death would not kill their first born. The *matzah* was unleavened, according to tradition, because the Israelites had to leave in such haste that there was no time for the bread to rise. The bitter herb (*maror*) represented the bitterness of slavery. Later the *haroset* (apples, nuts, cinnammon) symbolized the mortar with which the Israelites built the cities of Pithom and Rameses. The *carpas* (greens such as parsley) was a reminder that as the Jews were released from Egypt, so nature, with the arrival of Spring was released from the bondage of Winter. The sacrifice of the paschal lamb was linked to the Temple. After the Temple was destroyed by the Romans, a roasted egg (a symbol of life and re-birth) was introduced.

Scholars have attempted to place the events described in the Bible in a historic context. Many hold to the view that the Israelites (Joseph and his brothers) were welcomed into Egypt about 1700 BCE, during the rule of the Hyksos, who, themselves, were foreign to the natives of Egypt. In 1570, Pharaoh Ahmose liberated the Egyptians from the Hyksos. He could have been the Pharaoh "who knew not Joseph." According to Exodus 12:40, the Israelites lived in Egypt for 430 years. That would place the Exodus at about 1270, when Rameses II was Pharaoh. Recall that the Israelite slaves were said to have built the city of Rameses. The Hasidim commented that the real slavery of the Israelites in Egypt was that they had learned to endure it.

The narrative of the origins of the Israelites, how they came to Egypt, were enslaved, and how God sent Moses to lead them out of bondage, was written in the first version of the *Haggadah* ("telling") during the first century CE. Passages were added to the *Haggadah* during the Talmudic, Geonic, Medieval and Modern periods. (See the *Polychrome Historical Haggadah for Passover*, edited by Jacob Freedman.) Still today, modern *Haggadot* have been written, celebrating contemporary emancipations (e.g., of African-Americans, of women). The Central Conference of American (Reform) Rabbis has published a *Haggadah* that includes commentaries from a wide range of Jewish sources. A more universalist *Haggadah, Gates of Freedom*, has been edited by Chaim Stern. It includes not only Jewish commentaries but passages on the theme of freedom from philosophers and writers, from John Stuart Mill to Tolstoy. Also, its Hebrew passages are written both in Hebrew and transliteration, so that those who cannot read Hebrew can follow the service.

The Seder (literally, "order") is usually led by the most knowledgeable member of the family. His or her responsibility is to maintain some balance between the serious meanings and the lighter moments of the evening. Children enjoy asking the "four questions" and looking for the *afikomen*. This Greek word originally meant merry-making, a common practice of Greeks after their meals. Another meaning of the term is "dessert," the last food eaten at the Seder, which became the pieces of *matzah* hidden for the children to find after the meal. Some scholars hold that the Seder was based on the Greek *symposium* (or "talk-feast"), when students would gather around a festive meal, ask and answer philosophic questions. The questions Jews ask relate more to history and its moral meanings.

The main purpose of the Seder is to enable the participants to identify with the Israelite slaves in Egypt and so gain a deeper appreciation of freedom. Such identification should encourage us to have more compassion for all who are oppressed and to do whatever is in our power to create a world in which all will live in freedom and peace. It is worth noting that the *Haggadah* reads that "in each generation each *person* (*adam*)"—not every Jew but every human being—"is obligated to see oneself as though he/she had gone out of Egypt." It is considered praiseworthy to pause to discuss the relevance of the traditional meanings for our time.

It is helpful for the leader to interject into the reading of the *Haggadah* comments that may add understanding and a bit of humor to the proceedings. Some suggested commentaries follow:

1. Before beginning the Seder, the leader may announce three rules: a) It is forbidden to fall into a deep sleep during the reading of the *Haggadah*. b)While it is praiseworthy to discuss the meanings of the *Haggadah*, one must begin eating the meal by midnight. c)You are required to relax (wine may help) whether you feel like it or not.

2. One must drink four cups of wine, as a reminder of the four times that God, in the Torah, promised to redeem the Israelites from slavery. Some say there was a fifth promise of redemption and call for a fifth cup. One day Elijah will return and decide four or five.

3. Blessing over the greens are often introduced by verses from *Song of Songs*(to be read in the synagogue during Pesach): In celebrating the spring harvest, we rejoice that nature and love are born again.

4. *Yachatz* (breaking of *matzah*): Two *matzot* recall the double portion of manna collected by the Israelites in the wilderness before Shabbat. The third *matzah* is the "bread of affliction." Breaking it reminds us of the poor who do not have a whole piece of bread. The "*Ha lahma anya*"("this is the bread of affliction") was written in Aramaic(the language of the people) so all would understand its meaning. "Next year in Israel" is a prayer for the messianic age when, according to tradition, the Jewish people will return to Israel.

5. *Mah nishtanah* (Why is this night different?): When do we dip herbs twice? When we dip parsley in salt water (symbolizing tears of slaves) and when we dip the *maror* in the *haroset*.

6. The Civil Disobedience of Shiphrah and Puah: Two Hebrew midwives were ordered by Pharaoh to kill the infant males of the Israelites. They refused and told Pharoah that Hebrew women give birth before the midwives can come to them. Then Pharoah ordered all Egyptians to kill all male Israelite infants (Exodus: l:15-21).

7. Ten Plagues: The rabbis were saddened by the suffering caused by plagues and so diminished the joy of liberation by taking ten drops from the cup of wine. (Some contemporary *Haggadot* emphasize plagues-of-the-spirit that must be overcome if we are to live in a society of real freedom, justice, and peace.)

8. Freedom requires human initiative: According to a midrash, the Israelites were waiting for God to part the sea. As the Egyptians came nearer, Nachshon went into the sea and was followed by the other Israelites. They waded into the sea until the water was up to their noses. Only then did the sea part.

9. Another midrash: As the Egyptians were drowning, the

angels began to sing songs of praise, but God rebuked them saying: "My children are drowning and you sing praises!"

10. What is *hametz*? It is fermented dough, specifically, anything made of wheat, barley, spelt, oats or rye, which when ground into flour and mixed with water is allowed to ferment. *Matzah* is made usually from wheat but is cooked quickly before fermentation takes place (less than 18 minutes).

11. So what else is forbidden? The Ashkenazic rabbis prohibited the eating of rice, corn, beans, peas, and peanuts. They feared that the flour made from these foods could become mixed with the prohibited grains. This was a *s'yag*, a fence around the Torah. (If one observes the "fence," one will surely observe that which is within the fence.) Sephardic Jews do not observe this prohibition.

12. At some point during the Seder, the group may wish to sing "The *Matzah* Song,"to the tune of "Mother"(note the Ashkenazic pronuciation):

> M is for the many times I've munched you
> A is for your arid after-taste
> T is for the trouble to digest you
> Z is for my zest for bread displaced
> O is for the oldest Jewish pastry
> S is for your secret recipe
> Put them all together they spell MATZOS
> Manischewitz's gift to me.

13. The Cup of Elijah. One or more of the children may open the door and say: "For Elijah the prophet, we open the door. May he bring the world peace and love evermore." According to Jewish tradition, Elijah was to return to earth and announce the messianic age. Why Elijah? Why not Isaiah, who was more closely identified with peace? Because Elijah went up to heaven in a chariot of

fire, his descent to earth was more likely than if he had been buried. When Elijah returns, he will turn the hearts of parents and
children towards each other, and will resolve rabbinic dilemmas.
Why did Jews open the door? To show that despite persecution,
the Jews were not afraid. Others have suggested that the reason
was to let Christian neighbors see that the charge that Jews used
Christian blood to make *matzot* was false.

14. What is the connection between Passover and Easter? Both
are Spring festivals that signify hope in the future. However, Easter is concerned with redemption from sin and achieving salvation
in Heaven through the resurrection of Jesus. Passover is concerned
with redemption from oppression and injustice and achieving the
salvation of freedom, justice, and peace here on earth. The Last
Supper is considered by some to have been a Seder. However, according to Professor Michael Cook, this is not so; Jesus, in Matthew and Mark, was arrested *before* the holiday to prevent a riot.
The Greek word used for bread in the Last Supper clearly meant
leavened bread, not *matzah*.

16. *Had Gadya:* The "only kid" represents the Jewish people.
The song can be interpreted as a survey of the Jewish experience
with persecution: Then came the cat, Babylon; the dog, Persia; the
stick, Greece; fire, Rome; water, Barbarians; ox, Islam; Angel of
Death, Crusaders . . . but God will destroy all the oppressors.

SHAVUOT

According to Leviticus 23: 15-6, seven weeks after Passover
the Israelites would "bring an offering of new grain to the Lord."
In Exodus 23:16, we read that the Israelites would then celebrate
an agricultural festival (the *Hag Ha-katzir*) when they would thank
God for the Spring *katzir*, or harvest. In Deuteronomy 16:10-12,

we read, "You shall observe the feast of weeks (*Shavuot*) for the Lord your God, offering your freewill contribution according as the Lord your God has blessed you." After the destruction of the Temple by the Romans, the Jewish people were scattered throughout the Middle East and the Mediterranean world. They were linked not by land but by Jewish law. As most were no longer farmers, they needed another reason for celebrating Shavuot. So the rabbis reinterpreted the holiday as a commemoration of the giving of the Ten Commandments on Mt. Sinai.

A basis in the Torah for this reinterpretation was needed and easily found. In Exodus 19, we read that the Israelites reached Sinai in the third month after leaving Egypt. According to tradition, they left Egypt on Nisan 15th. The next two months were Iyar and Sivan. Shavuot falls seven weeks after Passover, so the date was Sivan 6th. The rabbis reasoned that this was the time, during the third month after leaving Egypt, that the Israelites arrived at Sinai and God revealed the Ten Commandments, or, according to Rabbinic Judaism, the entire Torah.

There was another reason why it made good moral sense to commemorate the giving of the Law seven weeks after Passover: It was not enough for the Israelites to have their freedom, Without some standards, rules, or laws, freedom could lead to anarchy. As Martin Buber wrote, "Freedom—I love its flashing face . . . I give my left hand to the rebel and my right to the heretic: forward! But I do not trust them. They know how to die, but that is not enough. I love freedom, but I do not believe in it. How could one believe in it after looking in its face? It is the flash of a significance comprising all meanings, of a possibility comprising all potentiality."

As explained in Chapter 3, God gave the Ten Commandments to the Jews, because they were willing to receive them. According to a midrash, God first offered the commandments to the Egyptians. They asked, "What do they command?" When told, "You shall not commit adultery," they refused. Then God offered the commandments to the Assyrians, who also asked, "What do they command?" When they were told, "You shall not steal," they refused to accept them. Finally, God offered the commandments to the Israelites. They did not even ask what was commanded. They simply said: "*Naaseh v'nishma,* We will do and we will hear," i.e., we promise to follow them; now let us hear what they command.

In Reform synagogues, Shavuot has become a time for Confirmation. Students after the age of *Bar/Bat Mitzvah,* usually after the tenth grade, take part in a synagogue service during which they affirm their personal commitment to Judaism. In some congregations, students will express in their own words those values in Judaism that they find most meaningful. No longer do adolescent Jews say, "we will do and we will hear." We are pleased if they are willing to say, "We will hear. We will listen to all the meanings that Judaism can have for the Jewish people. We will consider those meanings and then "we will do."

The *haftarah* for the morning of Shavuot is the book of Ruth. There we read the story of how, because of famine in the land, Naomi, her husband, Elimelech, and her two sons moved from Judah to the more fertile fields of Moab. Elimelech died, and the two sons, Mahlon and Chilion, married two Moabite women, Orpah and Ruth. Then the two sons died. Naomi decided to return to her land where she had family. She urged each of her two daughters-in-law to return to her mother's house. Orpah kissed Naomi and bid her farewell. Ruth, however, refused to leave. She said to Naomi, "Entreat me not to leave you, to turn back and not follow you. For wherever you go, I will go. Wherever you lodge, I will lodge; your people shall be my people, and your God, my God. Where you die, I will die and there I will be buried. Thus and more may the Lord do to me if anything but death parts me from you"(Ruth 1: 16-17).

' After Ruth returned to Judah with Naomi, she met and married a distant kinsman, Boaz. She gave birth to Obed, who was the father of Jesse (the father of David). Consider the implications: The Moabites were enemies of the Israelites. Yet the two young Jewish men married two daughters of their enemies. Then the Moabite Ruth returned to Judah with Naomi. Here we have the two "highest" forms of love: love of the enemy and love of the mother-in-law! From the union of a Moabite and an Israelite not only David but eventually the Messiah (descended from David) would be born—as universalist a message as you will find in the *Tanakh*.

According to Jewish tradition, Ruth was the first convert. There was no established ceremony. She accepted both the God of Israel and the people of Israel. Today, the essence of the conversion experience is still the acceptance of both the faith of Israel and the fellowship of the Jewish people. (For more on conversion, see Ch. 21.)

It has become customary for Jews to eat cheese dishes on Shavuot. As Gaster points out, "cheese-making was a common feature of Spring harvest festivals in many parts of the world." The rabbis had to stretch a bit to find a basis in the Bible. In Psalm 68:15, Mt. Sinai is referred to as *gabnumin*, a many-peaked mountain. *Gabnunim* sounds somewhat like *gevinah* (cheese). Enjoy your blintzes!

SUKKOT

The third harvest festival of the Biblical year falls on the fifteenth of the seventh month of Tishri, just five days after Yom Kippur. Sukkot, the Feast of Booths, celebrates the Fall harvest. Originally called, *Hag He-asif*, the Feast of Ingathering, Sukkot was and is a time of thanksgiving. However, exactly for what the Israelites were thankful changed from age to age even as the historic conditions of the Jewish people changed. According to Theodor Gaster, the evolution of this holiday can be illustrated by the different meanings given to its symbols.

The *sukkah* was originally the booth or hut under which the Israelite farmers took shelter during the Fall harvest. They may have waved branches of palms, citron trees, myrtles, and willows as a way of thanking God for the harvest (Leviticus 23:40). *Once the Israelites became a nation,* the *arba minim* (four species) came to represent their "founding fathers," Abraham, Isaac, Jacob, and Joseph. The *sukkah* then reminded them of the booths in which their ancestors had dwelled on their journey through the wilderness to their Promised Land (Leviticus 23:43). King Solomon dedicated the First Temple on Sukkot (I Kings 8:2-21), perhaps to assert that God's presence was in the Temple as it was with the Israelites in the desert. In the Mishnah we read that during the time of the Second Temple, there was a fourth-of-July-like celebration during which water was poured, trumpets were blown, songs were sung, and a giant menorah was lit. The Israelites had, in the language of the third verse of "The Star-Spangled Banner," "praised the Power that had made and preserved (them) a nation."

After the destruction of the Second Temple by the Romans, the symbols came to express more universal values, which we cherish to this day. The *sukkah,* in which one is expected to eat one meal each day, reminds us to thank God not just for the harvest but for all our blessings. For some the *sukkah* is a reminder of the poor who lived (and still live) in homes unfit for human habitation. Waving the *lulav* (palm branch), *etrog* (citron), willow, and myrtle to the north, south, east and west can be interpreted as a prayer that people everywhere will be blessed with abundance. Each of the species has been given a meaning. The myrtle leaf reminds us the of the eye. (May it appreciate the beauty of the world.) The willow leaf looks like a mouth. (May it speak words of caring and sensitivity, not of indifference and slander.) The *lulav* suggests one's spine. (May we stand straight and upright as we strive for justice.) The *etrog* symbolizes the heart, believed to be the seat of love and understanding.

For the rabbis, the *arba minim* also represent four kinds of personalities: The *etrog*, with smell and taste, represents those Jews who have knowledge of Torah and do good deeds. The palm, with taste but no aroma, suggests one who knows Torah but never brings it into his/her life. The myrtle, with aroma but no taste, is the ignoramus who, nonetheless, leads a good life. The willow, with neither aroma nor taste, symbolizes one who neither knows the Torah nor does good deeds.

The rabbis gave specific directions regarding building a *sukkah*. It is a temporary structure erected in the open air. It consists of four walls with an opening and a covering that must be made of material grown from the soil, such as branches and plants. There must be enough space between the branches so that one can see the stars. It is usually decorated with hanging fruits, vegetables, or flowers. Jewish men are expected to eat and sleep at least one night in the *sukkah*. Today it is customary for families to eat at least one meal in the *sukkah* during the holiday.

In recent years, Sukkot has become a time to pray and work for peace. There is, in Zechariah 14:16, a hint of a connection between Sukkot and the messianic age: "All who survive of all those nations that came up against Jerusalem shall make a pilgrimage year by year to bow low to the King, Lord of Hosts and to observe the Feast of Booths."

It is interesting that the meanings of Sukkot, while changing through the ages, seem to have returned to its earliest message of thanking God for the harvest and the earth from which it grew.

Sukkot has become the Jewish festival most closely associated with today's urgent concern for our planet and its environment. Genesis 2:15 reads: "The Lord God took man and placed him in the Garden of Eden to till and tend (i.e., care for) it." According to a midrash, God said to Adam, "I created many worlds and was not satisfied with any of them. This is the last world I will create. Take good care of it, for there will be none to follow"(based on *Eccles. Rabbah:* 7:28). Psalm 24 begins, "The earth is the Lord's and the fullness thereof." If God "owns" the earth, then humans have leased or borrowed it. According to the *Shulchan Arukh*, the borrower is obligated to return property in as good a condition as it was when he/she received it.

Rabbinic law recognizes the ill effects of pollution. To protect people from polluted air, one must remove from the city all threshing floors, cemeteries, tanneries, and kilns. No garbage plants were allowed in any part of Jerusalem, for the smoke would blacken the walls and cause the entire nation to be disgraced. According to the Jerusalem Talmud, "It is forbidden to live in a city that does not have a green garden." The rabbis extended the Biblical prohibition against destroying trees during a military operation (Deuteronomy 20:19) to the command, *Bal tash-cheet:* Do not destroy anything needlessly.

Surely the rabbis would have been deeply disturbed by the dangerous phenomenon of global warming. The scientific consensus is that the same humans who live on the earth are heating the planet. Bill McKibben, author of *The End of Nature*, has written: "Spring comes a week earlier across the Northern Hemisphere than it did just 30 years ago. Severe rainstorms have grown by almost 20%, precisely what you'd expect on a planet where warmer air can carry more water vapor . . . Glaciers are melting. Sea levels are rising." It is too late to prevent global warming, but it is in our power to slow the process. Fuel-economy standards for cars and trucks should be set and enforced. A new generation of renewable energy technologies is urgently needed.

Within the Jewish community there is an impressive effort to raise the consciousness of American Jews on environmental issues, and to develop actions we should take to help preserve the planet on which we all depend. The Coalition on the Environment and Jewish Life (COEJL) is an umbrella organization in which, at last count, twenty-eight national Jewish organizations participate, from the American Jewish Committee to the Shalom Center to Women's American ORT. COEJL initiated Operation Noah, based on the Torah text that tells how Noah protected at least two of every animal species, enabling all of God's creatures to make "safe passage from one era to the next." So we, in our generation, should protect endangered species. Maimonides provides a rabbinic basis for our concern in his *Guide to the Perplexed*: "It should not be believed that all beings exist for the sake of the existence of humanity. On the contrary, all the other beings too have been intended for their own sakes, and not for the sake of something else." In the Talmud (*Shabbat* 77b) one reads: "Nothing that the Lord created in the world was superfluous or in vain, hence all must be sustained."

At times, Sukkot is referred to as simply *He-hag, the* Festival, implying its special importance. Of all the festivals, only Sukkot is called *z'man simchataynu,* a time of rejoicing. The day after the seven days of Sukkot is called Sh'mini Atzeret, freely translated as the eighth day of solemn assembly. Gaster suggests that because the root of *atzeret* means "to restrain," it is possible that this was a day of austerity that marked "the end of the reaping and the real beginning of the new agricultural cycle." Sh'mini Atzeret is followed by (or in Reform Judaism, combined with) Simchat Torah, a time of rejoicing in the Torah. As mentioned in Chapter 2, the last verses of Deuteronomy are read, followed by the first verses of Genesis, to indicate that learning, especially study of the Torah, should never cease. Perhaps there is a connection with the harvest festival of Sukkot: According to the Talmud, "a student is like a seed in the ground. Once it sprouts, it grows toward Heaven."

Still another nature-holiday, Tu B'Shevat, has been revived in many synagogues, particularly those influenced by the movement for Jewish Renewal (See Chapter 18.) The fifteenth of the Hebrew month of Shevat was known as the New Year of the Trees. At the full moon, the sap began to flow from the roots of the fruit trees into their branches. In Biblical times, this marked the beginning of the fiscal year, when tithes would take place. Why were tithes given? According to Arthur Waskow in *Trees, Earth and Torah,* the Jews "did not carry on economic enterprise in a vacuum. Part of their success came from the whole society and even beyond—from earth and rain and sunshine, from the Unity called God. So they owed part of their income to the greater reality." Tithes were first used to pay for the upkeep of religious centers. By the seventh century BCE, every third year the tithe was kept in the local community and used to support its poor.

A rabbinic story for Tu B'Shevat: Hadrian, the Roman emperor, met an old Jew planting fig shoots. Hadrian asked: "Why should you, old man, (who will not see the seeds become trees) exhaust yourself for others?"

The man replied: "If I should merit it, I will eat of the fruit of my shoots; if not, my children will eat them." It was understandable that the old man should care about the well-being of his children. Environmentalists who care about the long-term effects of global warming must feel a connection not only with their children but with the human species through time.

In sixteenth century Tzefat, the Kabbalists revived the celebration of Tu B'Shevat. It became the New Year for the Tree of Life, whose roots are in Heaven and whose fruit is the world, itself.

Today there are Israeli and American Jews who hold Tu B'Shevat seders when they partake of the fruits and nuts of Israel and feel a special connection with the natural world. As the midrash in *Genesis Rabbah* reads: "All of the trees, plants and spirits that dwell in nature conversed with one another. The spirit that lives in the trees and nature conversed with humankind, for all of the beings in nature were created for mutual companionship with humans."

TOPICS FOR DISCUSSION

1. What do you consider ten "plagues" that afflict the world today?

2 . Do you believe that the descendants of religious, racial or ethnic groups that have been the victims of oppression and discrimination should be given any kind of preferential treatment today?

3. How would you balance the need for freedom and the need for standards or laws in the following situations: a) the freedom to buy and sell tobacco products versus the command to preserve life; b) the right to voice words of hatred toward particular groups versus the command not to slander.

4. How would you respond to someone who says: "I just don't care what will happen to this planet hundreds of years from now, so I am not going to favor major sacrifices to protect the environment."

RESOURCES

Elon, Ari, Naomi Hyman and Arthur Waskow (ed.). *Trees, Earth and Torah: A Tu B'Shvat Anthology.* Philadelphia, Jewish Publication Society, 1999.

Friedman, Jacob. *Polychrome Historical Haggadah for Passover.* Springfield, Mass., Jacob Friedman Liturgy Research Foundation, 1974.

Friedman, Ruth Gruber. *The Passover Seder: Afikomen in Exile.* Philadelphia, University of Pennsylvania Press, 1981.

Gaster, Theodor H. *Festivals of the Jewish Year.* New York, Morrow Quill Paperbacks, 1978.

Goodman, Philip (ed). *The Shavuot Anthology.* Philadelphia, Jewish Publication Society, 1974.

Goodman, Philip (ed). *The Sukkot and Simhat Torah Anthology.* Philadelphia, Jewish Publication Society, 1973.

Strassfeld, Michael. *The Jewish Holidays: A Guide and Commentary.* New York, Harper & Row, 1985.

Syme, Daniel. *The Jewish Home: A Guide for Jewish Living.* New York, UAHC Press, 1988.

Walzer, Michael. *Exodus and Revolution.* New York, Basic Books, 1984.

Waskow, Arthur. *Seasons of Our Joy.* New York, Bantam, 1982.

15.

HANUKKAH AND PURIM:

NOT FOR CHILDREN ONLY

Hanukkah and Purim have some characteristics in common. Both are viewed as holidays primarily for the children. Neither is a Yom Tov, a festival with its own services in the *Machzor* (festival prayer book). Both are based on stories of hostility against the Jews and Judaism and both have their own variations on two themes: the right to be different, and dedication to the heritage of Judaism.

HANUKKAH

How many of these questions can you answer? 1) In what book or books do we find the story of Hanukkah? 2) Where is the first mention of a flask of oil lasting for eight days? 3) Why did Antiochus ban the Jewish religion? 4) Why was Judah called "Maccabee?" 5) What finally happened to Judah Maccabee and how did he end his days? 6) What did he achieve for the Jewish people? 7)What did his brothers, Jonathan and Simon, achieve for the Jewish people? 8)What does the word, "Hanukkah" mean?

To answer these questions and to discover the adult meanings of Hanukkah, we first need some historical perspective. After the death of Alexander the Great (331 BCE), his empire was divided into two kingdoms: the Seleucid based in Syria and the Ptolemaic based in Egypt. Judea was part of the Ptolemaic kingdom until 201, when the Seleucid kings became its rulers. Meanwhile, Rome was becoming the dominant power in the region. Among the Jews in Palestine were the Hellenists and anti-Hellenists, those who accepted and those who rejected aspects of Greek culture. (See the Chronology of the Hellenistic Period.)

Antiochus IV (176-165 BCE) installed a Hellenist, Onias-Menelaus, as the high priest in Jerusalem. His brother, Lysimachus, raided the Temple treasury. When Antiochus was engaged in a military campaign in Egypt, anti-Hellenist Jews violently protested the oppressive taxation. Antiochus sent his forces into Jerusalem and massacred many of the rebels. In 169 BCE, Antiochus invaded Egypt again. This time Rome intervened on behalf of the Egyptians, captured Antiochus, and humiliated him in Rome. The anti-Hellenists, thinking Antiochus was either dead or powerless, made the anti-Hellenist, Joshua, the high priest, thus flouting the authority of Antiochus.

Infuriated, Antiochus left Rome and invaded the province of Judea, entered Jerusalem, and in 168 BCE, desecrated the Temple, putting in it the statue of a Greek god and letting pigs run through the building. Then he banned the practice of Judaism. The Jewish people, under Mattathias, united and revolted against the Seleucid (sometimes called Syrian) rule. Mattathias died in 167 BCE and his son, Judah, took command of the Jewish forces. He carried out a guerrilla war in the hills. While Judah was fighting against the Syrian General Lysias, Antiochus led an army to the northeast to suppress a revolt of the Parthians. During this campaign, Antiochus died, probably due to a mysterious illness (165 BCE). In that same year, Judah's forces recaptured the Temple and cleansed it. Judah made peace with Lysias (who had become the guardian of the child, Antiochus V). According to II Macabees, the Jews recaptured the temple on Heshvan 23rd, but waited a month until Kislev 25th to dedicate the Temple, perhaps because that was the date the Temple was desecrated. Others suggest that Kislev 25th was the day when peoples throughout the Mediterranean world celebrated the winter solstice. Perhaps Hanukkah was superimposed on an ancient pagan holiday.

Why eight days? The traditional explanation is found in the Talmud, written three or four centuries after the event: There was only enough oil to last one day, but miraculously it lasted for eight days. This is surely a legend. According to II Maccabees, the reason for the eight days was that during the eight days of Sukkot and Sh'mini Atzeret, the Jews were fighting in the hills, where they were not able to celebrate their thanksgiving holiday. So they postponed the Sukkot of 165 BCE until the Temple was cleansed and turned their thanksgiving celebration into a dedication (*hanukkah*) of the Temple. They marched through the streets carrying torches, acknowledging the winter solstice. Solomon Zeitlin, respected historian of this period, suggests that because Ezra dedicated the Temple for seven days, the Maccabees thought that a re-dedication should last eight days.

In 163, a peace settlement was arranged with Lysias, giving the Jews religious freedom. This was followed by Jews fighting Jews, the Hellenists versus the anti-Hellenists. Judah continued the armed struggle against the Seleucids, because he was not satisfied with religious freedom. He wanted political independence. However, he had little popular support for carrying on the armed struggle. After winning a battle against Nicanor (who had many elephants), Judah with only 800 soldiers confronted the army of

Bacchides, 20,000 strong. Judah never had a chance. His small army was overrun, and he was killed. Judah came to be known as the Maccabee. Some say that Maccabee was an acronym for *Mi Komocha Ba-aylim Adonai*("Who is like You among the gods, O Lord."), words sung by the Israelites after they had crossed the Red Sea to freedom. Zeitlin points out that heroes were often named after their physical characteristics. Because Judah's head resembled a hammer (*makabee*), he was called the Maccabee. Still another explanation: he hammered the foe, hence, the Maccabee.

After Judah's death, his brother, Jonathan, resumed the struggle for independence, not by warfare but by diplomatic means. He was appointed high priest by the Seleucid ruler, Alexander Balas. After Jonathan's death his brother, Simon, led the Jewish people. Through negotiations with the Seleucid ruler, Demetrius II, Simon gained political independence for the Jewish people. Because the family name of Judah and his brothers was Hasmonean, the free state of Judea was at times came to be called the Hasmonean state. Judea retained its independence until Pompey of Rome conquered the Jewish state in 63 BCE.

By now you should be able to answer almost all of the questions posed at the beginning of this chapter. One question remains: Why did Antiochus IV (called Epiphanes, or God Manifest) prohibit the practice of Judaism? Some suggest that he wanted to *unify his empire*. The best way to do this, so he thought, was to make all his peoples adopt the Hellenistic religion. The Jews had a history of rebellion, so they were first on his list. Also, his humiliation in Rome left him looking for a scapegoat.

Whatever the explanation, two major meanings have been found in Hanukkah. First, the Jewish people were demanding the right to be different. They refused to conform by rejecting the Hellenistic gods. In contemporary terms, they demanded the right first to religious freedom and then to national self-determination. So Hanukkah should be a time to celebrate all those who struggled for the right to be different, from Michael Schwerner to Martin Luther King, from Baruch Spinoza to Oliver Wendell Holmes, from Susan B. Anthony to her Jewish co-crusader, Ernestine Rose. In a sense, Hanukkah celebrates what is best about America. I have written a Hanukkah pledge of allegiance: "I pledge allegiance to America and to the differences for which she stands; differences in the color of our skin; different football teams we want to win; differences in what we say; different churches and synagogues where we pray; differences in how we talk; different ways we think Uncle Sam should walk. We pledge to protect the right to be different, so there will be liberty and justice for all."

This is so cool

The second major meaning of *Hanukkah* we find in the word, itself, which means Dedication. Despite overwhelming obstacles, the Jewish people, as a whole, remained dedicated to their Jewish heritage, not only by defying Antiochus but by rejecting all efforts to force them to give up their Judaism throughout the centuries. This value—continuity with an exceptional past—has been put into song by Peter Yarrow, of Peter, Paul, and Mary:

> Light one candle for the Maccabee children, with thanks
>   that their light didn't die.
> Light one candle for the pain they endured, when their
>   right to exist was denied.
> Light one candle for the terrible sacrifice, justice and free-
>   dom demand
> But light one candle for the wisdom to know, when the
>   peacemaker's time is at hand.
> Don't let the light go out, it's lasted for so many years
> Don't let the light go out, let it shine through our love and
>   our tears.

The candles (one the first night, two the second night, etc.) are placed from right to left and are kindled by the *shamas* candle from left to right. When I was a child, we simply lit candles and sang "Rock of Ages." Today in many Jewish families, children receive one present on each of the eight nights. If Jewish children, in addition, want presents on the Christian holiday of Christmas, I would not go into theological explanations about Jews' not accepting Jesus as the Messiah. I would simply say: Don't be greedy!

PURIM

Perhaps the holiday most enjoyed by children is Purim. They get to dress in costumes. They may put on a play ridiculing the villain, Haman. When they come to synagogue and the scroll of *Esther* is read or chanted, they wait eagerly for the name, Haman, so that they may twirl their *graggers* (noise makers), They may attend a Purim carnival. Young and old symbolically eat Haman by devouring hamantashen (the three-cornered Jewish pastry stuffed with poppy seed or prunes).

Some find the origin of this festivity in the pagan celebration of the Persian new year. Others suggest that the holiday was a time for the Jewish people to mock their oppressors. This catharsis must have been helpful to Jews who did not have the political or military power to overthrow those who persecuted them. They could release their hostility through ridicule and laughter.

Behind the mask of mockery there is a deadly serious side to Purim. The wicked Haman was intent on destroying the Jewish people in Persia. He was attempting genocide or at least, ethnic cleansing. What motivated Haman, and why did his plan nearly succeed?

Most scholars believe that the scroll of Esther was written when the Jews were ruled by the Seleucid kings. In contrast to the hostility of some Seleucid monarchs, Persian kings were generally tolerant of the Jews. Since the Persians ruled Palestine from 539 BCE. to 331 BCE., (when they were defeated by Alexander), one might conclude that the story, while written when Judea was part of the Greek Empire, was intentionally placed a few centuries earlier, to avoid antagonizing the Seleucid rulers.

The scroll is a kind of historical fiction. Some have suggested that the events make sense when viewed against the background of Persian history. Ahasuerus is Hebrew for Xerxes(from the root, "mighty man"), who ruled Persia from 486 to 465 BCE. The Purim story begins with a banquet in the third year of his reign. This could have been a farewell party for Persian troops who were engaged in putting down revolts in Egypt and Babylonia and then, in the fifth year of his reign (481 BCE), assembled to invade Greece in order to avenge the defeat of the Persian army at Marathon (490 BCE). Ahasuerus orders his wife, Vashti, to dance for the guys, but she says, in effect, "I won't dance; can't make me." The King did not make her dance but, on the advice of his counselors, expelled her from the palace, thus making Vashti one of the early heroines of Women's Liberation.

Themistocles, the Athenian general, evacuated Athens, which was then occupied by the Persians. Then, he lured the Persian fleet, still filled with soldiers, into the straits of Salamis, and the Athenian navy inflicted a crushing defeat. Xerxes had to flee back to Persia. However, he left behind a large infantry force that again captured and wrecked Athens. In 479 BCE (the seventh year of his reign), his infantry was defeated by the Spartans, his navy sunk by the Athenians, and the remnants of his forces returned to Persia in disgrace. The people of Persia must have felt totally humiliated. They may well have been in the mood to find a scapegoat. It was then, still in the seventh year of Xerxes or Ahasuerus' reign, that Mordecai, fearing hostility against the vulnerable Jews, made sure that his niece, Esther, entered the contest to become the new queen.

(This is further evidence that the story is fictional, for Persian queens were always chosen from noble families.) Haman was a bigot whose time had come. After the King appointed him the equivalent of prime minister, he behaved with arrogance, demanding that everyone bow down before him. Mordecai refused, and Haman remembered the Jew's defiance. His hatred of Mordecai was expanded to include all the Jews in the kingdom. He deceived the King by telling him that the Jews were disloyal, placing their laws above the law of the kingdom. He received the King's permission to deal with the Jews as he wished.

Haman is portrayed as a typical authoritarian bigot. While meek before the King, he demanded the subservience of all those "beneath him." As bigots will do, he generalized on the basis of one experience with Mordecai, and believed that all Jews were disloyal. Because the humiliated Persian people needed a scapegoat, Haman must have found support among the masses. He was so confident that he cast lots (*Purim*) to decide on the day when the Jews would all be slaughtered.

Esther won the King's favor and became his Queen. She had not told him that she was Jewish. Once Mordecai learned of Haman's evil plan, he told Esther to intervene. She was reluctant, because to come before the King without being invited or summoned was a capital offense. Mordecai warned her that if Haman succeeded, she would not be spared, and help would come from another place (a possible allusion to God, although "God" is never mentioned in the entire scroll.) Esther courageously decided to go before the king, saying, "If I perish, I perish."

Of course, Esther did not perish. The King received her and said that he would give her whatever she wanted up to half his kingdom. All she wanted was two banquet, with just Haman, Ahasuerus, and herself. At the second banquet she told the King that Haman was planning to kill all the Jews, including herself. (I imagine the King saying, "But you don't look Jewish.") The King was furious with Haman and condemned him to be impaled on the stake that he had planned to use for Mordecai. Unable to countermand orders already signed and sealed by the King, Ahasueras did allow the Jews to defend themselves. This they did with much success. However, the failure of Ahasueras to use his army to defend the Jews (thus leaving them to their own devices) suggests that he did not have effective control over his "empire." We often leave out the bloody end of this story when telling it to children. The Jews of Shushan celebrated. They "enjoyed light and gladness, happiness and honor."(Esther 8:16) Mordecai was given a prominent place in the government, wearing "a crown of gold and a mantle of fine linen and purple wool." He decreed that Jews should observe the 14th and 15th of Adar as a time of feasting, merry-making, and giving gifts to the poor(Esther 9:20). Today Purim is observed on Adar 14, except in walled cities (as Shushan was walled). Therefore, in Jerusalem, Purim is observed on Adar 15, and in cities that may or may not have been considered walled (e.g., Tzefat, Akko, Tiberias, and Lydda) the holiday is observed both on the 14th and 15th.

Behind the merry mask of Purim there is a serious significance. As interpreted above, Purim can give us insight into the nature of the bigot: an authoritarian personality who makes false generalizations and accusations of disloyalty. Assuming the historic context suggested above, Jews are most vulnerable to attack when they are living in a nation that is going through very difficult economic or political depression. In the words of Mordecai Kaplan, "It is appropriate to make of the Feast of Purim, and of the special Sabbath preceding it, an occasion for considering anew the difficulties that inhere in our position as a "people scattered and dispersed among the nations."

Purim reminds me of a midrash about a Roman Emperor and

two Jews. The Emperor was walking down the road and came upon a Jew, who said to his ruler, "Shalom (peace)."

The Emperor was furious. "How dare you, a mere Jew, address your Emperor before he has said a word to you! Off with his head!" The Emperor continued on his walk and came upon another Jew, who had heard the previous conversation. Needless to say, he did not greet the Emperor. This infuriated the Emperor, who demanded, "How dare you pass by the Emperor without so much as a greeting! Off with his head!"

An advisor to the Emperor asked him, "Your Excellency, how could you treat both Jews in the same way even though they behaved differently?" The Emperor exclaimed, "Who is to teach me how to deal with my enemies?" What does this story suggest about the effect of Jewish behavior on anti-Semitism? What if Mordecai *had* bowed down? Would Haman have still wanted to kill all the Jews?

TOPICS FOR DISCUSSION

1. How do you feel about Judah Maccabee's decision to continue fighting for political independence after the Jews had achieved religious freedom?

2. In what ways do you think that Jews should be different from the mainstream of American culture? How should we be similar to that mainstream? In other words, what should we accept and what should we reject from the larger culture in which we live?

3. In what ways is Hanukkah similar to and different from Christmas?

4. Why do you think that Purim was among the very last books included in the *Tanakh?*

5. Are there modern Hamans in the world today? Who?

6. Do you know any jokes in which Jews ridicule their adversaries, or make fun of themselves? How do you feel about ethnic humor that uses stereotypes to get a laugh?

7. Who was the most heroic: Vashti, Esther, or Mordecai? Why?

8. Discuss the story of the Emperor and Two Jews. How much effect do you believe Jewish behavior has on the attitude of the bigot?

RESOURCES

Bickerman, Elias. *Four Strange Books of the Bible.* ("The Scroll of Esther"). New York, Schocken, 1967.

Goodman, Philip (ed.). *The Hanukkah Anthology.* Philadelphia, Jewish Publication Society, 1976.

Goodman, Philip (ed.). *The Purim Anthology.* Philadelphia, Jewish Publication Society, 1988.

Grant, Michael. *The Founders of the Western World: A History of Greece and Rome.* New York, Charles Scribner's Sons, 1991.

Syme, Daniel. *The Jewish Home: A Guide for Jewish Living.* New York, UAHC Press, 1988.

Waskow, Arthur. *Seasons of Our Joy.* New York, Bantam, 1982.

Zeitlin, Solomon. *The Rise and Fall of the Judean State*, Vol. One. (Chap. Three) Philadelphia, Jewish Publication Society, 1968.

REFORM MOVEMENT	CONSERVATIVE AND RECON. MOVEMENTS
1810: Temple in Seesen, Germany. 1814: Israel Jacobson holds services in his home in Berlin. 1818: Hamburg Temple dedicated. 1820's: Zunz: Science of Judaism.	1808-1888: Neo-Orthodoxy of Samson Raphael Hirsch.
1825: Harby's Reformed Society of Israelites in Charleston.	1825: B'nai Jeshurun in New York.
1838: A. Geiger rabbi in Breslau.	
1841: Poznanski dedicates Beth Elohim in Charleston. 1844-46: Synods in Germany.	
	1845: Z. Frankel leaves Frankfurt Synod, forms "historical school."
1840-1860: Migration of German Jews to U.S. 1846: I.M. Wise arrives in Albany. 1857: Wise publishes *Minhag America.*	
	1860's: Historical School in U.S. led by Jastrow, Szold, and Morais.
1869: First American all-Reform Conference in Philadelphia. 1872: *Olat Tamid* prayerbook by David Einhorn.	1867-1873: Maimonides College, established by Isaac Leeser.
1873:Union of American Hebrew Congregations formed.	

1875: Wise establishes Hebrew Union College.	1880s: Alexander Kohut debates Kaufmann Kohler.
1883: Trefah banquet alienates more traditional rabbis.	
1885: Pittsburgh Platform.	
1889: Central Conference of American Rabbis formed.	1886: Jewish Theological Seminary founded. Morais, first president.
1894-5: Union Prayer Book published.	
	1901: Alumni Association founded, to become Rabbinical Assembly.
	1902: Solomon Schechter, president of JTS.
1903: Kohler. 2nd president of HUC.	
	1913: United Synagogue of America.
	1915: Cyrus Adler, president of JTS.
1918: Social Justice Commission.	
1922: Stephen Wise establishes Jewish Institute of Religion. Julian Morgenstern, pres. of HUC.	1902-1954:Louis Ginzberg taught rabbinics at JTS. Mordecai Kaplan developed his Reconstructionist philosophy.
1926: World Union for Progressive Judaism formed.	
	1934: Kaplan published *Judaism as a Civilization.*
	1935: Reconstructionist journal published.
1937: Columbus Platform supports Jewish homeland and sets broad requirements for Reform practice.	

1940: Louis Finkelstein, pres.,JTS
1941: Recon. publish *New Haggadah.*

1942: CCAR favors Jewish army to fight Nazis. American Council for Judaism formed.

1945: Recon. publish *Sabbath Prayer Book* as an alternative to the Conservative movement's *Shabbat and Festival Prayer Book.*

1947: Nelson Glueck, pres. of HUC.
1948:UAHC, led by Maurice Eisendrath, moves offices from Cincinnati to New York City.

1949: Kaplan publishes *The Future of the American Jew.*

1950: HUC and JIR merge.
1956: Leo Baeck College in London established to train Liberal and Reform rabbis.
1960: Religious Action Center established in Washington, D.C. by UAHC pres. Maurice Eisendrath.
Solomon Freehof publishes first of seven volumes of Reform Responsa.
1963:HUC-JIR campus in Jerusalem.

1968: Reconstructionist Rabbinical College opens in Philadelphia. Its presidents have been: Ira Eisenstein, Ira Silverman, Arthur Green and David Teutsch. Always admitted women as rabbinic students.

1971: Alfred Gottschalk,
president of HUC-JIR.
1972: Sally Preisand becomes first   1972: Gerson Cohen, pres. of
woman rabbi.   JTS.
1974: *New Passover Haggadah.*
1975: *Gates of Prayer* published;
Rabbi Schindler, Pres. of UAHC,
launches Outreach program.

1976: Centenary Perspective of
Reform Judaism(San Francisco).
1977: ARZA formed.
1978: *Gates of Repentance*
published.

1979: Masorti movement in
Israel established by
Conservatives.
1983: Rabbinical Assembly
agree to train women rabbis.
1986: Ismar Schorsch, pres. of
JTS.

1995: Sheldon Zimmerman,
pres., of HUC-JIR.
1999: New Pittsburgh Platform
adopted by CCAR.
2001: David Ellenson, pres. Of
HUC-JIR.

PART FIVE:

JUDAISM MEETS THE MODERN WORLD

16.

THE EVOLUTION OF REFORM JUDAISM

At the Hebrew Union College I was taught by Abraham Cronbach, spiritual humanist who has excelled in applying Jewish values to social issues, that Reform Judaism began with the prophets. Micah and Isaiah were the first to state that the essence of Judaism is one God as well as the moral principles of love, justice and peace. Ritual that does not lead to moral behavior is a meaningless mockery.

Then Ellis Rivkin, who gave me and many others a fresh perspective on Jewish history, pointed out that Uriel Acosta in early seventeenth century Amsterdam was the first Jew publicly to challenge the basic tenet of rabbinic Judaism: that Jewish law, both the Torah and its rabbinic interpretations, are ultimately from God and, therefore, are binding. Uriel was twice excommunicated, and in painful isolation wrote that what is true in the Torah is the law of love, rooted in human nature. Sort of a Jewish Deist, Acosta angrily rejected all tradition; today this would disqualify him from being a Reform Jew. Still, he was something of a hero to rabbinic students who thought of themselves as mavericks. Rivkin connected the rise of capitalism, which required that the individual be free to make economic choices, and the emergence of Reform Judaism, which affirmed the individual's freedom to make ideological choices.

Jacob Rader Marcus, dean of American Jewish historians, reminded his students that history is made up and moved not only by factors and forces but by fascinating personalities, their struggles and stories. For Dr. Marcus, history was not only enlightening but entertaining. I found this particularly true of the history of Reform Judaism. Finally, I must acknowledge Professor Michael A. Meyer, on whose thorough and thoughtful work, *Response to Modernity*, significant portions of this chapter are based.

A RELIGIOUS EVOLUTION

Because Moses Mendelssohn, the eighteenth-century philosopher, believed both that the entire Torah was revealed on Sinai and that Jews are bound to follow Jewish law, he is not considered "Reform." However, Mendelssohn contributed to the emergence of the Reform movement by liberating the Jewish mind. He believed that the free use of reason would lead thinking people to the basic tenets of Judaism: God, immortality of the soul and providence. He asserted that Judaism is "liberty in belief and conformity in acts." He also translated the Torah into German so German Jews could understand it, and he insisted on the separation of Church and State. The problem was that four of his six children took seriously the "liberty of belief"; their reason convinced them that conformity to Jewish law was not necessary, and they converted to Christianity. Grandson Felix was baptized and wrote the Reformation symphony, which was banned by the Nazis because of their claim that Felix had "Jewish blood."

Many German Jews converted to Christianity not necessarily because they believed in Christian doctrine. Some may have reasoned that both religions advocate the ethic of love. Because we do not accept the traditional theologies of either faith and because the only way we can be part of the cultural elite in Germany is to become Christian, we might as well do so. Heinrich Heine, who quipped, "How can one Jew believe in the divinity of another Jew," acknowledged that his conversion was "a ticket to European culture." In later years he regretted his decision.

In the early-nineteenth century, as the more integrated German Jews rejected Orthodoxy and craved acceptance in the larger culture, thousands converted to Christianity. It was then that Reform Judaism emerged, the response of those Jews who could accept neither Orthodox Judaism nor Christianity and were looking for another valid way to express their Jewish identity. The rabbi who first introduced liturgical reform by omitting several prayers, reading the service slowly so its meaning could be appreciated, and giving sermons on social justice was Izak Graanboom. He was a Swedish convert to Judaism, and his congregation, *Adath Jeshurun*, was organized in 1797, not in Germany but in Amsterdam. A Christian writer dubbed them "the remarkable reformed Jews of Holland." Why Holland? Because the French, under Napoleon, had conquered Holland and established the separation of church and state. This meant that the rabbis could no longer impose their authority on other Jews, a key condition for the rise of Reform.

So it was no coincidence that in Germany, the Reform movement took root in Westphalia, a region ruled by France. It was there that educators David Frankel and Joseph Wolf published the journal *Sulamit* , in which they asserted that ceremonies were but a means to help Jews grasp the divine. They also felt it was necessary to "separate the wheat from the chaff," i.e., the meaningful traditions from those that had lost their relevance. In 1803, Frankel introduced the first Confirmation ceremony. It was also in Westphalia that we meet the man often called the first Reform Jew, Israel Jacobson. A banker and financial advisor to Jerome

Bonaparte, Napoleon's younger brother, Jacobson contributed to Bonaparte's coffers. He was allowed to set up a consistory (a ruling body), made up of three rabbis, two laymen, and himself, which introduced some reforms. The most controversial was granting permission for Ashkenazic Jews to eat peas, beans, rice, and corn on Pesach, as the Sephardim do. The Assembly also spelled out the role of the rabbi: he was to be a moral example, a pastor (as were Christian clergy), and was to give on the holidays "appropriate brief sermons."

Meanwhile in France, in 1806, Napoleon convened an "Assembly of Jewish Notables" and presented them with questions meant to test their loyalty to France: Did Jewish marriage and divorce laws conflict with French law? In fact, did Jews even consider France their country? The "Notables" pledged their loyalty to France and French law. Their responses were ratified by a "Grand Sanhedrin" called by Napoleon. The effect of the Assembly and Sanhedrin may have been to foster a belief among the more integrated European Jews that their civil rights depended both on demonstrating absolute loyalty to the law of the land and on conforming to the national culture.

The Reform movement took institutional shape when Jacobson moved to Cassel and established a Jewish school. There, in 1810, in a Confirmation ceremony, 13-year-old boys demonstrated that they had learned the principles of Judaism. Also in 1810, in nearby Seesen, the first Temple was built for a Reform congregation. The *bima* was placed in front of the ark, so the rabbi could more easily preach, and an organ was introduced. However, the women were still confined behind a partition in the balcony. Jacobson revealed something of his motivations when in his dedication speech he advocated that Jewish ritual should be purged of those elements that were "rightfully offensive to reason and to our Christian friends." In 1813, when Napoleon was defeated, Jacobson moved to Berlin and brought his reforms with him.

In 1814, Jacobson held services in his home which accommo-
dated 400 worshippers. In the same year, girls were first included
in a Confirmation service, conducted in M. H. Bock's private
school. However, in 1815, the Prussian King Frederick William II
banned all Reform services in Berlin because he feared that if Judaism were modernized, Christian missionaries would have more
difficulty converting Jews. In 1817, Jacob Beer, Berlin's wealthiest
Jew, who made his money refining sugar, was allowed to hold services in his home. In what may have been the first ideological
liturgical change, *goel*, redeemer, was replaced by *geulah*, redemption, and so the concept of a personal messiah was replaced by
faith in a messianic age of peace. The authorities in Berlin once
again prohibited Reform services.

The Reformers had to move to more hospitable surroundings
and ended up in the commercial center of Hamburg where 6,000
Jews (the largest community in Germany) lived. Most were not
wealthy but were middle-class merchants. In 1818, the Hamburg
temple was dedicated. The women were still in the balcony, but
there was no partition. They could see what was happening and
demanded that some prayers be read in German so they could
understand the service. The women spoke, and Rabbi Edward Kley
listened. He developed the Hamburg prayerbook, which included
translation of prayers into German. This first comprehensive Reform liturgy eliminated prayers for restoring sacrifices, rebuilding
the Temple and returning to Zion. After all, was not Germany
their homeland?

Meanwhile, back in Berlin in the 1820's, scholars led by
Leopold Zunz formed the Society for the Scientific Study of Judaism (*Wissenschaft des Judentums*). They were influenced by the
early theories of evolution that held that only those organisms
which were able to adapt to their environment survived. Zunz
argued that historically, Judaism had survived because under the

Pharisees and Talmudic rabbis it did adapt to changing conditions. It was only in the later Middle Ages that adaptation ceased. So the Reformers saw themselves as returning to the essential principle of dynamism that made possible Jewish continuity. There was only one tiny problem: At what point would Judaism change or adapt so much that it was no longer Judaism? Zunz believed that by objective study of Jewish sources, one could determine what was essential to Judaism. For example, he demonstrated that the weekly sermon had an ancient history and so should be reinstituted.

The rabbi-scholar who was most influential in developing what came to be called "Classical Reform" was Abraham Geiger. A student of philology, philosophy, and history, he maintained that neither the Bible nor the Talmud was entirely from God, for in each age Jewish thought had been influenced by changing conditions. Every element of tradition could claim relative validity in that it revealed the religious consciousness of the time. While Geiger emphasized Judaism as a historical process, he did insist that the religious consciousness of each age was linked by a Jewish spirit, although never clearly defined. In a sermon in Breslau, Geiger preached that within Judaism there are certain "eternal elements" that he called "prophetic Judaism": concern for the poor, rejection of rituals devoid of spiritual or moral meaning, and peace for all humanity. Later he wrote that the "essence of Judaism" is not "abstract Deism" but faith in "the One holy and living God . . . who has imbued (humans) with reason and free will and has given us the privilege of communing with God and the function of loving our neighbor as ourselves." Geiger opposed the "abolition of all ceremonial law," but in a private letter he did characterize circumcision as a "barbaric bloody act which fills the father with fear." For Geiger and other Classical Reformers, those traditions that enabled Jews to realize the essence (i.e., to come closer to God and fellow-humans) should be retained. He even predicted that the moral message of the one eternal God preserved and propagated by the Jewish people would eventually become the religion of humanity!

The leaders of the Reform movement held conferences in Brunswick (1844), Frankfurt (1845), and Breslau (1846), where they debated which traditions should be dropped or retained and why. The "radical" wing was led by Samuel Holdheim who so emphasized the *idea* of Shabbat that he argued Shabbat could be observed on any day, including Sunday. Zechariah Frankel attended the Frankfurt conference, but was indignant when the majority of rabbis, while advocating that the service should include Hebrew, voted that on principle, one could hold a Jewish service without Hebrew. Frankel then became a critic of the Reformers and developed positive-historical Judaism, an early form of the Conservative movement.

In justifying their reforms, the rabbis at the conferences—and later at synods in Leipzig (1869) and Augsburg (1871)—often tried to demonstrate that their changes were consistent with Jewish law. At Frankfurt, Leopold Stein defended the use of the organ (common in Protestant churches) by interpreting the Talmud to the effect that Jews may imitate any worthwhile custom of the Gentiles. The law prohibiting imitating pagans in their attire applies only if the clothing relates to paganism itself. Therefore, the organ, not being pagan, could be adopted. However, it soon became evident that not all the changes advocated by the reformers could be justified by citing Jewish law. For example, the entire body of laws pertaining to mourning(*hilchot avelut*) was considered not law but custom, and so could not be required.

Those traditions that had spiritual and moral meaning for the current generation were retained. This meant, however, that certain values prized by mid-century German Jews influenced their decisions. Wanting a religion consistent with reason, the Reformers thought it was not rational to observe festivals for two days, because the reason for the practice (to make sure the holiday was observed outside of Palestine when it was being celebrated in Jerusalem) no longer had relevance. Wanting to conform to cultural norms (recall Napoleon's "Grand Sanhedrin"), the Reformers decided that in their culture taking off the hat was a sign of respect; so *yarmelkes* were not considered necessary. In their society, divorce had become a civil matter; so a *get* was not required. A less-recognized value was that of finding spirituality in simplicity (common to other religious reform movements). This value could have influenced some Reform Jews to consider the *tallit* superfluous. There is a problem with the rationale of relevance. What happens when a particular generation says, we don't find meaning in any of the traditions except the Seder, Hanukkah lights, and maybe *Kol Nidre*?

"ONLY IN AMERICA"

Toward the end of the nineteenth century, as German society became increasingly authoritarian, the Reform movement survived but did not flourish. It was "only in America" that Reformers found the fertile soil of individualism that made possible continual growth and creativity. The first seedling was Southern. In 1825, Charleston, South Carolina, boasted the largest Jewish community in America: 600 people. About 200 (most from English or Portugese background) broke from the Orthodoxy of Beth Elohim and, under journalist Isaac Harby, formed the Reformed Society of Israelites. Harby was committed to a Judaism free of superstition and an America free of prejudice. Michael Meyer unearthed a fascinating letter that Harby wrote to President Monroe after Mordecai Noah was fired from his job as consul to Tunis, because Noah was Jewish. In effect, Harby said: If we Jews cannot find liberty in America, we will go to Palestine. So, in 1825, *sixty years before Herzl*, the first American Reform Jew saw Palestine as a potential solution to anti-Semitism!

Harby and other leaders of the Society left Charleston to "go North," so the remaining members rejoined Beth Elohim. The synagogue's leaders imported from Hamburg Gustavus Poznanski, whom they believed to be Orthodox. For a couple of years, Poznanski made no reforms. Then he married the daughter of the wealthiest Jewish family in Charleston and introduced an <u>organ.</u> <u>Beth Elohim soon became America's first Reform temple.</u> In Poznanski's dedication sermon, he compared freedom in America with anti-Semitism in Europe and proclaimed: "This synagogue is our temple, this city our Jerusalem, this happy land our Palestine."

From 1825 to 1875, the Jewish population in America grew from 5,000 to 250,000. The overwhelming majority of newcomers came from German-speaking lands, and many brought with them the Reform Judaism they knew in Europe. To become a movement, American Reform Judaism needed a leader and found him in Isaac Mayer Wise, who, at 27, landed in New York in 1846. In Bohemia, he had antagonized Emperor Ferdinand by performing marriages for more Jews than the government allowed and by denouncing anti-Semitism on the Emperor's birthday. Wise brought with him his wife, a child and German Reform Judaism. Wise was elected rabbi of Beth-El in Albany, where he introduced Confirmation, and German and English hymns, and preached his philosophy of Reform: There was but one permanent revelation, the Ten Commandments given at Sinai. So insistent was Wise on the Decalogue that he forced a board member to resign because his business was open on the Sabbath.

The members of Beth El were divided on how Reform they wanted to be, so when Wise, in public debate announced his disbelief in a personal messiah and bodily resurrection, the Board met and fired him. Wise claimed a quorum was not present, so he appeared on the pulpit on Rosh Hashanah. The President, in Wise's words, "smites me with his fist so that my cap falls from my head." There was an uproar in the synagogue, with the young people supporting Wise. The "sheriff and his posse" were called and the Rabbi was taken to the police station and booked on Rosh Hashanah! What did Wise's supporters do? Naturally they formed another congregation: Anshe Emet (Men of Truth). In 1854, Wise moved on to Cincinnati where at Beth Yeshurun he became (in his words) "the only Jewish preacher in the West."

Wise had a dream, perhaps in response to the bitter divisions in Albany: *one* American Judaism . . . no "denominations." Wise assumed that, given the individualism in American culture, Judaism would eventually be Reform. Meanwhile, he was willing to compromise. So at a rabbinic conference in Cleveland, he, along with more traditional rabbis, signed a statement that Biblical laws should be practiced according to their Talmudic interpretation. So convinced was Wise of the future that he wrote in his journal, *The American Israelite*, that American Judaism would become "the religion of the (entire) civilized world."

Wise's willingness to compromise infuriated Rabbi David Einhorn of Baltimore, who called his rival "the Jewish pope." In contrast to the gregarious, dynamic Wise, Einhorn was scholarly, reserved, and intellectual. He believed that at Sinai the Jewish people accepted as their purpose to bring monotheism to the world by living those ideals of justice and love that flow from faith in a universal God. Einhorn practiced what he preached. Because he condemned slavery, Einhorn was forced to leave Baltimore for Philadelphia. Einhorn had his own prayer book, *Olat Tamid* (*Perpetual Offering*), which was to become the basis for the *Union Prayer Book*.

Meanwhile, Wise had published a more traditional prayerbook, called—significantly—*Minhag America*, a liturgy for all American Jews. It was Einhorn, who called the first all-Reform rabbinic conference in America. In 1869, in Philadelphia, the Reform rabbis set forth basic principles of their movement, emphasizing the concept (so dear to Einhorn) of Jews as a priest-people. Two years later, 1871, at a more ecumenical conference in Cincinnati, Wise shocked his colleagues by stating he believed in Spinoza's view of a God who is not personal but is eternal and infinite. He even claimed that belief in a personal God was not Jewish but a philosophic fiction intended to counter the Christian doctrine of incarnation!

After Wise's rabbinic colleagues denounced his radical theology, Wise turned to lay leaders to realize his dream of one American Judaism. In 1873, he encouraged Moritz Loth, president of Beth Yeshurun, and other laymen to form the Union of American Hebrew Congregations, open to all synagogues regardless of "denomination." In 1875, the UAHC established in Cincinnati the Hebrew Union College and made Wise its president. The first year there were nine students, ages 13 to 17. But at the first graduation ceremony of HUC, in 1883, Wise's dream of one American Judaism came to an abrupt end.

Graduation was held during the UAHC convention, attended by not only Reform rabbis but their colleagues who observed *halakhah*. For the festive banquet a Jewish caterer was hired. As an eye-witness reported, the best-laid plans "gang aft aglee." Shrimp, clams, and soft-shelled crabs (prohibited by the laws of *kashrut*) were served. The more traditional rabbis stormed out in anger. The "*trefah* banquet" has been considered a stimulus that gave rise to American Conservative Judaism.

Actually, the Conservative movement had its roots in the Historical School, led by Benjamin Szold, Morris Jastrow, and Sabato Morais, all of whom were committed to the Written and Oral Law, and who believed that changes could be made only by rabbis committed to *halakhah*. (See Chapter 17.) They found support from some of the Jewish immigrants from Russia and Poland who

had started arriving in America in the 1880's. Most of these Eastern European immigrants were either socialist atheists or Orthodox. In either case, they would not set foot in a Reform temple.
However, many would eventually be drawn to the emerging Conservative movement. It was Sabato Morais who established the Jewish Theological Seminary (JTS) "to train a new generation of rabbis who would respect traditional Judaism" as well as the "practical
realities of American life." When Morais died in 1897, the very
existence of JTS was in doubt. But the lay leaders of the Reform
movement (Schiff, Warburg, Marshall, and others) gave the financial support that enabled the new seminary to survive and flourish. These more integrated, well-established German Jews saw Conservative Judaism as a way of Americanizing the newcomers from
Eastern Europe, lest their alien ways provoke anti-Semitism.

Two years after the "*trefah* banquet" on November 16, 1885,
in Pittsburgh, 15 Reform rabbis, realizing that Wise's dream of
one American Judaism would not be realized in the foreseeable
future, produced the "Pittsburgh Platform," the American version
of Classical Reform. It maintained that ethical monotheism is the
essence of Judaism; that the Bible, while a "potent instrument of
religious and moral instruction" also reflects "primitive ideas of its
own age"; and we should consider binding "only the moral laws
and only such ceremonies as elevate and sanctify our lives." Israel
is defined as a religious community, not a nation. The Platform
held that Judaism is "a progressive religion" that strives to be "in
accord with the postulates of reason," and so while asserting that
the soul is immortal, denies "the belief in bodily resurrection."
These American rabbis emphasized more than most German reformers the social justice theme:

> "We deem it our duty to participate in the great task of
> modern times, to solve on the basis of justice and righteous-
> ness the problems presented by the contrasts and evils of the
> present organization of society."

The Pittsburgh Platform should be understood as a response both to the Ethical Culture Movement, founded by Felix Adler, son of Samuel Adler, Reform Rabbi of New York's Temple Emanu-El, and to the Historical School, soon to become the Conservative movement. It has been criticized for its negativity, as it states what one need not do (e.g., observe *kashrut)* and seems to leave it up to the individual to decide which traditions "elevate and sanctify" his/her life. Of course, one might expect that any movement that rebels against Orthodoxy would begin by emphasizing what is being rejected. The Platform has also been criticized for its rejection of Jewish nationalism. One should recall that it would be eleven years before Herzl wrote *The Jewish State* (1896), the first clear statement of political Zionism. The Reformers at Pittsburgh were rejecting the Orthodox concept that after God sent a messiah, the Jewish people would return to Zion. Still, the Platform's insistence that Jews are no longer a nation but a "religious community" reflects the fear, imported from Europe, that Jews would not be granted equality unless they shed their ethnic differences and national aspirations and were perceived as a religious denomination. Recall that the Napoleonic Sanhedrin in 1806, did indeed link Jewish rights to a rejection of all loyalties other than to France.

Two trends within Reform Judaism were represented by the two sons-in-law of David Einhorn, Emil G. Hirsch and Kaufmann Kohler. At Temple Sinai in Chicago, Hirsch was a vigorous proponent of social justice. He was also among 100 rabbis who all but eliminated Hebrew from the service and was among 20 who held services on Sunday instead of Saturday. This anti-traditional tendency was denounced by Rabbi Kohler, who in 1903, succeeded Rabbi Wise as president of the Hebrew Union College and whose main focus was Jewish theology. Today, Reform rabbis consider personal piety and social justice, the spiritual and ethical dimensions of Judaism inextricably linked. The real tension may be between those who are concerned with social justice within the larger community and those who focus almost exclusively on what directly affects the Jews.

The two brothers-in-law, Hirsch and Kohler, did unite: to help organize the Central Conference of American Rabbis, to defeat efforts of Rabbis Margolis and Enelow to establish an official creed for the Reform movement as well as a synod that would mandate required practices. Reform Jews were now reading the Victorian prose of the *Union Prayer Book* and singing lyrics written to church-like and classical music in the *Union Hymnal.* Those raised in the Classical Reform tradition had the memorable experience of singing to the stirring melody of the last movement of Beethoven's Ninth Symphony: "Onward brothers, march still onward, side by side and hand by hand. We are bound for God's true kingdom. We are an increasing band . . ."

DEBATING ZIONISM
AND RETURNING TO TRADITION

The most severe criticism of Classical Reform and the Pittsburgh Platform was voiced after the first World War and the Balfour Declaration. Political Zionism had begun attracting followers among American Jews, including Justice Louis Brandeis, who insisted that one could be both a loyal American and a Zionist. Because the Hebrew Union College, in 1922 (under its new president, Julian Morgenstern) still rejected a Zionist interpretation of Jewish life, Reform Rabbi Stephen Wise (who had rebuffed Temple Emanu-El's attempt to restrict freedom of the pulpit and had founded the Free Synagogue) established in New York City the Jewish Institute of Religion. Its students were presented with a more traditional and thoroughly Zionist approach to Judaism.

Between 1880 and 1924, about two-million Jews left behind

poverty and pogroms in Eastern Europe to come to the United States. The immigrants, if they were religious, tended to join Orthodox or Conservative synagogues. Many of their children and grandchildren preferred the greater autonomy allowed by Reform Judaism. However, when they joined Reform synagogues, they brought with them traditions that had been dropped by Classical Reform, a stronger sense of Jewish identity, and a recognition of the need for a homeland whose gates would always be open to Jews. They were greatly to influence the evolution of Reform Judaism toward more tradition and Zionism. This evolution was led by rabbis, most of whom also had roots in Eastern Europe.

With the rise of Hitler, the Nazi persecution of Jews, and the refusal of the democracies to open their gates to all but a token number of refugees, political Zionism became not a matter for philosophic debate but an urgent issue of life and death. In 1932, *Hatikvah*, the Zionist anthem, was included in the *Union Hymnal*. In 1937, the UAHC passed a resolution favoring a Jewish homeland in Palestine. In the same year, a majority of Reform rabbis at the CCAR in Columbus, Ohio, passed the "Columbus Platform." The Platform stated: "In the rehabilitation of Palestine, the land hallowed by memories and hopes, we behold the promise of renewed life for many of our brethren. We affirm the obligation of all Jewry to aid in its upbuilding as a Jewish homeland by endeavoring to make it not only a haven of refuge for the oppressed but also a center of Jewish culture and spiritual life."

The rabbis at Columbus were also concerned that too many Reform Jews were, in the idiom of the Pittsburgh Platform, concluding that hardly any ceremonies could "elevate and sanctify their lives." Because many Reform Jews had dropped practically all traditions, the Columbus Platform set limits, parameters within which Reform Jewish life should be observed: "Judaism as a way of life *requires* in addition to its moral and spiritual demands, the preservation of the Sabbath, festivals and holy days, the retention and development of such customs, symbols and ceremonies as possess inspirational value, the cultivation of distinctive forms of religious art and music and the use of Hebrew, together with the vernacular, in our worship and instruction."

This "return to tradition" led to the restoration or creation of customs now taken for granted: candle-lighting and *kiddush* at home and in the synagogue; the return of Bar Mitzvah and the introduction of Bat Mitzvah as a step toward Confirmation; the use of authentic Jewish music in place of Haydn and Beethoven and the emergence of the *hazan* (cantor) in many Reform synagogues; the use of more Hebrew in the service. Rabbis began wearing prayer-shawls(*atarot*) and eventually *talletim*. *Kipot* (also called *yarmelkes*) became optional. Some Classical Reformers complained that Reform was "becoming Orthodox, or at least Conservative." But even the Pittsburgh Platform states that we should observe those traditions that "elevate and sanctify our lives." Clearly, many members of Reform synagogues with roots in Eastern Europe had decided that the simplicity of Classical Reform was too abstract, and they did find spiritual meaning in the warmth of some traditions practiced by their parents or grandparents.

Some Classical Reform Jews were still opposed to Zionism. In 1942, the CCAR resolved that "the Jewish population of Palestine be given the privilege of establishing a military force which will fight under its own banner." This call for a "Jewish army" was understood as a more clearly nationalistic resolution than the 1937 call for a "homeland." So 90 rabbis, including Julian Morgenstern, president of HUC, signed a statement advocating "aid to (our Jewish) brothers in economic cultural and spiritual endeavors" but claimed that "Jewish nationalism confuses the role of the Jews in the world." These rabbis and like-minded congregants formed the American Council for Judaism, which, while advocating increased Jewish immigration to Palestine, opposed the establishment of a Jewish state.

When, in 1943, Maurice Eisendrath became Executive Director of the UAHC, he found a Reform movement that had stopped growing, even as the American Jewish population was expanding. Put simply: Reform Judaism, with its headquarters in Cincinnati, was not attracting enough of the thousands of Jews who had come from Eastern Europe and who were living in the large cities on the East Coast. In 1946, Eisendrath assumed the presidency of UAHC, the first time this was a salaried office. In 1948, against considerable opposition, he led and won the fight to move the Union's offices from Cincinnati to New York, closer to the mainstream of American Jewish life. He established regional offices throughout the country and so prevented the Reform movement from becoming a small sect within American Jewry.

Once Israel came into being in 1948, the American Council became insignificant as virtually all American Jews supported the Jewish state in its struggle for survival. In 1947, archaeologist Nelson Glueck succeeded Julian Morgenstern as president of the Hebrew Union College. In 1950, HUC merged with the Jewish Institute of Religion, forming the College-Institute (HUC-JIR). In 1954, the College-Institute opened a campus in Los Angeles, and in 1963, in Jerusalem. An important part of the College-Institute in New York is the School of Sacred Music, which trains cantors who bring both traditional and contemporary Jewish music to congregations. The College-Institute also provides professional training for religious school principals and teachers. One can receive more information on the Reform Jewish website, http://rj.org.

FROM SOCIAL ACTION TO
SPIRITUAL SEARCH

The 1960's was a decade of social action for the Reform movement. In 1961, under the leadership of its president, Maurice
Eisendrath, the UAHC voted to establish the Religious Action
Center (RAC) in Washington, D.C., so that Reform Jewish leaders might pursue "justice, justice" (for Jews and non-Jews alike) by
advocating those policies approved by the Social Action Commission, led by Albert Vorspan. These policies included support for
the civil rights movement and opposition to the war in Vietnam.
Rabbi/ attorney David Sapterstein is effectively leading RAC out
of the old millennium and into the new.

Meanwhile, as the number of Reform synagogues grew, the
number of Reform rabbis increased from less than 500 in 1943, to
1,150 in 1975, to 1,800 in 2000. As we enter the new millenium,
there are about 900 Reform congregations throughout North
America. The activities of the movement are coordinated by the
Reform Jewish "alphabet": WRJ (Women for Reform Judaism);
NFTB (National Federation of Temple Brotherhoods) which sponsors the JCS (Jewish Chatauqua Society); NFTY(National Federation of Temple Youth); NATE(National Association of Temple
Educators); NATA (National Association of Temple Administra-
tors); NOAM(National Organization of American Mohalim/ot);
WUPJ (World Union for Progressive Judaism); and ARZA (The
Association of Reform Zionists in America). When the World Union
was formed in 1926, among its inspirational leaders were Claude
Montefiore and Lily Montagu of England and Leo Baeck of Germany. From very small beginnings in Great Britain, Holland, Germany, Argentina and South Africa, the movement grew between
1940 and 1977 to 50 congregations with 30,000 members.

In London in 1956, the Leo Baeck College was named after

the inspiring rabbi-philosopher who remained with his people in Germany and survived the death camps. It continued the work of the Berlin *Hochschule* where Baeck had taught. The next generation of European-born rabbis included the charismatic Hugo Gryn and the eloquent, scholarly Albert Friedlander, who directed the College from 1967 to 1977 and is still its dean. Approximately 150 rabbis have been ordained at the College. They are serving 75 progressive congregations in Great Britain, as well as synagogues in Israel, Canada, and the U.S.A. In 1990, out of Great Britain's less than 300,000 Jews, 23% were affiliated with either Reform or Liberal congregations. (Reform in Britain is closer in its practices to "left-wing" American Conservatism, and Liberal is the British version of American Reform). Both the Liberal and Reform movements have produced new liturgies, among them, *Service of the Heart* (1967) and the *Gates of Repentance* (1973), which were to influence the new American Reform prayerbooks of the 1970's.

In 1973, when Richard Hirsch became executive director of WUPJ, he initiated the move of its headquarters from New York to Jerusalem. Rabbi Hirsch devoted much of his energy and effort to developing "Progressive" Judaism in Israel. Today, supported by WUPJ and ARZA, Progressive Judaism in Israel is engaged in a continual struggle to achieve the same rights given the Orthodox. There were in 2000, 23 congregations and two *kibbutzim* , *Yahel* and *Lotan.*

The 1970's was a decade of transition. In 1971, Alfred Gottschalk succeeded Nelson Glueck as president of HUC-JIR, and in that same year Joseph Glaser succeeded Sidney Regner as executive vice-president of the CCAR. In 1973, Alexander Schindler succeeded Eisendrath as president of the UAHC, and established the Outreach program to bring the message of a liberal Judaism not only to non-Jews who marry Jews but to all those (Jews and non-Jews) who are searching for a religious commitment. (See Chapter 21.) Also, during the 1970's, the CCAR concluded that

Reform Jews should be given more specific guides to enable them to practice Jewish traditions. Rabbi Solomon Freehof's volumes of "Responsa" had become widely respected by rabbis and laypersons. Freehof answered hundreds of questions from ritual practice to medical ethics by citing traditional sources and giving his Reform interpretation. However, there was some resistance to publishing a guide for Reform Jewish practice, lest it become a "Reform *Shulchan Arukh*," a code of required practice that would stigmatize non-conformists. In 1972, the *Shabbat Manual* was published. The *mitzvot* of Shabbat were presented not as requirements but as opportunities for greater spiritual fulfillment. Also in 1972, a major transition within the Reform rabbinate began. This was the year the first woman, Sally Preisand, was ordained as a rabbi. By the 1990's, about 40% of the students at the College-Institute were women, and in 2000, there were 350 women Reform rabbis.

The seventies was the decade of "the gates." In 1975, *Gates of Prayer* was published. With ten Shabbat evening services reflecting different themes and theological perspectives and containing more Hebrew, it was to replace the *Union Prayer Book*. The new High Holyday prayer book, *Gates of Repentance,* was published in 1978. Also in 1978, ways to observe life-cycle events were recommended in *Gates of Mitzvah*. This was followed in the 1980's by *Gates of the Seasons* and, in 1991, *Gates of Shabbat*. Most widely used was the *New Passover Haggadah* (1974). In 1988, the UAHC published Daniel Syme's *The Jewish Home: A Guide for Jewish Living.*

The philosophy behind this increased emphasis on Jewish tradition was set forth in the Centenary Perspective, whose chief author was Eugene Borowitz. Adopted in San Francisco by the CCAR in 1976, the Perspective states, "Within each area of Jewish observance Reform Jews are called upon to confront the claims of Jewish tradition, however differently perceived, and to exercise their individual autonomy, choosing and creating on the basis of commitment and knowledge."

CHALLENGING THE CLAIM OF *HALAKHAH*

Chapter 1 dealt with the resolution of the CCAR that recognized as Jews children of Jewish fathers and non-Jewish mothers, so long as there were "timely and formal acts of identification with the Jewish faith and people." Remember, Conservative and Orthodox Judaism hold to the halakhic definition based on matrilineal descent.

Another position of Reform Judaism that challenged the claim of Jewish tradition was taken in 1990, when the CCAR confronted the issue: Should the Reform movement should accept openly gay and lesbian rabbis? In the Torah we read, "Do not lie with a male as with a woman; it is an abhorrence" (Leviticus 18:20). However, this prohibition assumes that homosexuality is a matter of free choice. Today it is generally recognized that a homosexual orientation is either due to genetic factors or complex psychological factors beyond the individual's control, or both, and, hence, is not a sin. The Conference accepted the report of the Ad Hoc Committee on homosexuality that stated, "All human beings are created *betselem elohim* ("in the divine image") . . . Sexual orientation is irrelevant to the human worth of a person . . . The committee strongly endorses the view that all Jews are religiously equal regardless of their sexual orientation . . . the College-Institute considers sexual orientation of an applicant only within the context of a candidate's overall suitability for the rabbinate, his or her qualifications to serve the Jewish community effectively, and his or her capacity to find personal fulfillment within the rabbinate." In effect, openly gay and lesbian students have been and are being admitted to and are graduating from HUC-JIR, and are finding positions as rabbis within the Reform movement.

After a distinguished 23 years as president of the UAHC, Rabbi Schindler retired and passed the mantle of leadership to Rabbi

Eric Yoffie, who served first as director of ARZA and then as Vice President of the UAHC and Director of the Commission on Social Action of Reform Judaism. After the untimely death of Rabbi Joseph Glaser—the rabbis' rabbi—a worthy successor, Rabbi Paul Menitoff was in 1995 appointed as executive vice-president of the Central Conference of American Rabbis. He had been serving as Regional Director of the Northeast Council of the UAHC. In Cincinnati, Rabbi Alfred Gottschalk retired as president of the Hebrew Union College-Jewish Institute of Religion. In 1995, he was succeeded by Rabbi Sheldon Zimmerman, a former president of the Central Conference of American Rabbis, and rabbi of Temple Emanu-el in Dallas, Texas.

In May, 1999, at its Pittsburgh convention, the CCAR adopted a new Pittsburgh Platform. Originally drafted by CCAR president, Rabbi Richard Levy, the text underwent numerous revisions, based on feedback from rabbis and lay leaders throughout the country. In the first draft there was specific mention of the option of "wearing the *tallit* or *tefillin* for prayer, *kashrut* (dietary laws) and *mikveh* (ritual bath.)" While the authors specifically stated that this was not an attempt to "legislate a code of belief or conduct," the very mention of such options for Reform Jews was considered by some a rejection of "their kind of Reform Judaism." So the final draft of the principles expressed the concept or general rule behind any such choices: "We are committed to the ongoing study of the *whole array* of *mitzvot* and to the fulfillment of those that address us as individuals and as a community. Some of these *mitzvot*, sacred obligations, have long been observed by Reform Jews; others, both ancient and modern demand renewed attention as the result of the unique context of our own times." (Compare with the Centenary Perspective of 1976.)

Among the more innovative statements in the new Pittsburgh Principles is an affirmation of the openness of Reform Judaism: "We are an inclusive community, opening doors to Jewish life to people of all ages, to varied kinds of families, to all regardless of their sexual orientation, to *gerim*, those who have converted to Judaism, and to all individuals and families, including the intermarried, who strive to create a Jewish home . . . We believe that we must not only open doors for those ready to enter our faith, but also to actively encourage those who are seeking a spiritual home to find it in Judaism." (This reflects the policy of Outreach originally voiced by Rabbi Schindler.) Concern for the environment is given a religious foundation: "We regard with reverence all of God's creation and recognize our human responsibility for its preservation and protection."

In 2001, David Ellenson, a highly respected professor of Jewish religious thought at HUC-JIR in Los Angeles was appointed president of the College-Institute.

HOW TO BALANCE AUTONOMY AND AUTHORITY

The difficult issue of how to balance authority and autonomy is still being debated within the Reform movement. Among those advocating the greatest autonomy is Professor Alvin Reines, whose polydoxy holds that all beliefs and practices have a valid place within Reform Judaism so long as they do not claim authoritative revelation and are not imposed on others. Among those who advocate a return to a greater respect for authority are the advocates of a "liberal *halakhah*," led by Gunther Plaut and Walter Jacob. After rejecting the Orthodox concept of the divine origin of the Law, they set forth certain principles of interpretation. Regarding the crucial issue of authority, Rabbi Jacob advocates that the Reform movement needs "governance," not "guidance." John Rayner, also an advocate of "progressive *halakhah*," may be more realistic when he asks, "Although the *halakhah* does not have decisive authority for us, may it not have an *advisory* authority as a source of wisdom?" Rabbi Plaut hopes that "our own people will carefully con-

sider our(the Responsa Committee's) decisions" that "are not sermons but are cast in a legal framework." Few Reform rabbis or
laypersons object to being "advised" by a Responsa Committee or
carefully considering traditional precedents. Anyone may choose
to accept the authority of a liberal *halakhah*, but so long as other
Reform Jews (without being stigmatized) may choose to reject
that authority, it would seem that Reform Judaism still respects
the autonomy of its adherents.

From the perspective of his Covenant Theology, Borowitz's response is that if a Jew fully participates in the Jewish people's
historical relation with God, if he or she is personally involved
with God and with the land, language, and tradition of the people,
then Jewish law and lore will become the best source of guidance
for life. Borowitz would judge Jewish authenticity less by the extent of observance than by the genuineness of effort to ground
one's life in the Covenant. Espousing Jewish pluralism, he considers "a communal life-style, richly personal yet Jewishly grounded"
as the "Jewish self's equivalent of *halakhah*." Assuming that our
sense of responsibility is crucially influenced by multiple interac-
tions since birth with parents, teachers, the media, and exposure
to the cultural diversity in America today, one may find it difficult
to determine to what degree the decisions of American Jews—even
the most conscientious participants in the Covenant—are influenced by encounters with God, Torah, and the Jewish people and
to what degree by non-Jewish factors. Whatever the multiple
sources of obligation, after all the encounters it is still the Jews
who choose.

Could there be a middle ground between the polydox and
halakhists? Is it possible to recognize that as Reform Jews, we need
a sense of spiritual, moral, and traditional commonality if we are
to function effectively for our own sake and for Jewish continuity?
Might we find a consensus in certain fundamental beliefs that

have persisted, with very few exceptions, throughout the evolution of Reform Judaism? These beliefs are:

1) a faith in one God, and an acceptance of a wide variety of ways of conceiving or experiencing God.

2) the ethical principles that flow from the unity of God, and a commitment to search together to understand what love and justice require in this complex world.

3) A commitment not only to search but to act in order to achieve *tikkun olam* , to repair our world and so bring nearer the messianic age.

4) A commitment to the preservation of the Jewish people. (Since 1948, this has meant the security of Israel.)

5) We may differ over the relation between God and the Jewish people (are we the chosen, the choosing, or both?), but we do find not only in faith but in Jewish historic experience motivation for the values of family, education and justice. We are also aware that ethnicity can become ethnocentrism if it is not guided by principles of universal morality.

6) the practice and preservation of those traditions that enable Reform Jews to preserve and identify with their religious community (The Columbus Platform with its requirement of preserving Shabbat , festivals and Holydays; Hebrew and authentic Jewish music still seems relevant.)

7) Within this framework, the most urgent Reform Jewish imperative is: Thou shalt search—through guides, study of Jewish sources, and prayer—to bring God, ethics, and tradition into your life that you may better find for yourself, your family, the Jewish people and humanity "the ways of pleasantness and the paths of peace."

JEWISH POPULATION BY DENOMINATION

According to the 1990 National Jewish Population Study, the Core Jewish Population (born Jews who affirm the Jewish religion; Jews by choice; born Jews with no religion) is: 5,515,000. Of these about 40% are affiliated with synagogues (2,200,000). Of affiliated Jews, 16% are Orthodox (355,000); 43% are Conservative (890,000); 35% are Reform (760,000); 2% are Reconstructionist (50,000); 4% are Other(*havurot,* Hasidic: *100,000).*

Of Jewish households with a denominational preference, Orthodox, 6.8%; Conservative, 40.4%; Reform, 41.4%; Reconstructionist: 3.2%; Traditional, 3.2%; "Just Jewish," 5.2%; Miscellaneous Jewish, 1.4%

TOPICS FOR DISCUSSION:

Which kind of Reform Judaism do you find most meaningful?

1. A Judaism that allows you to hold any religious belief or practice so long as you do not claim that it was revealed by God and so long as you do not consider your belief or practice binding on others.

2. A Judaism that requires the belief in one God and the moral principles of justice and love, and which gives you the freedom to follow whatever traditions have spiritual or moral value for you.

3. A Judaism that requires the belief in one God and the moral prnciples of justice and love, and which requires

that you preserve the Sabbath festivals and holidays and retain Hebrew and authentic Jewish music in the service. Within these limits you may choose those traditions that are most meaningful to you.

4. A Judaism that requires you to pray to God, to become familiar with the vast array of Jewish tradition, to study Jewish law and lore, to consider your responsibility to the Jewish people and through these encounters with God-Torah-Israel, to discover your moral and ritual responsibilities.

Give reasons for your choice. Try to identify which statement of principles or theologian is represented by each of the above choices.

RESOURCES

Borowitz, Eugene. *Liberal Judaism*. New York, UAHC Press, 1984.

Borowitz, Eugene. *Reform Judaism Today.*Vol. I, II, III. New York, Behrman House, 1977-8.

Borowitz, Eugene. *Renewing the Covenant*. Philadelphia, Jewish Publication Society, 1991.

Cohen, Henry. "The Limits of Autonomy in Reform Judaism: Hello Columbus!" in *CCAR Journal*, New York, Fall, 1991.

Freehof, Solomon. *Reform Jewish Practice*, Vol. I and II. New York, Ktav, 1976.

Jacob, Walter and Moshe Zemer(ed.). *Progressive Halakhah*. Pittsburgh, Rodef Shalom Press, 1988.

Jacob, Walter(ed.). *Contemporary American Reform Responsa*. New York, CCAR, 1987.

Marcus, Jacob Rader. *Israel Jacobson: The Founder of the Reform Movement in Judaism*. Cincinnati, HUC Press, 1972.

Martin, Bernard(ed.). *Contemporary Reform Jewish Thought*. New York, Quadrangle, 1968.

Meyer, Michael A. *Response to Modernity: A History of the Reform Movement in Judaism*. New York, Oxford University Press, 1988.

Plaut, Gunther. *Rise of Reform Judaism*. New York, World Union for Progressive Judaism, 1963.

Plaut, Gunther. *The Growth of Reform Judaism*. New York. World Union for Progressive Judaism, 1965.

Plaut, Gunther and Mark Washofsky (ed.). *Teshuvot for the Nineties: Reform Judaism's Answers for Today's Dilemmas*. New York, Central Conference of American Rabbis, 1997.

Wiener, Max. *Abraham Geiger and Liberal Judaism*. Philadelphia, Jewish Publication Society, 1962.

Zola, Gary (ed.). *Women Rabbis: Exploration and Celebration*. Cincinnati, HUC-JIR Rabbinic Alumni Association Press, 1996.

17.

THE EVOLUTION OF

CONSERVATIVE JUDAISM

There are significant similarities between Reform and Conservative Judaism. Both had their roots in nineteenth-century Germany. Both view Judaism as an ongoing historical process. Both have, among their rabbis, advocates of a more strict and a less strict interpretation of Jewish law. Both allow men and women to sit together. As some Reform congregations have returned to more traditional practices (e.g., *kipah*, more Hebrew), and as some Conservative congregations have a more liberal approach to Jewish tradition, an outsider may not be sure if he/she has entered a Reform or Conservative synagogue. The fundamental difference between the two movements is not how many traditions one observes, but let's not get ahead of ourselves.

First, a flashback to Frankfurt, Germany, in 1845. A synod of Reform rabbis had held that, in principle, one can have a Jewish service without Hebrew. Zechariah Frankel was so outraged that he left the Reformers and began developing his "positive historical" Judaism. He agreed with the Reformers that for the past three centuries Judaism had become too rigid. Like the Reformers, he

also did not believe in the divine revelation of all Jewish law. To
him, "a tradition of Moses from Sinai" meant an ordinance of unknown origin. He favored, as did the Reformers, the scientific study
of Judaism as a method of change.

But Frankel contended that the Reform rabbis had gone too
far beyond the "total popular will" of the Jewish people. In the
past, rabbinic scholars had been attuned to the needs of the whole
people, and their legal interpretations reflected that will. The Reform leaders had lost touch with the vast majority of the Jewish
people and were reflecting the opinions of a relatively small group
of rabbis. Frankel was confident that the people, themselves, would
preserve Judaism. He wrote:

> "Judaism demands religious activity, but the people is not al-
> together clay to be molded by the will of theologians and scholars.
> In religious activities, as in those of ordinary life, (the people) de-
> cides for itself. This right was conceded by Judaism to the people
> When the people allows certain practices to fall into disuse, then
> the practices cease to exist. There is no such danger for faith. A
> people used to activity will not hurt itself and will not destroy its
> practices. Its own sense of religiosity warns against it. Only those
> practices from which it is entirely estranged and which yield it no
> satisfaction will be abandoned and will thus die of themselves."

Meanwhile in 1825, the very year that the first American Reformers established the Reformed Society of Israelites, the first
step toward Conservative Judaism was taken when some members
of Shearit Israel, America's oldest synagogue, found its practices
too rigid and formed B'nai Jeshurun, later to become an outstand-
ing Conservative synagogue in New York City. In most of the nineteenth century, the rabbis and congregants who observed more
traditions than did the Reformers called themselves not "conservative" but adherents of "the historical school." Much as the Orthodox Moses Mendelssohn prepared the way for Reform, so the Or-

thodox *hazan* (cantor) of *Mikveh Israel* in Philadelphia, Isaac Leeser, prepared the way for the historical school. Leeser translated the Bible into English. With Morris Raphall, he published an English translation of the prayers for women. (Recall that the Hamburg Reform prayer book was also published in response to the request of women.) He denounced the Reformers in Charleston when they rejected the belief in a personal messiah and the resurrection of the dead. Leeser insisted that any change to be made must be justified by the *halakhah.* In 1867, in Philadelphia, Leeser helped establish Maimonides College, in order to teach and ordain American rabbis. Only four rabbis graduated. Because of lack of support, the College was closed in 1873.

In the 1860's, the Historical School was led by Marcus Jastrow (who published his own prayer book), Benjamin Szold (who formed the first Zionist group in America), and Sabato Morais(who was the first president of the Jewish Theological Seminary.) In 1879, they asserted an ideology that differed from Orthodoxy by stating that much of the *Shulchan Arukh* had outlived its usefulness . They differed from the Reformers by insisting that Judaism in America should return to the method of halakhic interpretations developed in Talmudic times. Some, not wanting to divide American Judaism, had with their congregations joined the Union of American Hebrew congregations. However, after the "*trefah* banquet" in 1883, Jastrow and others resigned. After the Pittsburgh platform of 1885 (which renounced such traditions as *kashrut),* the Historical School established the Jewish Theological Seminary (JTS). In its preamble it proclaimed "fidelity and devotion to Jewish law." The Seminary was dedicated to "the preservation in America of the knowledge and practice of historical Judaism as ordained in the Law of Moses expounded by the prophets and sages in Israel in Biblical and Talmudic writings." JTS, from its inception, was supported by eleven congregations, from the more traditional *Mikveh Israel (*led by Sabato Morais) to the less traditional *Oheb Shalom* in Baltimore (led by Benjamin Szold). As noted in the previous chapter, wealthy Reform Jews were the major financial contributors to JTS, because (as noted in the previous chapter) they viewed it as a way to acculturate the immigrants from Eastern Europe who were coming to America by the thousands. The Alumni Association of JTS, organized in 1901, eventually became the Rabbinical Assembly.

In 1902, the highly regarded scholar, Solomon Schechter, became president of JTS. Born in Romania, where he had studied in a traditional *yeshiva*, Schechter had also, with Leopold Zunz, been a disciple of the Scientific Study of Judaism. He saw historic Judaism as an "evolving organism." In his inaugural address, he recognized the importance of the eighteenth-century Enlightenment, but he insisted that "the teaching in the Seminary will be . . . confined to the exposition and elucidation of historical Judaism in its various manifestations. There is no other Jewish religion but that taught by the Torah and confirmed by history and tradition, and sunk into the conscience of Catholic Israel." The phrase, "Catholic Israel" refers to the will of *K'lal Yisrael*, the entire Jewish people, a reflection of the philosophy of Zechariah Frankel. Schechter stated that the new theology should include the best of Geiger and Zunz, as well as the mysticism of the Baal Shem Tov, and should promote "a love for Israel's nationality" as expressed by Theodor Herzl and Ahad Ha-Am." (See Chapter 19.) Sabato Morais opposed a Jewish state but believed that Palestine should be a "center of spiritual truth." However, most members of the Historical School were ardent Zionists. Schechter saw Zionism as "the great bulwark against assimilation." An organization of "Young American Zionists" was formed, based on Isaiah 1:27: "*Tzion bamishpat tipadeh*, Zion shall be redeemed with justice." This may be the origin of the ZBT fraternity.

Schechter believed that traditional interpretations of the Bible should be based on "the collective conscience of Catholic Israel as embodied in the Universal Synagogue." Like Isaac Mayer Wise, Schechter hoped that there would emerge one American Judaism, although his kind of American Judaism differed significantly from that of Wise. Schechter, as a historian, did recognize that Judaism had dogmas, including belief in bodily resurrection, the advent of the Messiah, the election of Israel, and the immutability of the Law. However, belief in these dogmas did not help one achieve salvation. All of these "dogmas" were not accepted by all rabbis in the Historical School; Szold and Jastrow, for instance, rejected bodily resurrection and believed in the immortality of the soul.

In the 1880's there were great debates between the Reform theologian, Kaufmann Kohler, and the emerging leader of the Historical School, Alexander Kohut. The *American Hebrew*, journal of the Historical School, and the *American Israelite*, edited by Isaac Mayer Wise, reported on these debates and published an outpouring of reactions to them. The Reform Pittsburgh Platform was formulated, in part, as a response to Kohut and his insistence that the survival of Judaism depended on accepting the divine origin of the Torah and the authority of the *halakhah*.

By 1913, Schechter recognized the need for a religious movement consisting of all groups "who have not accepted the (Reform) Union Prayer Book nor performed religious devotion with uncovered head." So he established the United Synagogue of America, and Conservative Judaism was on its way to becoming a "movement" within America. He stated that the purpose of the United Synagogue would be to advance the cause of Judaism in America and to maintain Jewish tradition in its historical continuity; "to assert and establish loyalty to the Torah and its historical expositions, to further the observance of the Sabbath and the dietary laws; to preserve in the service the reference to Israel's past and the hopes for Israel's restoration . . ." According to Conservative theologian Neil Gillman, this was an early attempt at a statement of principles, although it omitted any reference to God, revelation, or the reason for the authority of the *halakhah*.

While Schechter did not spell out his own ideology, Gillman has extracted from Schechter's writings several beliefs:

1) America will protect religious freedom.
2) Judaism can deal with modernity.
3) The study of Judaism should be carried out through critical and scientific analysis.
4) History can teach what in Judaism has remained unchanged.
5) Change should be decided by a consensus of caring committed Jews.
6) Hebrew is the language of the Jewish people.
7) Zionism should be encouraged.
8) *Halakhah* is the pre-eminent form of Jewish self-expression.
9) *Halakhah* changes to meet new situations in the more superficial areas of Jewish life and under the guidance of recognized authorities in Jewish law.

After Schechter's death in 1915, Cyrus Adler became first the acting and then the designated president of JTS. While he had a doctorate in Semitics from Johns Hopkins, Adler became known less as a scholar and more as an administrator and builder of institutions. Though he, himself, adhered to the more traditional branch of the Conservative movement, he insisted on allowing academic freedom within the Seminary and despite much opposition, allowed the future founder of Reconstructionism, Mordecai Kaplan, to remain on the faculty. When Kaplan resigned in 1963, to promote the Reconstructionist movement, he was still considered professor *emeritus* at JTS. Unlike almost all of the faculty, Adler was not a Zionist. Like some German Reform Jews, he feared that Zionism would compromise American Jews' loyalty to the United States. He resigned his position as president of the United Synagogue of America in 1917, after it adopted a statement that endorsed the Zionist movement.

During Adler's administration, the most influential professor was Louis Ginzberg, who taught rabbinics from 1902 to 1954. As an ardent traditionalist, Ginzberg discouraged but did not condemn men and women sitting together. He contended that the Conservative movement was allowing the individual Jew too much autonomy and needed an authoritative body to interpret Jewish law. Of *halakhah* he stated, "as its meaning, 'conduct' indicates, (it) comprises life in all its manifestations—religion, worship, law, economics, politics, ethics and so forth. It gives us a picture of life in its totality and not of some of its fragments." He also asserted that "the dietary laws are not incumbent upon us because they conduce to moderation . . . The law as a whole is not the means to an end but the end itself." Ginzberg inspired his students to have a "veneration of the Law."

After the death of Cyrus Adler in 1940, Louis Finkelstein became president of JTS and was Chancellor from 1951 until his retirement in 1972. He was, in Gillman's words, "the intellectualized model of Jewish piety." He believed that the authentic Jew was the studying Jew. Worth repeating is his statement: "When I pray, I speak to God. When I study, God speaks to me." In 1944, Finkelstein created the prize-winning "Eternal Light" program on the radio. Until 1948, the Committee on Interpretation of Jewish Law limited its interpretations to those that could be justified strictly by the precedents and methods of *halakhah*. After 1948, no formula was imposed on the method of interpretation so that extra-legal considerations could be taken into account. For example, the question, "Should women be counted in a *minyan* (the ten adults required for public prayer)?" was posed to the Law Committe. The traditionalists argued that the term, *minyan*, refers to the number of Jews required to follow a particular law. Because unlike men, women are not *required* to pray three times a day, they could not, therefore, be counted in the *minyan*. The more liberal rabbis (the majority) took into account an extra-legal consideration—the spiritual equality of men and women—and held that women could be counted in a *minyan*. Because there was such a division within the Law Committee, the decision could be made by each Conservative rabbi. If there was overwhelming consensus on the Committe, *its* decision was binding. If as many as six out of 25 votes held to a minority opinion, that view could be considered acceptable by the individual rabbi, who was the authority in each congregation.

Among the decisions: Individual congregations could refrain from observing the second day of festivals, except for Rosh Hashanah. Rabbis had the right to nullify Jewish marriages if the groom refused to give his wife a *get*, the Jewish divorce certificate. Also, Conservative Jews were permitted to use electricity on the Sabbath and to drive cars so long as they were going to synagogue. The Committee agreed with the Orthodox that embalming of a corpse is not permitted. When a vote was overwhelming (e.g., the insistence on matrilineal descent to determine who is a Jew), the ruling can become a "standard of rabbinic practice." Violation by a rabbi could lead to expulsion from the Rabbinical Assembly, if 75% of its rabbis so concurred. It is noteworthy that the Committee on Law never considered abrogating the dietary laws (except for allowing swordfish to be eaten). (A clear summary of the laws of *kashrut* and the reasons for observing them may be found in the Chapter,"What Jews Eat," in *Living a Jewish Life*, by Anita Diamant with Howard Cooper.) Also, the Committee did not significantly amend Shabbat observance: While one could drive to synagogue, one could not go shopping, play golf, mow the lawn, or pay bills. The consensus of the Rabbinical Assembly held that Conservative Judaism reveres tradition and acknowledges the authority of the *halakhah* without ascribing to it divine sanction in the literal sense. (See below, the Statement of Principles, *Emet Ve-Emunah*.) The most authoritative guide to Conservative Jewish Religious Practice has been written by Rabbi Isaac Klein. (See Resources.)

Ginzberg's most articulate opponent on the JTS faculty was Mordecai Kaplan. According to Herbert Parzen's *Architects of Con-*

servative Judaism, Ginzberg insisted that whatever modern thoughts do not fit in with the tradition should be abandoned. Kaplan held the opposite view: Those traditions that could not be harmonized with modern views could be discarded. While Kaplan created a radically new prayer book, the Conservative movement published its own *Shabbat and Festival Prayer Book*, which made few changes in the traditional liturgy. (It did eliminate the prayer in which men praised God "for not making me a woman.") The most recent Conservative prayer book is *Siddur Sim Shalom*. Gillman states that because of the Ginsberg-Kaplan controversies, there were before World War II, "two Conservative Judaisms."

The following chapter will be devoted primarily to Mordecai Kaplan and the Reconstructionist Movement. To balance the "transnaturalism" of Kaplan, the students were influenced by Abraham Joshua Heschel, "a Hasid in a faculty that looked askance at his style of being Jewish."(See Chapter 4.)

After World War II, the Conservative movement grew significantly. According to sociologist Marshall Sklare, Conservative Judaism appealed to those Jews who had moved to their "second settlement" (i.e., the second neighborhood in which they lived after arriving in America.) Sklare also pointed out the wide gap between the positions of the rabbis at JTS and the traditional practices—or lack thereof—among the laity. Only 15% of Conservative Jews observe the dietary laws. Sklare commented that Conservative Judaism consisted of "an Orthodox faculty teaching Conservative rabbis to minister to Reform Jews." Still the Conservative movement experienced enormous growth. By 1990, 43% of all affiliated Jews belonged to the Conservative movement. Like the Reform movement, it has programs for all ages, such as excellent summer camps (*Ramah),* an active youth program (USY), a Men's Club and a Women's League.

In 1972, Dr. Finkelstein retired and Gerson Cohen became

president and chancellor of JTS. While Finkelstein focused on the perpetuation of Jewish scholarship in America, Cohen turned his attention to the issues facing the Conservative movement. In 1979, he established the Masorti (traditional) movement in Israel, which included 40 congregations affiliated with Conservative Judaism. Like the Reform movement, Conservative Judaism has a campus in Jerusalem (*Neve Schechter*), and has established a *kibbutz (Hanaton)*.

In 1973, the United Synagogue of America urged the ordination of women, and 10 years later 75% of the Rabbinical Assembly agreed. They were influenced by Rabbi Joel Roth's argument that while women were not bound by *halakhah* to obey those positive commandments that had to be done at a specific time, they could take on themselves the obligation to do so, and thus become rabbis. By the year 2000, 120 women had been ordained by JTS. In reaction to this leap forward, some of the more traditional rabbis formed the Union for Traditional Conservative Judaism. By 1990, this Union was for all practical purposes no longer part of the Conservative movement.

Since the 1950's modern Orthodoxy, led by Norman Lamm, president of Yeshiva University, had become more of a presence on the American scene. Also, the Reform movement—after having adopted the Columbus Platform that affirmed Zionism and stated that Judaism *required* the preservation of the Sabbath and Festivals, the use of Hebrew in the service, and authentic Jewish music—was returning to more traditional practices. These developments led the Conservative movement to give more serious thought as to just what were its fundamental principles.

There could be a tension between Frankel's reliance on the will of the people *(k'lal yisrael)* to determine which traditions should be retained and the Rabbinical Assembly's insistence on allowing only those changes that were acceptable to the Committee on Jewish Law and Standards. This tension was resolved by Rabbi Robert

Gordis who reasoned that to modify Jewish law to conform to the way of life of nonobservant Jews would be "tantamount to amending the Constitution of the United States so as to harmonize it with the viewpoint of an anarchist. Only Jews who accept the concept of Jewish law and seek to observe it can help determine its direction. When the Talmud told the rabbis, 'Go, see how the people conduct themselves,' the people as a whole did believe in and follow the law. The rabbis would never have consulted Sabbath violators to determine how the Sabbath should be observed." A generation later, Robert Gordis's son, Daniel, wrote, in *God Was Not in the Fire*, that observing the law as a result of one's free choice is on a lower level than observing the law out of obedience. By acting purely out of obedience, one comes closer to God.

It was understandable that Gerson Cohen, chancellor of JTS, and Alex Shapiro, president of the Rabbinical Assembly, would appoint Rabbi Robert Gordis to chair a joint committee that would develop a statement of principles for the Conservative movement. Cohen resigned in 1986 and was succeeded by Ismar Schorsch, noted for his scholarship in Jewish history. Just one year into his administration, in 1987, the Conservative movement adopted its very first comprehensive Statement of Principles, *Emet Ve-Emuna* ("True and Faithful"). Theologian Gillman has written that its statement about God articulates two different positions on God's nature: a traditionalist image . . . as "a supreme, supernatural being" who "has the power to command and control the world through His will," and a more Kaplanian image of God as "not a being to whom we can point" but rather "a presence and a power that transcends us," a God who is "present when we look for meaning in the world, when we work for morality, for justice and for future redemption."

The primary difference with Reform Judaism is found in the section of *Emet Ve-Emunah* titled, "*Halakhah.*" According to this Statement of Principles, "For many Conservative Jews, *Halakhah* is indispensable because it is what the Jewish community understands God's will to be. This divine election of Jewish law is understood in varying ways within the Conservative community, but, however it is understood, it is for many the primary rationale for obeying *Halakhah* . . . It is a means of identifying and preserving the Jewish people and its traditions . . . Each individual cannot be empowered to make changes in the law, for that would undermine its authority and coherence; only the rabbinic leaders . . . because of their knowledge of *Halakhah*, are authorized by Jewish tradition to make the necessary changes, although they must keep the custom and needs of the community in mind as they deliberate . . .

"Authority for religious practice in each congregation resides in its rabbi . . . In making decisions rabbis may consult the Committee on Law and Standards consisting of representatives of the Rabbinical Assembly, the JTS of America and the United Synagogue of America. The Committee on Jewish Law and Standards issues rulings shaping the practice of the Conservative community. Parameters set by that Committee and at Rabbinical Assembly conventions *govern* (author's italics) all of the rabbis of the Rabbinical Assembly, but within those bounds there are variations of practice recognized as both legitimate and, in many cases, contributory to the richness of Jewish life."

Gillman explains that the statement on *Halakhah* legitimizes two approaches to dealing with laws that are not susceptible to the normative processes of legal change: "Some within the Conservative community are prepared to amend the existing law by means of a formal procedure of legislation." Others "are willing to make a change only when they find it justified by sources in the halakhic literature." One of the recent decisions occurred in 1992, when the Rabbinical Assembly prohibited Conservative rabbis from performing commitment ceremonies between gay or lesbian couples. (The Reform movement left this decision to the conscience of the individual rabbi.) Avowed homosexuals are not admitted to the Conservative rabbinate or allowed to become cantors. (This, too, differs from the view of Reform Judaism, as indicated in the previous chapter.) However, individual congregations could decide for themselves how homosexuals could function in either the professional or lay leadership of the synagogue.

Another difference between the Conservative and the Reform movements is that the Rabbinical Assembly prohibits any of its members from officiating at a mixed marriage (between a Jew and a non-Jew). In the 1973 CCAR convention in Atlanta, this resolution was adopted: "The CCAR, recalling its stand adopted in 1909, 'that mixed marriage is contrary to the Jewish tradition and should be discouraged,' now declares its opposition to participation by its members in any ceremony which solemnizes a mixed marriage. Recognizing that historically the CCAR encompasses members holding divergent interpretations of Jewish tradition, the Conference calls upon those members who dissent from this declaration: to refrain from officiating at a mixed marriage unless the couple agrees to undertake, prior to marriage, a course of study of Judaism equivalent to that required for conversion . . . to refrain from co-officiating or sharing with non-Jewish clergy in the solemnization of a mixed marriage . . ." (After surveying the surveys, I would estimate that about 40% of American Reform rabbis will, under certain conditions, officiate at a wedding of a Jew and non-Jew.) Also the Conservative movement requires a convert to appear before a *bet din* (a court of usually three rabbis), go to a *mikveh,* and, if a male, be circumcised or, if already circumcised, have a *tipat dam(*a drop of blood) taken from the penis. Reform rabbis vary in the requirements that they make of one who converts. Of course, a period of study is required as is a conversion ceremony. Today Reform rabbis are more likely than in the past to encourage or require *mikveh, bet din,* and even *tipat dam.*

How one views the relation between the Reform and Conservative movements depends on whether one emphasizes similarities or differences. It is my impression that most of the Reform rabbinic consensus summarized at the end of the previous chapter would be shared by most Conservative rabbis. The primary difference would be the attitude toward *Halakhah.* I would suggest that Gillman's definition of an "Ideal Conservative Jew" would be quite acceptable to many Reform rabbis: a "willing Jew," because Jewish commitment involves a decision to "refract all aspects of life through the prism of one's Jewishness"; a "learning" Jew, because one cannot be whole as a Jew without commitment to serious and ongoing study of the tradition; and a "striving" Jew because "what is needed is an openness to those observances one has yet to perform and the desire to grapple with those issues and texts one has yet to confront."

TOPICS FOR DISCUSSION

1. What do you consider to be the most fundamental difference between Reform and Conservative Judaism?

2. Which do you favor? 1) considering the Law as a guide and, after much study, allowing Jews to choose which traditions to follow, so long as they preserve Shabbat and the festivals, use Hebrew in their services, and return to authentic Jewish music; 2) considering the Law, as interpreted by the Committee on Jewish Law and Standards, to be authoritative as it sets parameters (e.g., observing *kashrut,* getting a *get* when one is divorced), but within those parameters, consulting one's rabbi to learn which traditions are required.

3. Do you see any basis or way that the Reform and Conservative movements could merge? If so, how? If not, what areas of

cooperation between the two movements could be further developed?

4. What do you consider the strengths and weaknesses of the Conservative movement?

RESOURCES

Davis, Moshe. *The Emergence of Conservative Judaism.* Philadelphia, Jewish Publication Society, 1963.

Diamant, Anita with Howard Cooper. *Living a Jewish Life.* (Chapter on "What Jews Eat"). New York, Harvard Perennial, 1976.

Gillman, Neil. *Conservative Judaism: The New Century.* New York, Behrman House, 1993.

Klein, Isaac. *A Guide to Jewish Religious Practice.* New York, JTS, 1979.

Parzen, Herbert. *Architects of Conservative Judaism.* New York, Jonathan David, 1964.

Sklare, Marshall. *Conservative Judaism: An American Religious Movement.* Glencoe, Illinois, Free Press, 1955.

18.

RECONSTRUCTIONISM,

RENEWAL, AND FEMINISM

It has been said that on the spectrum of Jewish "denominations," the Reconstructionist Movement lies somewhere between the Reform and Conservative ideologies. There is a grain, but just a grain, of truth in this too-convenient labeling. The Reconstructionists are similar to Reform Jews in that they do not accept the *Halakhah* as binding. They are similar to Conservative Jews in that their services often have a traditional sound and mood that is closer to Conservative services than to Reform and their theology has some adherents among both Conservative and Reform rabbis.

Let us begin at the beginning. The founder and guiding spirit of the Reconstructionist philosophy was Mordecai Kaplan. Born 1881, in Vilna, he was raised in an Orthodox home during the Enlightenment (*Haskalah*). As a young man he was influenced by Yehuda Leib Gordon who counseled, "Be a man in the streets and a Jew at home," perhaps suggesting to Kaplan to live in two civilizations simultaneously.

After his father had come with Mordecai to America to serve as a rabbi in the New York Orthodox *kehillah(*organized Jewish community*)*, Kaplan was enrolled in the Orthodox Yitzhak Elhanan Theological Seminary. At the same time he attended classes at CCNY (again, two civilizations). Among his non-Jewish influences were Herbert Spencer (in order to survive, one's violent instincts must be held in check by reason); Frank Giddings (his "social mind" became for Kaplan the collective consciousness of the community); and Matthew Arnold (God is a Power not ourselves that makes for righteousness). The Jewish thinker who most influenced him was Ahad Ha-Am, who held that an ethical Jewish nationalism was needed to preserve Judaism. However, Kaplan did not agree with Ahad Ha-Am's dismissal of the synagogue and indifference to theology.

Scholars differ as to how influential were the ideas of sociologist Emile Durkheim. Like Kaplan, Durkheim saw religion as essential for group cohesion and survival. They both emphasized the "collective consciousness" of the community as the foundation of moral imperatives. Mel Scult in his biography of Kaplan (*Judaism Faces the Twentieth Century*) offers evidence to indicate that Kaplan had arrived at these ideas before he became acquainted with Durkheim. However, once Kaplan read Durkheim, he may have been influenced, to some degree, by the French scholar.

Kaplan was a major force on the faculty of the Jewish Theological Seminary for 57 years. As noted in the previous chapter, even though his ideas were considered radical by his colleagues on the faculty, the president, Cyrus Adler, insisted on Kaplan's right to express his views. In 1922, Kaplan was invited by his friend, Reform Rabbi Stephen Wise, to be on the faculty of the newly established Jewish Institute of Religion. While feeling ambivalent about the offer, he turned it down, perhaps because he might then be branded even more radical and heterodox, or because he felt a loyalty to the JTS where he was allowed to speak his mind and engage in stimulating debate with Ginzberg and other colleagues.

It was at JTS that Kaplan developed the foundation of what came to be his Reconstructionist philosophy: that Judaism should be interpreted less as a religion and more as a broad civilization encompassing "language, folkways, patterns of social organization, social habits and standards, (and) spiritual ideals, (all of) which give individuality to a people and distinguish it from other peoples." In 1922, he founded the Society for the Advancement of Judaism, "a religious fellowship of Jewish men and women who want Judaism to act as an ethical influence in their lives. Most people associate Judaism with dogmas which are either self-evident or unacceptable, and with ceremonies which are honored more in the breach than in the observance . . . They ought to know that Judaism once embraced the whole of life; that it consisted of a language, a literature, a code of laws, an ethical system, a community life and a public opinion—that it was, in fact, a whole civilization." Chapters of the SAJ were established in several cities, from Scranton to Brooklyn.

Kaplan set forth this philosophy in 1934, in his most influential book, *Judaism as a Civilization.* He explained that the crisis of the modern Jew has been caused by the breakdown of ethnic or national identity due to the rise and success of democracy, and the breakdown of faith due to the rise of science. For Kaplan, the challenge was to find a way for the Jewish people to continue to function as a social organism. His solution was to recognize that Judaism is a religious civilization, which includes a sense of common past and future, a common language (Hebrew), and a collective consciousness that points the way the community should go to make life worthwhile.

Every civilization has its own religion, which is in Kaplan's words, "the conscious quest for salvation or life worthwhile; those institutions, places, historic events, heroes and all other objects of popular reverence to which superlative importance or sanctity is ascribed." This implies that the United States has its own religion, with such sacred documents as the Declaration of Independence and the Constitution, such sacred places and objects as Independence Hall in Philadelphia and the Liberty Bell, and such holidays as the Fourth of July and Thanksgiving. Among the early publications of the Reconstructionist movement was a book entitled *The Faith of America*, which provided readings for each of the holidays of the American religion. The American Jew, therefore, had the privilege of participating in both the American and Jewish civilizations. Kaplan also gave a more psychological definition of religion: "that part of the collective consciousness that deals with fundamental and ultimate concerns about human nature, self-fulfillment and our obligations to others."

Kaplan's concept of God was summarized in Chapter 4. God is whatever Power makes for salvation. Kaplan defined salvation as the "progressive perfection of the human personality and the establishment of a free, just and cooperative social order." As stated earlier, this Power can be found in our own inner tendencies toward, growth, moral responsibility, love and integrity. Because these tendencies are linked to processes *throughout* nature that support our quest for the life abundant, Kaplan is often called a "transnaturalist." Kaplan doubted the possibility of discovering eternal truths. Because religion is the highest expression of group life, beliefs are "true" if they function beneficially for the group. Still, Kaplan believed there are some absolute ethical standards built into the structure of the universe.

For Kaplan, the solution to the crisis confronting the modern Jew is to develop fully the Jewish civilization even as one lives in the civilization of the surrounding culture. He wrote, "To be a Jew means to participate in some form of Jewish community life where the standards of right and wrong are to be clearly formulated and

accepted." Kaplan advocated developing an "organic Jewish community," in which all elements of civilization play a role in the life
of the individual Jew; a group that worships together but does
nothing else together will not endure. So Kaplan was among the
creators of the Jewish center. For him, the "synagogue-center" was
ideal, because religion is the core of the Jewish civilization. He
later advocated the creation of a *kehillah,* a Jewish community,
that would pass laws, establish the qualifications of its rabbis and
cantors, have a voice in the selection of rituals to be observed, and
establish ethical rules for its members.

Kaplan accepted the findings of modern Biblical scholarship.
For him, the Torah represents the search of the Jewish people for
meaning and value. To the degree that it expresses spiritual and
moral forces in Jewish life, the Torah is divine. To state that God
created the world is to affirm that the world will function for our
benefit if we follow the laws of love and justice. *Halakhah,* in the
sense of Jewish law as developed by the rabbis, is not binding.
However, traditions and folkways serve the function of enabling
the Jewish people to survive and the individual Jew to find personal fulfillment.

As stated in Chapter 3, Kaplan considered the belief that Jews
are the "chosen people" as chauvinistic, and he rejected it. However, he did hold that it is the "vocation" of the Jewish people, as it
should be the vocation of all peoples, to bring nearer God's kingdom of justice and peace on earth. Kaplan did not believe that the
Jewish people needed a rationale for surviving. He asserted that no
justification is needed for a civilization to persist. It will survive, if
it is a viable culture, if its idea of God does not conflict with reason
and if it gives primacy to humane values.

In 1935, the *Reconstructionist,* a journal expressing the views of
Kaplan and his followers, was published by Kaplan with the aid of
his son-in-law, Rabbi Ira Eisenstein. In 1941, *The New Haggadah*

was published by Kaplan, Eisenstein, and Eugene Kohn. Kaplan's most controversial publication was, in 1945, the Reconstructionist *Sabbath Prayer Book*. Its purpose was to reflect what Jews actually believed. It was severely criticized by some of Kaplan's colleagues at JTS, notably Louis Ginzberg. The Union of Orthodox Rabbis of the U.S. and Canada issued a ban (*herem*) against Kaplan and had the Prayer Book burned. In 1949, Kaplan published *The Future of the American Jew*, in which he elaborated on the idea of the chosen people, the nature of religion, Jewish law and the status of women. There may be no better image that captures Kaplan's life and thought than that reported by Ira Eisenstein when he, his wife, Judith, and the Kaplans were spending a summer at the Jersey shore. Eisenstein came upon Kaplan one morning, with *tallit* and *tefillin*, but instead of praying, he was reading from Ahad Ha-Am and John Dewey!

For Ahad Ha-Am, Zion is the center of the Jewish world, and the Diaspora is the periphery. For Kaplan, "Palestine was the only place where an original Jewish civilization could flourish." However, a Jewish state must "look to the dispersed communities of the Jewish people for the re-emergence of genuine ethnic-religious societies where Jews would live in two civilizations."

While Kaplan had wanted the Reconstructionist philosophy to bring together and influence Jews of every movement (particularly, Reform and Conservative), this dream of unification could not be achieved, primarily because his theology and liturgical works were clearly out of the mainstream of non-Orthodox rabbinic thought. However, sociologist Charles Liebman has contended that the Reconstructionist philosophy is, in fact, the "folk-religion" of American Jews. That is, although most affiliated American Jews join Reform and Conservative synagogues where personal theism is expressed in their worship, these same Jews in their beliefs and practices are, in fact, closer to the beliefs and practices of the Reconstructionist movement!

Ira Eisenstein realized that if the Reconstructionist movement was to survive, it required a rabbinical seminary and Reconstructionist congregations. Kaplan grudgingly agreed with this view, and in 1968, the Reconstructionist Rabbinical College was opened on Broad Street, near Temple University, in Philadelphia. The College has flourished under its presidents. Ira Eisenstein, who founded the College, was succeeded by Ira Silverman, who oversaw the move from Philadelphia to the suburb of Wyncote. He was succceeded by Arthur Green, whose book, *Seek My Face, Speak My Name*, influenced students and non-Orthodox rabbis to take more seriously the perspective of Jewish mysticism. (See Chapter 4.) David Teutsch, as president, led the College into the new millenium, as he raised its profile in the community, holding institutes on spiritual and ethical issues. The College accepted openly gay and lesbian students even before the Reform seminaries adopted that policy. As of the year, 2000 most of its 232 graduates (97 of them women) are serving Reform, Conservative or Reconstructionist congregations, or *havurot* (fellowships). Others hold academic positions in Jewish studies programs or are serving as Hillel rabbis, hospital chaplains, or leaders in other Jewish communal organizations.

JEWISH RENEWAL

In 1993, the P'nai Or Fellowship and the Shalom Center merged into ALEPH: The Alliance for Jewish Renewal. My experience with Renewal, this relatively new movement in Jewish life had been, marginal. In the 1970's, I had heard that a unique spiritual experience could be had at the home of Rabbi Zalman Schachter-Shalomi in the Mt. Airy neighborhood of Philadelphia. So I went. I was in my early forties, twice as old as most people there. We sat in a circle on pillows on the floor. I remember wine and a sturdy wooden ark like one I imagined could have been found in the wooden synagogues of Poland. Reb Zalman made his entrance, coming downstairs, dressed in a caftan(a long tan robe.) He began singing a *niggun,* a melody without words associated with a particular Hasid. We all joined the singing. Then he told stories, perhaps originally told by the Hasid to his followers two centuries ago; something of the Hasid's spirit was with us. Reb Zalman then spoke. As I recall, he encouraged us to find the oneness in our hearts, the oneness in the room, the Oneness in the universe. We meditated. Then he asked us to make up our own *niggun* on the theme of majesty. We did, each in his or her own voice. When I left, I felt uplifted, but the feeling did not last. Still, I remember.

I did not return. I did send to Reb Zalman young Jews who had lost their way going from one ashram to another. Some of them found through Reb Zalman a new way of being Jewish. Had I become part of the embryonic movement for Jewish Renewal, I would have joined a *havurah,* a fellowship of Jews searching together for new ways of bringing God and Torah into their lives. Its members pray and sing, meditate and dance and study Torah and Kabbalah, each becoming a rebbe and finding his or her own meaning in the text.

I was fortunate in that the spirit of my synagogue had been created by the remarkable Rabbi Sam Markowitz, whose eleventh commandment was: "Thou shalt participate—or else find another congregation." We formed our own *havurot,* one for study, another for supporting a young man, Roberto, who had fled persecution in Guatamala.

In 1994, Michael Lerner's book, *Jewish Renewal,* was published. According to Lerner, the essence of Judaism is the possibility of healing and transforming ourselves and the world (as in *tikkun olam*). (Lerner is the editor of the journal, *Tikkun,* the progressives' answer to *Commentary.*) For Lerner, God is the force that makes possible this transformation. The "Renewalist" strives for transcendence, to bring into the world aspects of ourselves and reality to which we have been deaf, and to re-establish contact with a deeper level of being.

A major difference from the so-called "New Age" religious groups is that Jewish Renewal requires political struggle. The basis for political activism is the recognition of the interconnectedness of all people and things. We experience this connection by becoming aware of the spiritual energy that permeates the universe. Millions of people have responded to this energy, which is God's presence in the world. We recognize each other's authenticity when we realize that we both have in common God's Being, manifest through this spiritual energy. It is expressed through our unconscious drive toward spiritual and moral health, which can overcome patterns of the past.

There is no single interpretation of Jewish Renewal. Arthur Waskow, the most prolific leader of Renewal, whose books range from *God-Wrestling—Round Two* to *Judaism and Ecology*, taught me that Renewal is both a continuation of and a challenge to the Reconstructionist movement. Like Kaplan, Zalman Schachter-Shalomi believed that Judaism is historically self-changing. However, unlike Kaplan, Reb Zalman sees God changing not because of new human conceptions of the Divine but because God calls forth the change. It was Reb Zalman who coined the term, "eco-kosher." Based on such rabbinic concepts as *bal tashcheet* (do not destroy needlessly), keeping eco-kosher could mean not eating vegetables that were grown by drenching the earth with pesticides, or not eating meat from animals raised in superproductive factory farms, or protecting one's body from carcinogens.

Arthur Waskow, founder and still director of the Shalom Center, a division of ALEPH, has offered a "definition-in-process" of Jewish Renewal. At its heart is "a renewed encounter with God and an understanding of Jewish history as a series of renewed encounters with God. These encounters have followed crises during which God has been eclipsed; yet, each crisis has resulted in the emergence of a more or less deeply transformed version of Judaism. Through prayer, study, and action, Jewish Renewal seeks to nurture the rebbe-spark in everyone without fearing its emergence in different ways . . . in different people; to nurture communities that dance and wrestle with God, that are intimate, participatory, and egalitarian, and that create a 'field of rebbetude'; and to assist the spiritual growth and healing of individuals, communities, whole societies, and the planet."

Waskow continued: "Jewish Renewal is rooted in a midrashic response to Torah, drawing on ancient wisdom without getting stuck in it, particularly on the wisdom of Kabbalah and Hasidism as well as the Prophets and Rabbis . . . Women and men are fully equal and participatory in shaping the future of Judaism, as are gay men and lesbians . . . There is respect for and often learning from other spiritual paths (e.g., Buddhism, Sufi) . . . Jewish renewal . . . applies Judaism in many down-to-earth-dimensions (food, money, sex, health, politics, etc.) as well as to prayer, festivals and Torah-study." Jewish Renewal is deeply connected to feminist Judaism (to be discussed in the next section).

In his eloquent booklet, *Restoring the Aleph: Judaism for the Contemporary Seeker,* Arthur Green writes that participants in Jewish Renewal "have sought to create a 'maximalist' version of liberal Judaism, as intense as Orthodoxy in its demands but more universalistic in perspective, emphasizing a renewed prophetic commitment and Judaism's demand for justice and care for the downtrodden as key portions of that maximalist agenda. Whether such a 'muscular' and demanding liberal Judaism can take hold is a key question in thinking about our collective future."

JEWISH FEMINISM

For me and many other rabbis of my generation, Jewish feminism meant welcoming women rabbis as equal colleagues, and
changing the English wording in the prayer book as we led services: from "brotherhood" to "humanity," from "King" to "Sovereign," and from "Lord" to "God." I admit to being a latecomer to
the richness of Jewish feminist theology and practice.

The first major work of Jewish feminism was Judith Plaskow's
Standing Again at Sinai, published in 1990. Its very first sentence
is powerful: "The need for a feminist Judaism begins with hearing
silence." The silence is, of course, the absence of women's voices in
the formation and development of Judaism, and the recognition
that Jewish theology and law were written by men and, naturally,
from a male perspective.

We might begin with Plaskow's beautifully written midrash
on a midrash about Adam, Eve, and Lilith. Briefly, according to
the original midrash, Lilith was Adam's first wife, but she demanded
equality and so was banished to the river where she became a demon, forever after trying to do evil to women giving birth. Eve,
made from Adam's rib, became his willing subservient helpmate.
In Plaskow's version, Lilith becomes not a demon but the first
liberated woman. Trying to return to the Garden of Eden, she was
turned back by Adam but caught a glimpse of Eve. Eve was no
longer willing to be subservient, so she climbed over the garden's
wall, met Lilith, and they became great friends. To Adam's puzzle-
ment, they would meet from time to time and learn from each
other. (Read the original by Plaskow in Umansky and Ashton's
Sourcebook, *Four Centuries of Jewish Women's Spirituality.*)

It is easy to find examples of discrimination against women in
the Bible. While the matriarchs, Sarah, Rebecca, Rachel and Leah,
were strong personalities, they were not considered part of the

covenant (circumcised) community. If a man marries a woman, and she is not a virgin, and he complains to her parents, she would be stoned to death! (Deuteronomy 22:13-21). Apologists might say that such killings never happened, but that the law was put in the Bible to emphasize the value of virginity. Discrimination against women in rabbinic divorce law and the prayer praising God "for not making me a woman" have already been noted. There are more than enough reasons for Jewish feminists to be angry at Jewish tradition.

What is remarkable are the positive directions into which that anger has been channeled. One direction is the development of feminist theology, which is based on the personal experience of women rather than on an intellectual attempt to discover eternal truths. For Plaskow, God is not a supernatural Other Being but is the "energy of the physical universe," the ground of being rather than Being, itself. Changing the social order is participating in God. For the social ethicist, Rachel Adler, God is personal, not a process, and authority is found by reflecting on the ongoing human-Divine relationship. She would accept a dynamic *halakhah* that is open to reinterpretation. Ellen Umansky also believes in God as a personal Being capable of commanding and revealing religious teaching, but as a Reform Jew, will not sacrifice autonomy to even a progressive *halakhah*. Some aspects of these theologies may remind one of the writings of Borowitz, Green, and Lerner. (Recall Chapter 4.) However, the uniqueness of Jewish feminist theology is the emphasis on God as immanent as opposed to transcendent and the new language created to express the Divine. Poet Marcia Falk refers to God as the "Source of life," the "Flower of life," the "Breath of all living things."

There is a close connection between Jewish Renewal and Jewish Feminism. Each influences the other. This becomes especially evident in a D'var Torah (word of Torah) that Arthur Waskow wrote for *The Jerusalem Report*. After linguistic analysis he concludes that the Hebrew, "Shaddai," has not been accurately rendered as "the Almighty." "If we look back at the blessing Jacob gives to Joseph, it is inescapable that the poet who wrote those lines meant: Shaddai is the Breasted One. (Genesis 48:3) Why else would the quatrain of this blessing so connect Shaddai with shadai-im (breasts)?"If this interpretation is correct, then "God is seen as Infinite Mother, pouring forth blessings from the Breasts Above and the Womb Below, from the heavens that pour forth nourishing rain, from the ocean deeps that birth new life."

The challenge of Jewish feminism is how to affect change in a religious tradition that has been so thoroughly permeated by a male perspective. The most creative efforts have been made by Marcia Falk in *The Book of Blessings*. Perhaps the most challenging change made by Falk is the elimination of "Blessed are You, O Lord, our God, King of the universe" by simply, "N'vareykh et eyn hahayim," "Let us bless the source of life." The blessing continues, "hamotzi'ah lechem min ha-aretz," "that brings forth bread from the earth." The blessing before reading the Torah totally elimi- nates reference to God as King who has chosen us (the Jews) from all peoples in order to give us the Torah. Falk prefers: "Let us bless the source of life . . . as we bless the source of life so may we be blessed. May our hearts be lifted, our spirits refreshed, our under- standing deepened by the study of Torah." Her blessing has more meaning for me than does the traditional Torah blessing. How- ever, when parents and grandparents are called up to the Torah for *aliyot*, how many will be willing or able to discard the Torah bless- ing they have known since childhood? Perhaps we should begin with the *motzi*.

TOPICS FOR DISCUSSION

1. What are the similarities and differences between Reform Judaism and the Reconstructionist movement?

2. What are the similarities and differences between Conservative Judaism and the Reconstructionist movement?

3. What aspects of Reconstructionist thought and practice appeal to you?

4. Do you believe one can have a spiritual experience without believing in God? How would you define a spiritual experience?

5. What is your opinion of Liebman's thesis that Reconstructionism is the "folk-religion" of the Jewish people?

6. What aspects of the Jewish civilization are a part of your life?

7. Would you like to become part of a *havurah,* whose members pray, sing, meditate, dance, and study together? Why or why not?

8. Are you willing to nurture the "rebbe-spark" within you?

9. If you are a woman, have you felt excluded from full participation in the past and present of Judaism?

10. How do you feel about the masculine words (e.g., Lord, King, brotherhood) sprinkled through Jewish liturgy? What changes would you like to see made?

RESOURCES

Adler, Rachel. *Engendering Judaism.* Boston, Beacon Press, 1998.

Buxbaum, Yitzhak. *Jewish Spiritual Practice.* Northvale, N.J., Jason Aronson, 1990.

Falk, Marcia. *The Book of Blessings.* San Francisco, Harper, 1996.

Goldsmith, Emanuel, Mel Scult, and Robert M. Seltzer. *The American Judaism of Mordecai M. Kaplan.* New York, New York University Press, 1990.

Green, Arthur. *Seek My Face, Speak My Name: A Contemporary Jewish Theology.* Northvale, N.J., Jason Aronson, 1990.

Heschel, Susannah (ed.). *On Being a Jewish Feminist.* New York, Schocken, 1983.

Kaplan, Mordecai M. *Basic Values in Jewish Religion.* Ann Arbor, Reconstructionist Press, 1963.

Kaplan, Mordecai M. *Judaism as a Civilization.* New York, Reconstructionist Press, 1957.

Kaplan, Mordecai M. *Judaism without Supernaturalism.* New York, Reconstructionist Press, 1967.

Kaplan, Mordecai M. *The Meaning of God in Modern Jewish Religion.* New York, Reconstructionist Foundation, 1947.

Kushner, Larry. *The River of Light: Spirituality, Judaism, Consciousness.* Woodstock, VT., Jewish Lights Publishing, 1993.

Liebman, Charles. "The Religion of American Jews," in *The Jew in American Society*, edited by Marshall Sklare, New York, Behrman House, 1974.

Lerner, Michael. *Jewish Renewal*. New York, Groesset/Putnam, 1994.

Plaskow, Judith. *Standing Again at Sinai: Judaism from a Feminist Perspective*. San Francisco, Harper & Row, 1990.

Schachter-Shalomi, Zalman. *Paradigm Shift*. Northvale, N.J., Jason Aronson, 1993.

Scult, Mel. *Judaism Faces the 20th Century: A Biography of Mordecai M. Kaplan*. Detroit, Wayne University Press, 1994.

Umansky, Ellen and Dianne Ashton(ed.). *Four Centuries of Jewish Women's Spirituality: A Sourcebook*. Boston, Beacon Press, 1992.

Umansky, Ellen. "Jewish Feminist Theology," in Eugene Borowitz, *Choices in Modern Jewish Thought*. West Orange, N.J., Behrman House, 1995.

Waskow, Arthur. *Down to Earth Judaism: Food, Money, Sex and the Rest of Life*. William Morrow & Co., New York, 1995.

Waskow, Arthur (ed.). *Torah of the Earth*, 2 Vol., Woodstock, Vermont, Jewish Lights, 2000.

Waskow, Arthur. "The God Who Nurtures at the Breast," in *The Jerusalem Report*, Jan. 15, 2001.

ZIONISM, THE HOLOCAUST, AND ISRAEL

1862: Moses Hess: *Rome and Jerusalem.*

1882: Leon Pinsker: *Auto-emancipation.*

1889: Ahad Ha-Am: "This Is Not the Way."

1896: Theodor Herzl: *The Jewish State.*

1897: First Zionist Congress.

1905: Ber Borochov: "The National Question and the Class Struggle."

1907: Second *Aliyah.*

1915: Jabotinsky advocates a Jewish legion.

1917: Weizmann encourages British to issue Balfour Declaration.

1919: Third *Aliyah* begins (through 1924).

1921: First partition: Transjordan separated from Palestine.

1923: Jabotinsky advocates maximalist Zionism(Revisionism). Publication of *Mein Kampf.*

1929: Massacre of Jews in Hebron.

1930: National Socialists in Germany receive 23% of the vote.

1931: Etzel (Irgun Tz'vi L'Umi) breaks from Haganah.

1932: National Socialists receive a plurality (33%). Hitler made Chancellor.

1933: Reichstag fire. National Socialists receive 44% of vote. Reichstag passes Enabling Act giving Hitler total power.

1935: Nuremberg Laws to protect "purity" of German blood. German-Jewish leaders urge Jews to flee. By 1938, 350,000 of 500,000 remain.

1936: Arabs attack Jewish settlements.

1937: Britain's Peel Commission proposes partition.

1938: Evian Conference does nothing for refugees. Nov. 9-10: Krystallnacht.

1939: Jan. 30: Hitler warns that war will mean destruction of "Jewish race."
May 17: British drastically restrict Jewish immigration to Palestine.
June: 954 Jews on liner St. Louis not admitted to Cuba or U.S.
Sept. 1: Hitler invades Poland. World War II begins.
Sept. 27: Germany and Russia divide Poland. Jews moved to cities.

1940: Polish Jews forced into ghettos: first Lodz, then Warsaw.

1941: June: Hitler's troops invade Russia.
September: *Einsatzgruppen* begin massacre of Jews in Russia.
December: *Struma* sinks, drowning 768 Jews.

1942: Jan. 20: At Wannsee, plan for genocide given to chain of command.
August: Riegner gives U.S. consul in Switzerland German plan for

killing of all Jews. Corroborated by Red Cross. Rabbi Stephen
Wise holds news conference reporting on massacres.

December: Rabbi Wise gives Roosevelt "Blueprint for Extermination."

Revolt in Warsaw Ghetto begins.

1943: Feb.: Allies refuse Romania's offer to free 70,000 Jews.
April: Bermuda: Britain and U.S. reaffirm closed-door policy.
May 12: Zygelboym commits suicide to protest world's apathy.
May 16: Resistance in Warsaw Ghetto crushed.
June: Romania again offers to release 75,000 Jews. Authorization
of U.S. funds to rescue Jews buried in State Department.

1943: October: Jews of Denmark rescued by fellow Danes. De-
portation of Jews from Rome. Rebellion of Jews at Sobibor.

1944: Morgenthau discovers State Department's obstruction and
tells FDR.
Feb.: Roosevelt establishes War Refugee Board(200,000 Jews saved.)
July: War Dept. refuses to bomb railways or crematory at Auschwitz.

1945: May: Germany surrenders.

1946: British government under Atlee and Bevan still refuse to
allow Jewish survivors into Palestine. *Aliyah Bet* brings in some
illegally.
Etzel sets off bomb in King David Hotel.

1947: Refugees on *Exodus* sent back to Europe.
UNSCOP first international group to advocate partition.
Nov. 29: Partition Plan approved by U.N. Accepted by Jews. Re-
jected by Arabs who immediately attack Jews from Haifa to
Jerusalem.

1948: Atrocities by both sides: Deir Yassin and Kfar Etzion.

May 14: State of Israel established.
Arab armies attack. 538,000-700,000 Arabs leave.

1949: April 3: Rhodes Armistice signed. August: Israel accepted at the U.N.

1950: Law of Return enacted; migration of 700,000 Jews from Arab lands.

1953: An exhausted Ben Gurion resigns; Moshe Sharett becomes prime minister.

1955: Egypt trains *fedayeen* to infiltrate and attack Israelis. Ben Gurion returns as prime minister.

1956: Sinai Campaign coordinated with Britain and France. Withdrawal followed by U.N. presence in Sinai.

1963: Levi Eshkol becomes prime minister.

1964: PLO established.

1967: U.N., at Nasser's demand, leaves Sinai, and Nasser sends in troops. Egypt blockades straits of Tiran. June: Six Day War.
August: Khartoum Conference rejects Israel's peace offer.
Nov.: U.N. Resolution 242 calls for return of territories for peace.

1968: PLO Covenant calls for destruction of Israel through armed struggle.
Yasser Arafat becomes chairman of the PLO.

1969: Golda Meir prime minister. Illegal settlers allowed to stay in Hebron.

1970: Hussein's army kills many Palestinians and expels PLO from Jordan.

1972: Black September terrorists kill Israeli Olympic athletes in Munich.

1973: Yom Kippur War: Egypt and Syria attack. Gush Emunim formed.

1974: PLO terrorists kill civilians in Kiryat Shmona and children in Maalot.

1975: U.N. brands Zionism as racism.

1977: Menachem Begin becomes prime minister as Likud defeats Labor.
Settlements expand into heavily populated Arab areas.
Egypt's President Anwar Sadat comes to Jerusalem.

1978: Camp David Accords signed by Sadat and Begin. Peace Now formed.

1982: Israeli-Lebanese War; Sabra/ Shatila massacres; PLO moves to Tunis.

1983: Yithak Shamir prime minister of Unity government.

1984: Shimon Peres prime minister of Unity government.

1986: Shamir prime minister of Likud-led government.

1987: First Intifada begins in Gaza, spreads to West Bank.

1990: Iraq invades Kuwait; Persian Gulf War; scuds fall on Israel.

1991: Almost one million Jews migrate over nine years from former Soviet Union. Peace talks held in Madrid.

1992: Yitzhak Rabin prime minister.

1993: Secret negotiations in Oslo lead to Rabin-Arafat handshake.

1994: Arabs killed in Hebron mosque; Hamas retaliates.

1995: Assassination of Yitzhak Rabin; Peres becomes prime minister

1996: Suicide bombers in Jerusalem. Netanyahu elected prime minister.

1999: Barak becomes prime minister.

2000: Meeting with Arafat produces no agreement. Sept: Second Intifada.

2001: Barak resigns. In February, Israelis choose Sharon over Barak to be prime minister.

19.

THE HOLOCAUST: WHAT CAN WE LEARN?

What was unique about the horror of the Holocaust? There have been all too many horrors—all too many genocides. The massacre of the Armenians by the Turks. The killing fields of Cambodia. African slaves who died on their brutal journey to America. Nothing can be gained by comparing genocides: "Mine was worse than yours." However, it is helpful to understand what there was about the Holocaust that can explain the enormous impact it had and still has on Jews and Judaism. In starkest terms: Adolf Hitler planned to murder every single Jew on this planet. If the Nazis had been the first to develop the atomic bomb, I would not be alive to write this chapter.

Israeli historian Yehuda Bauer used the term, "Holocaust," to refer to the total elimination of a people. It is an extreme form of genocide, by which Bauer meant that it was total and global in scope and was driven by ideology. In contrast, the Turks' mass murder of Armenians was confined to ethnically Turkish areas. The Armenians in Jerusalem, which was part of the Ottoman Empire, were not targeted. The Turks' motive was pragmatic: political expansion, confiscation of riches, and the elimination of economic competition. The motive behind the Nazi's genocide was primarily ideological. Bauer acknowledged that the suffering of other victims of genocide was no less than that of the Jews.

The world had fair warning. In 1923, in *Mein Kampf,* Hitler wrote that Germany's mission was to dominate all non-Aryans and to crush the greatest threat to the Aryan race, the Jew. Jewish blood was a carrier of filth and disease, death and destruction. Because of their racial characteristics, Jews were the power of evil striving for domination of all nations and using Bolshevism as a front. Inconsistently, Hitler also considered the Jews rich capitalists who caused Germany's defeat and reaped great profits in World War I. Twenty years later, Nazi doctors rationalized that Jews had to be eliminated for the health of the social organism. The patient was the *volk,* the German people, so Jews could be killed in the name of healing.

Perhaps the most frightening aspect of the Holocaust, other than the barbarity of the mass killings, was the fact that *Hitler was given absolute power by the democratically elected representatives of the German people!* In 1932, the German voters gave Hitler's National Socialists a plurality, 33% of the popular vote. Paul von Hindenberg, President of the German Republic, appointed Hitler as Chancellor, perhaps hoping to curb his extremism. The Nazis set fire to the Reichstag (parliament) and blamed the Communists. In an atmosphere of fear, Hitler won his highest plurality, 44%. Then the Catholic Center party joined the National Socialists in passing the Enabling Act, which gave Hitler the power to ignore the Constitution and become the dictator of Germany. Thus, through a legal and democratic process, the German people chose fascism.

Before the Holocaust there was an invidious increase in discrimination and persecution. In 1935, the Nuremberg laws prohibited the marriage of Jews to other Germans. Only persons of "German blood" were considered citizens. Therefore, the Jews could not vote, nor could they rely on police protection. If one grandparent was a Jew, the grandchild was registered as a *mischling* (of mixed blood). (That is why to this day the Law of Return in Israel allows any person with one Jewish grandparent to be accepted as an Israeli citizen.) In 1938, all Jewish businesses were taken over by Aryans. Those Polish Jews who had been living in Germany were expelled to the frontier between Germany and Poland, where they lived in miserable conditions. The son of one such Polish family, Herschl Grynszpan, in protest, killed Ernst Von Rath, secretary of the German embassy in Paris. The Nazis seized on this act as an excuse for a nationwide pogrom on November 9, 1938, when Nazi storm troopers led mobs in the burning of hundreds of synagogues, thousands of shops and businesses; hence, *Krystallnacht*, the night of broken glass. 91 Jews were killed, 20,000 were sent to concentration camps, and the Jewish community was fined one billion marks for "atonement."

One purpose of *Krystallnacht* was to encourage Jews to leave Germany. By 1938, 350,000 out of 500,000 remained. However, during that crucial period between November, 1938, and September, 1939, the Jews had great difficulty finding any country (including the Western democracies) that would accept them as refugees. On January 30, 1939, Hitler, speaking to the Reichstag, warned that "if international finance Jewry should succeed once more in plunging the peoples into a world war, then the consequence will be . . . the destruction of the Jewish race in Europe."

On May 17, 1939, the British government issued a White Paper, drastically limiting Jewish immigration to Palestine to 10,000 refugees for each of the next five years, after which 75,000 would be permitted, but then no more without Arab acquiescence. In June, the German liner, *St. Louis*, left Hamburg for Cuba with almost 1,000 Jews, all of whom had been given landing permits. During their voyage the landing permits were revoked retroactively. Unable to land in Cuba, the *St. Louis* sailed slowly by the

Florida coast. Telegrams were sent to President Roosevelt urging him to admit the refugees to the United States. The telegrams were not answered. 287 Jews were fortunate to be admitted in England. All others were returned to Belgium and France. 667 were killed in the Holocaust.

On September 1, Hitler's armies invaded Poland. Germany occupied the western portion and Russia the eastern portion of Poland. In 1940, Polish Jews were rounded up and forced into ghettos, first in Lodz, then in Warsaw. In 1941, Germany declared war on Russia and quickly captured the Ukraine. A mobile killing unit, the *Einsatzgruppen*, began the massacre of Jews. Reinhard Heydrich instructed the officers in charge to keep in strict secrecy the "planned overall measures." Adolph Eichmann later confirmed that these officers understood this to mean the murder of all Jews. About 35,000 were killed at Babi Yar, outside of Kiev. In December, a small Romanian vessel, the *Struma*, eluded the Nazis and escaped to the port of Istanbul with 769 Jews. Turkey refused them entry. When the British would not give the *Struma* permission to proceed to Palestine, the Turkish government ordered the overcrowded boat to leave its port. Heading toward Bulgaria, the *Struma* sunk in the Mediterranean. There was one survivor.

The most explicit orders to murder all Jews were given at the Wannsee Conference outside of Berlin on January 20, 1942. In August, Gerhardt Reigner, an official of the World Jewish Congress, through a German industrialist, learned of the "final solution" and reported his horrific news to the United States consul in Switzerland. He was not believed, but when the Red Cross corroborated his report, the Assistant Secretary of State, Sumner Welles became convinced. Welles told Rabbi Stephen Wise that the Rabbi's worst fears were confirmed. On November 24, 1942, Wise held a news conference to gain public support for rescue efforts. The *New York Times* published a brief account of Wise's remarks on page 20.

Among American periodicals, only *The Nation* and *The New Republic* gave prominence to reliable reports that the mass murder of all Jews was actually happening. In December, Rabbi Wise delivered to President Roosevelt the "Blueprint for Extermination." Nothing was done.

In February, 1943, the Romanian government offered to move 70,000 Jews to any place of refuge chosen by the Allies, just for the cost of travel. Probably the Romanians realized that Germany would lose the war and wanted to be treated leniently by the Allies. Both the British Foreign Office and the U.S. State Department viewed the offer as a bribe and, again, did nothing. Within the American Jewish community, most leaders were working behind the scenes to influence the government's policies. However, a group of Revisionists(ardent Zionists, to be discussed in the next chapter), led by playwright Ben Hecht, put an ad in the *New York Times* that screamed: "For Sale to Humanity—70,000 Jews."

The Jewish establishment was embarrassed by Hecht's "sensationalism" but held its own rally demanding that approaches be made not only to Romania but to Hungary and Italy. Rabbi Wise and Judge Joseph Proskauer of the American Jewish Committee met with British foreign secretary Anthony Eden. Eden's response was that rescue attempts would not work. However, when Eden discussed the matter with U.S. Secretary of State Cordell Hull and President Roosevelt, he told them that Hitler might take us up on our offer, and there are not enough ships available. Neither Hull nor FDR responded to this preposterous excuse. In his *Abandonment of the Jews,* David Wyman suggests that Eden's real objection was his concern that more Jews might insist on going to Palestine, a situation that would disrupt the British Middle East policy of not antagonizing the Arabs. Perhaps FDR feared that if rescue efforts succeeded, there would be great pressure for the admission of thousands of Jews into the United States, and American public opinion, led by the labor unions, opposed such large-scale immigration.

As pressure was mounting, Britain and the U.S. called a conference on refugees in Bermuda. No Jewish delegates were admitted. The Bermuda Conference simply came up with more reasons why the Allies could not help. This led a member of the Polish government-in-exile, Shmuel Zygelboym, to commit suicide as a protest against the indifference of the free world to the mass murder of Jews. He left behind these words, "Let my death be an energetic cry of protest against the indifference of the world which witnesses the extermination of the Jewish people without taking any steps to prevent it."

Finally, when the Romanian government once again offered to deliver Jews at no cost to itself, the World Jewish Congress raised the funds and obtained clearance from the Treasury Department, which was in charge of immigration. However, the State Department held up the process for eight months. Mid-level non-Jewish Treasury officials could not understand why there was such a delay. They reported the obstruction to Henry Morgenthau, Secretary of Treasury, a Jew and a friend the President. Morgenthau told FDR, who did order the State Department to act, but by this time the Romanian offer had been withdrawn. Before this scandal could become public, President Roosevelt, in February, 1944, at long last appointed the War Refugee Board.

Through the WRB, 46,000 Jews were rescued from Romania. Its President Cretzianu asked: Why did you (the Allies) not come sooner? You could have saved more lives. Among the difficulties facing the WRB was the small number of nations that would accept significant numbers of Jews. In the United States, only one refugee camp accommodating 1,000 Jews was opened. In Hungary, the WRB worked with Raoul Wallenberg, a heroic Swedish diplomat, to rescue 20,000 Jews. The WRB, as well as the partisan underground in Europe, urged the Allies to bomb the crematoria at Auschwitz. This request was refused on the grounds that doing so would interfere with the war effort, even though factories five miles from Auschwitz were bombed. All in all, the War Refugee Board was able to save about 200,000. Imagine how many more could have been rescued had attempts been made earlier.

There were a few notable exceptions to the world-wide policy of indifference. In October, 1943, thousands of Denmark's Jews were hidden by their fellow-Danes and were then smuggled across the sea to safety in Sweden. There were individual Germans who helped Jews survive, the best known being the the industrialist Oskar Schindler, most of whose Jewish workers were spared. There were exceptional religious leaders, such as Martin Niemoeller, a pastor in the German Confessing Church, whose protests caused him to spend over eight years in a concentration camp. He wrote these oft-quoted words:

"First they came for the Communists, and I did not speak out, because I was not a Communist. Then they came for the Socialists, and I did not speak out, because I was not a Socialist. Then they came for the trade unionists, and I did not speak out, because I was not a trade unionist. Then they came for the Jews and I did not speak out, because I was not a Jew. Then they came for me, and there was no one left to speak out for me."

The role of Pope Pius XII has been widely debated. He did open monasteries and convents in Italy to Jewish refugees. Unfortunately, few took advantage, believing themselves safe, because the Germans did not occupy Italy until September, 1943. The main criticism of the Pope is that he never specifically condemned the crime of genocide. He did deplore all atrocities committed by both sides. Three reasons have been suggested for the papal policy: First, because Communism was considered as great a threat to civilization as Fascism, the Pope may have been "even-handed" for fear of being considered "soft on Communism;" second, the Pope feared that a direct condemnation of the Nazis would put Catholics in Germany at risk; and third, the Pope believed that his protests would not change Nazi policy.

After remembering the six-million Jews who were slaughtered, painful questions cry out for answers. How could such a horror have happened? Could the Jews have done more to resist the Nazis and save themselves? What has been the impact of the Holocaust on Jews and Judaism? What can be done to prevent genocides in the future?

1) Who or what caused the Holocaust?

The Holocaust would never have happened were it not for a painful history of anti-Semitism in Europe. In the Middle Ages, some churchmen predicted that a Jewish leader, the anti-Christ, would arise and lead an army of Jews out of the East. They would be destroyed by the forces of Christendom. This fantasy is eerily similar to Hitler's claim that the Jews would lead the forces of Bolshevism out of the East, only to be destroyed by the Aryan saviors of civilization. Hitler's initial actions against the Jews had been employed centuries before by the Church: e.g., yellow badges, confinement in ghettos, confiscation of property. The anti-Jewish persecution of the late Middle Ages was transformed into a racial doctrine. The very term, anti-Semitism, was first used in 1879, by Wilhelm Marr in his pamphlet, "The Victory of Judaism over Germanism." His racist ideas were spread throughout Europe by Houston Stewart Chamberlain and by the fabrication known as "The Protocols of Zion," a forgery that alleged the Jews had formed a world-wide conspiracy to control all social institutions, from governments to the media. So when Hitler began to plant the seeds of bigotry, Germany and much of Europe was fertile ground.

A second major factor was the dire economic crisis in Germany. After the first World War, the Germans were forced to pay the Allies 32-billion dollars and cede the mineral-rich Saar Valley. The German economy collapsed due to soaring inflation and high unemployment. The Social Democrats running the Weimar Republic could not solve the economic crisis, and German industrialists, fearing the rise of Communism, turned to the National Socialists who promised to restore to Germany pride, glory, and prosperity. When the Nazis gained power, re-took the Saar Valley, and re-built the German war machine, unemployment dropped dramatically, the industrialists prospered, and many Germans felt pride in the promised restoration of national glory.

Of course, the Holocaust would never have happened without a paranoid leader such as Hitler, who for whatever psychological reasons viewed the Jews as enemies bent on the world's destruction and who, therefore, had to be destroyed. But Hitler could not have carried out the genocide without first eliminating and silencing, by murder and terror, tens of thousands of opponents of Nazism in the 1930's. Then Hitler required the support of what Yehuda Bauer, in a 1998 address to the German Bundestag (House of Representatives), called "the layer of intellectuals—the academicians, the teachers, the students, the bureaucrats, the doctors, the lawyers, the churchmen, the engineers—(who) joined the Nazi party because it promised them a future and a status." Many were making a meager living and so were willing to buy into the National Socialists' utopianism. That this goal called for the mass murder of Jews was accepted as part of the movement toward a greater Germany. These "lumpen-intellectuals" so identified with the Nazi party that they transferred moral responsibility to the Fuhrer.

Bauer did not charge, as did Daniel Goldhagen in his *Hitler's Willing Executioners* that the "ordinary Germans" espoused a "virulent and violent . . . eliminationist anti-Semitism . . . which called for the elimination of Jewish influence or of Jews themselves from

German society." Like most historians who have dealt with the Holocaust, Bauer was critical of Goldhagen's analysis. In *Rethinking the Holocaust,* Bauer pointed out that in Germany until 1930, the anti-anti-Semitic parties (Social Democrats, Communists, Democrats) formed a clear majority in the Reichstag. The constitution of the Weimar Republic was written by a Jew, Hugo Preuss. Bauer considered Goldhagen's thesis simplistic, not seriously taking into account the deep despair of the German people after their defeat in the first World War. Finally, Bauer maintained that "eliminationist anti-Semitism" was not a special characteristic of German society but was more prevalent in other parts of Europe, such as Croatia, Romania, and Russia.

The question remains: How could enough Germans be found to carry out the mass murders? Bauer's response was that the layer of intellectuals provided "a justification for ordinary folks to participate in the genocidal program." He added that "even among the non-anti-Semitic or even anti-anti-Semitic . . . (there was) a queasiness regarding the Jews," an "unease" that could also be found throughout Europe. "This queasiness made it practically impossible for a general protest against the murder of Jews to develop." In contrast, a mass protest against the murder of handicapped Germans did bring about the end of the "so-called euthanasia program."

Richard Rubenstein, in *The Cunning of History,* observed that the German leaders had perfected organizational techniques of rational control, a vast bureaucracy that could have no conscience, because if one individual refused to act, another would surely do so. Yet, even with all these historic, economic, psychological, and political explanations, the question—but how could human beings bring themselves to sanction and participate in the attempted total destruction of all Jews from the face of the earth—somehow is not fully answered. After quoting Sigmund Freud and Erich Fromm, Bauer concluded that "humans veer between the urge for life and the life-destroying urge." Long before Freud and Fromm, the Torah quoted God as saying, "I have put before you life and death, blessing and curse. Choose life, if you and your offspring would live (Deuteronomy 30:19).

2) Could the Jews have done more to save themselves?

Some have wondered: Why did not more Jews attempt to resist the Nazis. or to escape? The psychoanalyst, Bruno Bettelheim, who spent some time in Buchenwald, has argued that Europe's Jews were the victims of "ghetto thinking." After centuries of being passive in the ghetto, Jews tended to be passive when they were threatened with mass murder. Most Holocaust scholars consider this nonsense. First, the Jews could not conceive of the inconceivable. Until the Nazis' Final Solution, no anti-Jewish tyrant (other than the fictional Haman) had ever attempted to kill all Jews. In Elie Wiesel's moving memoir, *Night,* which recounts his experience as an adolescent in Auschwitz, he reports that in his Hungarian village of Sighet, a Jew named Moche escaped from the Nazis and returned to Sighet to warn the people of the mass murder that awaited them. He was simply not believed. Wiesel wrote, "I did not believe him myself . . . I felt only pity for him." Also, consider the time frame. When it was still possible for Jews to leave Germany, they viewed such anti-Jewish attacks as *Krystallnacht* to be more extreme forms of the persecution Jews had endured in the late Middle Ages. Many of those who tried to leave in 1938-9 could find no country that would accept them. Once the War had begun, it was difficult if not impossible to escape Nazi-dominated Europe.

A couple who tried to escape Poland were Vladek Spiegelman and his wife, Anna. Their story has been preserved in the remarkable cartoon memoir, *Maus,* by their son, Art, who depicted the

Jews as mice, the Nazis as cats, and the Poles as pigs. Vladek and Anna could not conceive of the annihilation that awaited Jews, but they knew the future for Jews in Poland would be extremely dark. They managed to escape the Nazis but had nowhere to hide. They paid smugglers to help them leave the country but the smugglers betrayed them, and they were captured and sent to Auschwitz—hardly passive "ghetto thinking."

Art asked his father, once you knew that Auschwitz was a death camp, why did you not at least try to resist? Vladek's answer: "It wasn't easy like you think . . . in some spots people did fight. But you can kill maybe one German before they kill fast a hundred from you." Jewish inmates had to weigh the certainty of death if they resisted against the slight possibility of living until the camps were liberated.

Gideon Hausner, prosecutor at the trial of Adolph Eichmann, wrote that once the Jews were totally at the mercy of the Nazis, they behaved no differently from non-Jews in similar circumstances. "Over a million Soviet prisoners of war were exterminated by shooting, with only one recorded case of rebellion . . ." What of earlier, when there was a slight chance of escaping the ghettos? Hausner responded, the Jews lacked weapons and a central organization. It was dangerous to join the partisans. Anti-Semitic Ukrainian partisans often killed Jews on sight. Polish partisans allowed Jews to join them only if they had guns, which they could acquire only by killing Nazis at the risk of their own lives and triggering mass reprisals. Soviet partisans and the French underground were more likely to accept Jews but were located further from the ghettos. Despite these dangers, 100,000 Jews did join the partisans; 60,000-70,000 were killed. There were, of course, desperate revolts in the Warsaw ghetto and the Sobibor death camp. Hausner concluded, the miracle is that, given the circumstances, so many Jews did resist.

3) What was the impact of the Holocaust on Jews and Judaism?

One might think that many Jews would feel that if the future holds more horrific persecution, even genocide, let us completely assimilate. But this was not the Jewish reaction. On the contrary, after the Holocaust, Jews throughout the world felt a stronger sense of Jewish identity. Theologian Emil Fackenheim stated that after Auschwitz, the Jewish people heard a 614th commandment: "The authentic Jew of today is forbidden to hand Hitler . . . a posthumous victory." By assimilating, Jews would willingly be completing Hitler's plan of putting an end to the Jewish people. Fackenheim suggested that this commandment came from God. Others might look to psychological explanations. If being Jewish is a core part of your being, then you may naturally resist any attempt to eliminate what is part of your very identity.

Elie Wiesel insisted that the Jewish people are obliged to survive as witness to such an incredible evil. There must be Jews to remind the world of how deeply humans may sink into barbarism. This obligation to witness has become even more necessary since a small group of pseudo-scholars have contended that the Holocaust never happened. Due to the efforts of Jewish scholars, courses on the Holocaust are offered on many college campuses. Michael Berenbaum, project director of the U.S. Holocaust Memorial Museum in Washington, D.C., reports that when he offered a course on the Holocaust at Weslyan University in 1973, there were five students, all Jews. In 1997, his course was one of the best attended in the University, and 80% of the students were not Jewish. He also reports that of the 14 million visitors to the Holocaust Museum, almost eight out of ten are not Jewish. Yes, the Jews have been witnesses so that the world will never forget.

The memory of the Holocaust has had somewhat contradictory effects on Jewish attitudes toward the non-Jewish world. As discussed in Chapter 2, members of groups with a history of persecution tend to be either more compassionate or less compassionate than the average person toward other victims of prejudice and oppression. Some Jews may believe that a Jew can never fully trust the non-Jewish world. They may even grumble, "Nobody helped us. Why should we help them?" This obviously contradicts the prophetic message of Judaism: "Are you not as the children of the Ethiopians unto Me, saith the Lord?" (Amos 9:7) If we Jews have been outraged at the indifference of most of the non-Jewish world during the Holocaust, how dare we be indifferent when others are victims!

The impact of the Holocaust on Jewish theology has been to sharpen the dilemma of theodicy: How could an all-powerful righteous God allow so many innocents to be murdered? The issue is as old as the book of *Job*. In Chapter 4, a variety of responses were given. Among them, God did not create fascism; human beings did. This, however, leads to a more contemporary question: Can we, after Auschwitz and Cambodia and Rwanda, still have faith in the human capacity for reason and compassion? Rabbi Jack Bemporad in an essay, "The Concept of Man after Auschwitz," has written that according to Judaism, "man is by nature neither good nor evil" but has the freedom to move in either direction. What the Holocaust should teach is not that nothing has meaning but that so much that has meaning could be lost. The memory of the Holocaust should cause us to strive all the more to value the love, beauty, and reason that gives life its significance, to use our freedom to choose life that we may more fully live.

While Wiesel's *Night* has posed the theological issues faced by a religious Jew after Auschwitz, Primo Levi's *Survival in Auschwitz* confronts the dilemmas that must be faced by a secular humanist. Levi was an Italian chemist who was deported to Auschwitz. Once freed by the Russians, he joined a band of partisans fighting the Nazis until, after the War, Levi returned to his home in Turin.

Concerned with what happens to humane values when humans try to survive under horrific conditions, he wrote that the minority who survived usually served some function in the camp, as cook, tailor, musician, chemist. Often the survivors lived by the law, "eat your own bread and the bread of your neighbor." However, Levi wrote that the reason he survived was the compassion shown him by Lorenzo, an Italian civilian worker who took great risk to bring Levi a piece of bread each day for six months, who gave him a vest, and who wrote a post-card to Levi's girl-friend so she could tell his family that he was alive. Levi wrote: "Because of Lorenzo I am alive today, not because of the material aid but because Lorenzo reminded me that there still does exist a just world outside the camp. Lorenzo made me feel there is still a remote possibility of good for which it is worth surviving . . . Thanks to Lorenzo, I managed not to forget that I, myself, was a man."

4) What can we do to prevent future genocides?

Yehuda Bauer concluded his address to the Bundestag by stating that we have not as yet learned much from the Holocaust. Otherwise, the international community would have promptly put a stop to the mass murders in Bosnia and Rwanda. Still, Bauer does have hope that we can learn. Remembering is only the first step. Our next reponsibility is to teach and study not only the Holocaust, but also "everything that transpired during the Second World War and thereafter involving racism, anti-Semitism, and xenophobia." Finally, we should add to the Ten Commandments three additional ones: "You, your children, and your children's children shall never become perpetrators . . . shall never allow yourselves to become victims . . . shall never, *never*, be passive onlookers to mass murder, genocide, or (may it never be repeated) a Holocaust-like tragedy."

TOPICS FOR DISCUSSION

1. Since the Holocaust there have been other genocides. We have cried "Never again," but cries are not enough. What can we do, and what policies should our government adopt, so that more genocides do not occur again?

2. Some have suggested that Jews have placed too much emphasis on the Holocaust and, in so doing, have given their children only negative reasons for being Jewish. What should be the place of the Holocaust in Jewish education?

3. What are the lessons of the Holocaust for the larger community?

4. Read Wiesel's *Night* and Levi's *Survival at Auschwitz*. Compare and contrast their responses to the horror.

RESOURCES

Davidowicz, Lucy. *The War against the Jews, 1933-1945*. New York, Holt, Rinehart & Winston, 1975.

Davidowicz, Lucy. *What Is the Use of History?* New York, Schocken, 1992.

Frank, Ann. *The Diary of a Young Girl*. New York, Doubleday. 1952.

Friedlander, Albert (ed.). *Out of the Whirlwind*. New York, UAHC Press, 1968.

Goldhagen, Daniel. *Hitler's Willing Executioners*. New York, Knopf, 1996.

Hausner, Gideon. *Justice in Jerusalem*. New York, Harper & Row, 1966.

Hilberg, Raul. *The Destruction of European Jews*. Chicago, Quadrangle, 1971.

Levi, Primo. *Survival at Auschwitz*. New York, Macmillan, 1986.

Levi, Primo. *The Drowned and the Saved*. New York, Summit Books, 1986.

Levin, Nora. *The Holocaust: The Destruction of European Jewry, 1933-1945*. New York, Cromwell, 1968.

Lifton, Robert Jay. *The Nazi Doctors: Medical Killing and the Psychology of Genocide*. New York, Basic Books, 1986.

Littell, Franklin. *The Crucifixion of the Jews: The Failure of Christians to Understand the Jewish Experience*. New York, Harper & Row, 1975.

Rubenstein, Richard. *The Cunning of History*. New York, Harper & Row, 1975.

Spiegelman, Art. *Maus*. New York, Pantheon Books, 1986.

Suhl, Yuri. *They Fought Back*. New York, Schocken, 1975.

Yahil, Levi. *The Rescue of Danish Jewry: Test of a Democracy*. Philadelphia, Jewish Publication Society, 1969.

Wiesel, Elie. *Night*. New York, Bantam, 1982.

Wyman, David. *Abandonment of the Jews: America and the Holocaust: 1941-1945.* New York, Pantheon Books, 1984.

Film: *Genocide.* Anti-Defamation League, 315 Lexington Ave., New York, N.Y., 10016.

20.

ZIONISM, THE ISRAELI-ARAB CONFLICT

AND AMERICAN JEWS

In November, 1974, when Yasser Arafat was appearing before the United Nations, I was one of a delegation of 22 Jewish and Christian clergy, led by Rabbi A. James Rudin of the American Jewish Committee, who were visiting Lebanon, Jordan, and Israel on a "journey for peace." When in Beirut we were taken in a car through the winding streets to the Palestine Liberation Organization headquarters where we met with Yasser Abed Rabbo, head of the PLO's Information Department. (Today he is still the PLO's minister of information.) Rabbo presented the PLO position: Establish a Palestinian state on the West Bank, and then negotiate with Israel to merge into a single "democratic secular state." I asked him, "What if the Israelis choose to retain their own state?" Rabbo replied, "That will be determined by the future, itself." I responded, "Must the establishment of a Palestinian state be at the expense of another people's self-determination?" Rabbo's response was, "You are interested in discussing a question which will arise maybe 15 or 20 years ahead. I am interested in discussing today."

There are so many questions and issues to be raised today

about Israel, the Palestinians, and American Jews. Why do so many Arabs believe that Israel has no moral right to exist? How do Israelis justify their moral right to their own state? Can there ever be lasting peace between Israel and the Palestinians and the larger Arab world? What is, or what should be, the relationship between American Jews and Israel? If there were a conflict between U.S. interests and Israeli interests, where would American Jews stand? Do American Jews have a right to speak out against the policies of an Israeli government if they believe that government is acting against the prospect of peace in the region?

VARIETIES OF ZIONISM

Before dealing with such questions, one needs some historical background, from the origins of Zionism to the desperate dilemmas facing Israel today. Zionism is based on the right of the Jewish people to have a nation in Palestine, a nation whose gates will always be open to Jews who wish or need to live there. For the Orthodox, this right is based on God's promise to Abraham: "Unto thy seed will I give this land." (Genesis 12:7) Orthodox Judaism has held that this Jewish nation will be re-established once the Messiah comes. That is why most Orthodox Jews in the nineteenth century did not support a political Zionism that would substitute human effort for God's power. Today, most, but not all, Orthodox Jews view the modern state of Israel as a step toward the creation of a new Israel to which all Jews will return and will live under the laws of the Torah.

The great majority of Zionists justify Israel's existence by citing not God's promise to Abraham but the Jewish people's historic connection with the land. Jews (or Israelites) were the majority of the inhabitants from about the twelfth century BCE to the second century CE, when, after the disastrous Bar Kochba revolt, much of Jerusalem was destroyed by the Romans. Wherever Jews have lived, they have echoed the words of the Psalmist, "If I forget thee, O Jerusalem, may my right hand forget its cunning"(*Psalm* 137). In the daily service and in the blessing chanted after each meal, there are prayers for rebuilding Jerusalem. Each year on the fast day of Tisha B'Av (the ninth of the month of Av), Jews have mourned the destruction of the Temple. Abraham Heschel has written how Jews asserted their claim to the land: "Our protest was not heard in the public squares of large cities. It was offered in our homes, in our sanctuaries, in our books, in our prayers. Indeed, our very existence as a people was a proclamation of our link to the land, of our certainty of return."

As modern Zionism emerged in the nineteenth century, there developed two main schools of thought. Leon Pinsker in Russia and Theodor Herzl in Vienna saw political Zionism as the solution to anti-Semitism. Both Pinsker and Herzl were raised when they believed the Jewish people were about to be given their freedom in Europe. Pinsker was a son of the Haskalah (Enlightenment). Beginning with Moses Mendelssohn in Germany, the maskilim (enlightened ones) developed secular Hebrew literature and insisted that Jews be educated in modern language, literature, and science. So it was that Pinsker came to study law and medicine at the University of Odessa. However, the pogroms of 1881 shattered his faith that Jews could be accepted in Russian society, and led him to write the pamphlet, *Auto-emancipation,* which held that the Jews must develop pride in their heritage and free themselves. He initially considered purchasing land in the American West! When this fantasy had no followers, he turned to Palestine as the place for a homeland and formed the *Hov'vei Tzion* (Lovers of Zion*)*. His efforts led to the first *aliyah (*"going up" to the land) in 1882.

Herzl was a cosmopolitan journalist and playwright in Vienna. As a reporter, he covered the Dreyfus Case. A captain on the French

General Staff, Dreyfus was falsely accused of treason and was sent to Devil's Island. Eventually he was exonerated, but the case unleashed a torrent of anti-Semitism in France. Herzl concluded that if such anti-Jewish hatred could flourish in "enlightened" France, then the Jewish people could never be safe in Europe. So in 1896, he wrote *The Jewish State,* and set in motion the movement of political Zionism. After a pogrom in Kishineff (1903), Herzl believed the plight of Russian Jewry was so desperate that he proposed, as a first step, buying Uganda from the British and beginning the Jewish state there. However, not only the British but the Russian Jews rejected the idea. Said Herzl, "With a rope around their necks, they still refuse." Herzl tried to raise money to buy Palestine from Turkey. Wealthy European Jews would not contribute to building a nation that they believed would be a permanent charity case, and the Sultan of Turkey was not interested in selling: "Too much Turkish blood has been spilled." Herzl's main achievement was convening the first Zionist Conference in Basel (1907), where he predicted that a Jewish state would be established in 50 years. (He was just one year off.) In Herzl's *Old-New Land,* he described his vision of a Jewish state as a utopia in which factories would be run by workers and consumers, several European languages (but not Hebrew) would be spoken, and the best of European culture would be represented. What of the Arabs? At that time there were only 200,000 in Palestine, and Herzl believed they would welcome the modern state the Jews would create.

An alternate philosophy of Zionism envisioned the Jewish state as the place where the Jewish spirit would flourish. This idea was first expressed in 1862 by Moses Hess, a cosmopolitan German Jewish Marxist who became disillusioned after the Revolution of 1848 restored the Junkers(army and monarchy) to power. In *Rome and Jerusalem,* Hess argued that if the Italians could establish their national spirit in Rome, then the Jews could do so in Jerusalem. For Hess that spirit was the belief that there is a Oneness behind all things.

Much more influential was Ahad Ha-Am ("one of the people"), whose actual name was Asher Ginzberg. In his 1889 essay, *Lo Zeh Ha-derech* ("This is not the way"), he argued against Pinsker that Zionism was not the answer to anti-Semitism. He became Herzl's main adversary within the Zionist movement. He wrote that Palestine could not hold all the Jews, and those remaining in the Diaspora would still be subjected to anti-Semitism depending on economic conditions. So why Zionism?

For Ahad Ha-Am, Zionism would solve not the political but the spiritual problem of the Jewish people. Orthodox Jews were too rigid and Reform Jews were too assimilated. However, once the Jews had their own nation, the spirit of the Jewish people could be fully expressed, a spirit of justice that would refuse to worship power. His emphasis on the moral essence of the Jewish spirit led him to be quite critical of those Diaspora Jews who believed that the Arabs were a "donkey-like, uncivilized desert people." In 1913, when he heard reports of Jews abusing Arab workers, Ahad Ha-Am wrote: "If this is the way it is now, how will we treat other people if indeed one day we become the dominant power in Eretz Yisrael? If this is the Messiah, let him come, but let me not live to see him."

In Russia, by the first decade of the twentieth century, many Jews had joined the revolutionary movement against the Czar. However, in 1903, Russian workers and peasants (supposedly their "comrades") turned against the Jews and joined the pogroms that attacked Jewish villages in southern Russia. Many of these Jewish Marxists concluded that the only place that the Jews could have a socialist revolution would be in their own country. So began Labor Zionism (*Poale Tzion*). In Palestine, the Jews would build a nation run not by the bourgeoisie but by the workers and farmers. In 1905, Ber Borochov expressed these ideas in "The National Question and the Class Struggle." He even thought the term, Zionism, was too *bourgeois,* so he initially called his movement "Palestinism." The ideas of Borochov, Nahum Syrkin, and Y.L. Gordon shaped the thinking of the "founding fathers and mothers" of Israel, whose migration to Palestine in 1907 was the second *aliyah.* Their socialist ideals were communally expressed in the *kibbutz* movement of farm collectives. While some Arabs condemned Zionism as an extension of imperialism, these pioneers (*halutzim*), such as David Ben Gurion, saw themselves as adversaries of both capitalism and imperialism. Ben Gurion, born David Green in Plonsk, Poland, at 17, was already a co-founder of the *Poale Tzion* of Poland. Later he became the first prime minister of Israel.

During the First World War, a Russian-Jewish writer and journalist, Vladimir Jabotinsky, saw the War as an opportunity to take Palestine away from Turkey. He tried to establish a Jewish legion for the liberation of the Holy Land but received no support. After the War, Jabotinsky advocated a "maximalist" Zionism, which envisioned a Jewish majority not only west but east of the Jordan river. A Revisionist Jewish state would oppose socialism and emphasize economic individualism. The youth movement of Revisionism was *Betar.* Some members of today's Likud party (e.g., Yitzhak Shamir) were members. Revisionism gave birth to the Irgun and the Stern Gang, which were later to carry out attacks against the British and the Arabs in the 1940's. What was Jabotinsky's response to the opposition of the Arabs? They had many other lands to call their own. The Jews had only Palestine.

For secular non-socialists, there was an alternative to Revisionism. A movement known as "General Zionism" appealed to middle-class Jews in the United States and Great Britain. The most prominent Zionist leader in Britain was Chaim Weizmann. Born in Russia, Weizmann moved to England in 1904 and became a prominent research chemist. As a Zionist, he became involved in settling Jews in Palestine. In November, 1917, Weizmann encouraged the British foreign secretary, Lord Balfour to issue the "Balfour Declaration," which stated that the British government favored "the establishment in Palestine of a national home for the Jewish people and will use their best endeavors to facilitate the achievement of this object, it being clearly understood that nothing shall be done which may prejudice the civil and religious rights of existing non-Jewish communities in Palestine." Some historians state that this was an effort by the British to retain dominance in one part of the Middle East, while the French would be dominant in Lebanon.

The initial Arab response was surprisingly positive. In March, 1919, Hashemite leader, Emir Feisal, wrote to Felix Frankfurter, who later became a Supreme Court justice: "We feel that the Arabs and Jews are cousins in race, suffering similar oppression at the hands of powers stronger than themselves. We Arabs, especially the educated among us, look with the deepest sympathy on the Zionist movement . . . We will wish the Jews a most hearty welcome home . . . We are working together for a revived and reformed Near East. . . . The Jewish Movement is national and not imperialistic. Our movement is national and not imperialistic; and there is room in Syria(which encompassed Palestine) for both. Indeed, I think that neither can be a real success without the other . . ."

Why such support from a prominent Arab? Feisal was interested in taking control of Syria from the French. Perhaps he believed he could make a deal with the Jews: You help us push out the French, and we will help you secure a Jewish state. Of course, the Jews could not act against the French, for that would endanger the Jews' relations with the British. When the Zionists did not respond to Feisal's proposition, the willingness of some Arabs to cooperate turned into bitter resistance to the very concept of a Jewish state in Palestine.

In 1920, the chief rabbi of Palestine, Avraham Kook, advocated a religious Zionism, which took political form in the Mizrachi party. He chose to fight for Torah within Zionism rather than outside it. One can now recognize that some of the current religious and political factions within Israel today have roots traceable to these early Zionists. The Labor Party (which split into One Israel and Meretz) could be traced back to the Labor Zionism of Borochov and Syrkin. The Likud party could trace its roots back to both the General Zionists and the Revisionists. The National Religious Party emerged from Mizrachi and its spiritual founder, Rabbi Kook.

THE ARAB-ZIONIST CONFLICT AND THE BIRTH OF ISRAEL

From 1919 through 1924, the third *aliyah* brought more Jews from Russia into Palestine. They purchased 92% of their land from wealthy Arab landowners and 8% from the British mandatory government. (In 1921, the British divided Palestine into two parts: East of the Jordan river, the land was called Transjordan; west of the Jordan, Palestine). During this period, not only did the Jews not drive the Arabs out of Palestine; rather the Jewish immigration had the effect of *increasing* the Arab population. In 1881, there were 260,000 Arabs in Palestine; by 1946, 1,200,000. Much of this increase occurred because the Jews had developed the land economically and so provided more jobs for Arabs from the surrounding nations.

However, the Arabs were more concerned about the growth of the Jewish population in Palestine, from 24,000 in 1881, to 620,00 in 1946. Their hostility led to the massacre of Jews in Hebron in 1929. Then, in 1936, Arabs attacked Jewish settlements throughout Palestine. The Jews defended themselves with their armed force, the Haganah. By this time the Revisionist militias, Etzel (*Irgun Tz'vai L'umi*), and the Stern gang were operating independently.

In 1937, the Peel Commission in England made a proposal that was to create sharp divisions between Arabs and Zionists and among the Zionists, themselves. Abba Eban credits Dr. Reginald Coupland, professor of colonial history at Oxford, for proposing the Partition Principle. Coupland recognized that because of deep cultural differences between Arabs and Jews, a united Palestine (between the Jordan and the Mediterranean) would be possible only with the domination of one group by the other. He stated, "Peace and order and good government can only be maintained in a unitary Palestine . . . by a rigorous system of suppression." Chaim Weizmann understood this and so agreed that the partition of the land (one entity controlled by the Jews; the other, by the Arabs) would be "the lesser injustice." Ben Gurion believed that the Jewish people had a moral right to the land up to the Jordan, but he agreed to accept partition, as a stage toward the achievement of the Zionist dream. He hoped that after the partition, with the increase in Jewish population, the Arabs would agree voluntarily to move east of the Jordan. The Arabs totally rejected the concept of partition, believing that because they were in the majority, Palestine belonged to them.

Abba Eban, a disciple of Weizmann, agreed with his mentor that both Arabs and Jews had just claims to the land. He wrote, "To deny the Zionist claim (to a Jewish state) would have been the affirmation that Arabs must be free and sovereign everywhere and the Jews nowhere . . ." He was later to argue at the United Nations that there were a dozen nations where the Arabs of Palestine could be at home with their cultural cousins. Note that at this time there was no organized Palestinian National Movement, but the Arabs living in Palestine considered themselves to be part of a Greater Syria and the larger pan-Arab nation. At the same time, Eban recognized, "To assert that thousands of years of Jewish connection totally eliminated thirteen centuries of Arab-Muslim history would be to apply a discriminatory standard to historic experience . . ." In retrospect, he saw armed conflict as inevitable: "If they (the Arabs) had submitted to Zionism with docility, they would have been the first people in history to have voluntarily renounced their majority rule."

Martin Buber believed there was a mystical connection, a dialogue between the land and the Jewish people. He also maintained that both Arabs and Jews have legitimate rights to a state in Palestine. His personal preference was a federation between the Jewish community and its neighbors. The small *Ichud* party of which he was a member favored a bi-national state. Both proposals were rejected by both sides. As Buber was later to write, "History has decided against either solution."

By the end of the Second World War, the international community gradually came to accept the partition principle. The horrific mass murder of six million Jews, the refusal of the free world to allow more than a trickle of refugees into their lands, the British White Paper that prohibited any significant Jewish immigration into Palestine, all these factors forced most nations to realize that the Jewish people did have a justified need for some land whose gates would always be open to Jews—and that the only land in which the Jewish people had deep historic roots was Palestine. At the same time, most nations also understood that the Arabs in Palestine, although they had not developed a Palestinian national movement, were still the majority in the land and were attached to the villages where they had roots. Therefore, both communities, the Arabs and the Jews of Palestine, had legitimate claims to the land. This was one of the rare times in the post-war world when the United States and the Soviet Union agreed. The British were all too eager to be out of Palestine: *Aliyah Bet* was bringing in Jews illegally from Europe. Etzel set off a bomb in British headquarters at the King David Hotel. Jewish refugees on a boat called *Exodus* were, unlike in the film, captured by the British and returned to Europe. UNSCOP (the United Nations Special Committee on Palestine) became the first international group to advocate partition.

So on November 29, 1947, the Partition Plan was approved by the General Assembly of the United Nations. The Jews of Palestine rejoiced when they learned of the UN's decision. Although they had dreamed of a Jewish state from the Jordan to the Sea, they were quite willing to accept a compromise, a "lesser injustice." (In the Jewish state, according to the Partition Plan, there would be 538,000 Jews and 397,000 Arabs. The Arab state would contain 804,000 Arabs and 10,000 Jews.) However, the Arabs of Palestine refused to accept partition. According to British historian, Christopher Sykes, "On the 30th of November, the day after the UN vote, there were Arab attacks on Jews, with considerable loss of life in Haifa, Tel Aviv, Jaffa, Lydda, Jerusalem, and on the roads . . ." The Mufti of Jerusalem declared a general strike which immediately became violent. From Cairo, Moslem leaders declared a holy war against the Jews. During the fighting between the Arabs and Jews of Palestine, some atrocities were committed on both sides. At the Arab village of Deir Yassin, Etzel killed more than 200 Arab men, women, and children. The Arabs massacred all Jews living in Kfar Etzion. On May 14, the British withdrew from Palestine. Ben Gurion declared the independence of the state of Israel. Arab armies from Egypt, Syria, Lebanon, Jordan, and Iraq invaded Israel with the aim of destroying the embryonic state.

During the fighting, between 538,000 and 720,000 Arabs fled the land. The first to leave were the middle-class Arab leaders who wanted to avoid the warfare and who believed they would return to their homes after an Arab victory. Without leadership, the Arab peasants fended for themselves. Some were frightened into leaving by reports of the Deir Yassin massacre. There were reports that others were encouraged to leave by Arab leaders who wished to show that no Arabs would live under Jewish sovereignty. Still other Arabs were driven out of their villages by the Haganah, particularly in the area around Lod and Ramle. (In contrast, the Jewish mayor of Haifa urged its Arab citizens to stay.) While the reasons for the Arab exodus are many and complex, there is no doubt that there would have been no Arab refugee problem if the Arabs had not attacked the embryonic Jewish state, if they would have been willing to accept the compromise of partition. Abba Eban was later to state, "The Arabs have never missed an opportunity to miss an opportunity."

On April 3, 1949, the Rhodes Armistice Agreement was signed, giving Israel control of about 8,000 square miles, 21% more land than had been allotted under the partition plan. In August, Israel was accepted as a state by the United Nations. Since May, 1948, the K'nesset (parliament) had been meeting in Tel Aviv. Golda Meir wanted the capital to be in Haifa; Ben Gurion, in the Negev. He was soon to change his mind. In the summer of 1949, at the UN, delegates from predominantly Catholic nations, following the lead of the Vatican, proposed that Jerusalem become an internationalized territory. On December 9, a majority of the General Assembly rejected this plan. The K'nesset was immediately moved to Jerusalem, and on January 23, 1950, the K'nesset proclaimed that the Holy City had "always" been the capital of the Jewish nation.

In 1950, the Law of Return was enacted, enabling anyone who had one Jewish grandparent, and who was no threat to the state to immigrate to Israel. The Palestinian Arabs were not the only ones who became refugees as a result of the conflict. Some 700,000 Jews from Arab countries left for Israel. Economic discrimination, physical attacks and governmental pressure convinced them that they had no future in Arab countries.

WAR AND MORALITY

According to Jewish law, one is permitted, perhaps required to fight a war in defense of one's self and one's country. This is called a *milhemet mitzvah*, a war that is a commandment. If one accepts the partition principle as valid, then the Jews did have a right to defend the very existence of Israel from 1947 to 1949. The rabbis also stipulated the way even wars of self-defense should be waged: e.g., one is forbidden to destroy the fruit-bearing trees of the enemy. A relatively small number of American Jews support the Jewish Peace Fellowship, which is committed to total non-violence, citing the Mishnaic statement that if you kill one person, it is as though you caused the entire world to perish.

Since 1949, Israel has engaged in four wars. In 1955, President Nasser of Egypt trained *fedayeen* (self-sacrificers), who infiltrated Israel killing civilians and triggering Israeli reprisals. Egypt was receiving massive arms from the Soviet Union, and, according to Benny Morris' history of the conflict, *Righteous Victims,* Ben Gurion and Moshe Dayan wanted to make a pre-emptive strike against Egypt before its army could absorb the new weapons. (Morris is one of the controversial "new Israeli historians" who have reported events not included in the earlier Zionist histories.) Egypt then blockaded the straits of Tiran, effectively cutting off Israeli trade through the port of Eilat. Nasser also nationalized the Suez Canal, creating a convergence of British, French and Israeli interests. In June, 1956, Nasser proclaimed, "We must be strong in order to regain the rights of the Palestinians by force." France, Britain and Israel coordinated the attack that resulted in Israeli troops at the Canal. Worldwide pressure forced the withdrawal of British, French and Israeli troops. A United Nations Expeditionary Force (UNEF) was stationed in the Gaza Strip and at Sharm el Sheik, supposedly to remain there until a permanent peace was arranged between Israel and Egypt.

In June, 1967, Israel fought a war because its very survival was at stake. Nasser demanded immediate withdrawal of the UNEF, and the United Nations complied. Nasser then blockaded the Gulf of Akaba and, with Syria, threatened a war that would destroy Israel. Israel's pre-emptive strike led to her victory in the Six-Day War. Because Jordan had entered the war, Israel was able to capture the eastern sector of Jerusalem (including the Western Wall) and the West Bank of the Jordan. In *The Seventh Day,* an eye-witness reported that at least one company of the Israeli army actually tried to follow rabbinic law. An officer from a religious *kibbutz* learned that his soldiers had looted the Jordanian village of Jenin. The eye-witness wrote, "(The officer) got the whole company together (and) started quoting them chapter and verse of the Bible: 'Thou shalt not plunder . . . ' After he'd finished, one of the storemen got up and asked him, 'What about the bit in the Bible: "And when Jehosephat and his men came to take away the spoil," what do you make of that? . . . ' So the CO (commanding officer) began to explain that Rashi, commenting on the verse, says that it should be taken to mean that a conquering army takes only what it really needs during the fighting . . . I stood in the corner and I thought to myself, 'What a peculiar army this is, standing there and listening to all this stuff . . . ' But there really was something in it."

At a conference in Khartoum the Arabs rejected Israel's offer to return territory for a full and permanent peace. The United Nations General Assembly passed Resolution 242 calling for a return of territory for peace. However, in 1969, when Golda Meir became prime minister, religious Israelis established an illegal settlement in Hebron and were allowed to stay there.

There were two important consequences of the Six Day War for the Palestinians. First of all, about 230,000 Arabs crossed from the West to the East Bank, preferring the reign of King Hussein to that of the Israelis. Secondly, Israel found itself occupying land on which lived 1,500,000 Palestinian Arabs. While the Palestine Liberation Organization had been founded in 1964, the 1967 War gave rise to a more ardent form of Palestinian nationalism, as expressed in the 1968 Covenant, which stated that armed struggle is "a strategy and not tactics." This signified the Palestinian intent to use violence to destroy what they called the "Zionist entity." In 1969, Yasser Arafat assumed leadership of the PLO and initiated terrorist attacks directed from bases in Jordan. Fearing that the PLO would undermine his government, King Hussein of Jordan sent his army against the Palestinians, killing hundreds of them, eliminating their bases from Jordan and forcing them to shift their activities to Lebanon. It was from Beirut that the PLO then directed its activities. In 1972, PLO terrorists entered the Olympic village in Munich and murdered eleven members of the Israeli Olympic team.

On Yom Kippur, 1973, Egyptian and Syrian forces launched a surprise attack against Israeli troops east of the Suez Canal and on the Golan Heights. As soon as the Israelis regained the initiative, but before they could win a decisive victory, they were forced by the United States and the Soviet Union to accept a cease-fire. Still, the crossing of the Canal by Egyptian forces raised the morale of the Arab world and gave President Sadat of Egypt the ability, in 1978, to go to Jerusalem and begin the process that led to a meeting at Camp David where President Carter was host to Sadat and Menahem Begin, who had become Israel's prime minister in 1977. There it was that Israel concluded its first peace agreement with an Arab nation, but Sadat was to pay with his life for becoming a peacemaker.

However, prior to that agreement, in the years between 1974 and 1978, PLO terrorists killed 24 schoolchildren at Maalot in northern Israel. The United Nations branded Zionism as racism. After Menahem Begin became Israel's prime minister, more settlements on the West Bank were established led by Gush Emunim(the bloc of the faithful) in heavily populated Arab areas. Of the 140,000 settlers, 17% were Jewish immigrants from the United States.

Once the Camp David Accords were signed, in a hopeful spirit, *Shalom Achshav* (Peace Now) was formed. However, rockets were launched against Israeli villages south of Lebanon. This provided the rationale for Israel's invasion of Lebanon, ostensibly to establish a security zone along the border. However, General Ariel Sharon ordered the troops north to Beirut. Meanwhile, the Lebanese were engaged in their own civil war. After the assassination of Bashir Gemayel, the Christian Phalangist president of Lebanon, the Phalangists were eager for revenge. So in September, 1982, these Christian Lebanese massacred Palestinians in the camps at Sabra and Shatilla. Because this was an area that the Israelis controlled, 400,000 Israelis in Tel Aviv protested that the Israeli command had allowed the massacre to take place. A commission, led by Supreme Court Justice Yitzhak Kahan, concluded that General Sharon, one of Israel's military heroes, was indirectly responsible, and he was forced to resign as defense minister. He was soon back in the cabinet as minister without portfolio. The PLO leaders in Beirut escaped the Israelis by moving their headquarters to Tunis. Israel retained a security zone north of the Lebanese border, patrolled by the Southern Lebanese Army (SLA). Meanwhile, Syria had become the dominant power in Lebanon.

In 1984, a Unity Government in Israel was led for two years by Shimon Peres of the Labor Party and for the next two years by Yitzhak Shamir of the Likud. In 1987, the first Intifada(uprising) began in Gaza and spread to the West Bank. Hundreds of young Palestinians, including children, showered Israeli settlers and soldiers with stones. Yitzhak Rabin was put in charge of suppressing the Intifada. He was quoted as ordering his soldiers to "break their bones." This response was intended to be less harsh than shooting live bullets. Israel's ambivalence (sense of humanity versus the need for self-defense) was, according to Yaron Ezrahi, symbolized by the extensive use of "rubber bullets" that were supposed to stop the stone-throwers without killing them. For almost five years the policy of suppression was tried, but the Intifada would not be suppressed.

In 1988, the Palestinian National Council (PNC) met in Algiers and approved the Palestinian Declaration of Independence based on the 1947 partition resolution. That 1947 resolution had recognized the legitimacy of the division of Palestine into a Jewish state and an Arab state.

In 1990, Iraq invaded Kuwait, and in 1991, the United States led a coalition of forces against Iraq. During this Persian Gulf War, Iraqi scud missiles fell on Israel, but the Israelis, at the urging of the United States, did not retaliate and left the fighting to the anti-Iraq coalition. As scuds were falling on Israel, the Palestinians cheered. Arafat sided with Iraq and succeeded in isolating himself from most of the Arab world that had been giving him financial support. In 1991, Prime Minister Shamir reluctantly agreed to peace talks between Palestinians and Israelis in Madrid.

In 1992, the Labor Party defeated Likud and formed a government under Yitzhak Rabin, who by this time had realized that the Intifada could not be suppressed by force. After peace talks in Madrid produced no progress, secret negotiations were undertaken in Oslo between an Israeli team led by Uri Savir in close consultation with foreign minister Shimon Peres, and representatives of the PLO. This led, in 1993, to the famous Rabin-Arafat handshake on the White House lawn, with President Clinton beaming. A Declaration of Principles was announced, and Israel began direct negotiations with the PLO. Extremists on both sides opposed the peace process. In 1994, an Israeli, Baruch Goldstein killed Arabs in a mosque in Hebron. Palestinian extremists, under Hamas, retaliated. In November, 1995, Primer Minister Rabin was assassinated by Yigal Amir, a 27 year old ultra-religious law student at Bar-Ilan University, and all of Israel as well as Jews throughout the world were shocked and shaken.

Shimon Peres succeeded Rabin as prime minister but had to face elections in May, 1996. Prior to the elections, suicide bombers brought death to the streets of Jerusalem. Although the Palestinians claimed that they would delete those portions of their Covenant that called for the destruction of Israel, the Israeli electorate, shaken by the suicide bombers, chose Benjamin Netanyahu, of the Likud party, to be prime minister. According to the Oslo Accords, Israel was gradually to withdraw from parts of the West Bank. Before the elections, Israel had turned over to the PLO Jericho and Gaza. After the elections, little progress toward peace was made, except for turning over Hebron to the Palestinian Authority without evacuating the Israeli settlers there, who required protection by the Israeli army.

Hopes for peace were raised in May, 1999, when General Ehud Barak defeated Netanyahu by 56% to 44%. Barak's One Israel party won only 26 out of 120 seats in the K'nesset, but this was still a plurality and enabled Barak to find enough coalition partners to establish a government without the Likud. Keeping his election promise, Barak ordered the withdrawal of Israeli troops from the security zone in southern Lebanon. Hopes were raised even more after President Clinton hosted a meeting at Camp David with Chairman Arafat and Prime Minister Barak.

For the first time both sides confronted fundamental issues such as the status of Jerusalem, the right of return of the Palestinian refugees, and the extent of Israeli withdrawal from the West Bank. Barak surprised many Israelis when he apparently agreed that Israel would withdraw from 90-92% of the West Bank, perhaps ceding to the Palestinians a small slice of Israeli territory. Of the West Bank settlers, 80% were already living near the pre-1967 border(the"Green Line"). They would be incorporated into Israel. The rest of the settlers would be given the option of receiving compensation for their homes or living under Palestinian rule. About 10,000 Palestinian refugees could return, perhaps to re-unite families, but funds would be paid to compensate others and settle them elsewhere. Barak rejected the Palestinian demand that Israel accept moral responsibility for the plight of the refugees. Even regarding the toughest issue, Jerusalem, there was talk of Palestinians having administrative control over parts of East Jerusalem, including Moslem religious sites, and establishing the capital of a Palestinian state on the outskirts of the city. Full Palestinian sovereignty would be confined to the outlying Arab neighborhoods and villages.

Arafat insisted on full Palestinian sovereignty over East Jerusalem, including the Jewish Quarter and the Western Wall. While he would make some concessions to allow an ongoing Jewish-Muslim presence at the Wall, he wanted full sovereignty over the Temple Mount. Barak countered that the nature of sovereignty over the Temple Mount must recognize Jewish historic-religious claims. Arafat demanded the return of the entire West Bank. Any adjustment would have to be on acre-to-acre basis. Arafat did agree with the security arrangements that Israel demanded, consisting of early warning stations on the West Bank mountain ridge, and an Israeli military presence(alongside Palestinians) in about 15% of the Jordan Valley for a certain period of time. The Palestinian state would have no air force, navy, or armor. (This account of negotiations is based on a report of Joseph Alpher, former head of the Center for Strategic Studies at Tel Aviv University, who was an advisor to Prime Minister Barak during and after the Camp David summit.)

The two sides seemed so close that many believed there really was a realistic hope for the long-awaited peace with the Palestinians. Sadly, this was not so. On September 28, 2000, General

Sharon, after being given permission by the Israeli government, visited the Temple Mount, accompanied by about 1,000 Israeli soldiers. This sparked an intense Palestinian reaction that became the second Intifada. Israelis pointed out that outbreaks of Palestinian violence had preceded the Sharon visit, and contended that the Palestinian response was an extreme overreaction. This second uprising became known as the Al-Aqsa Intifada, because the Islamic movement in Israel claimed that the Al-Aqsa mosque was in danger. Not only were Palestinian youth throwing stones, but the *Tanzim,* an armed militia of the PLO's Fatah wing, were shooting at Israeli soldiers and civilians, prompting Israeli attacks from soldiers and helicopter gunships, intended to eliminate the source of the Palestinian attacks.

Members of the Israeli "peace camp" were shocked and depressed. How close they had come! Was this the latest instance of the Palestinians never missing an opportunity to miss an opportunity? Barak resigned and called for new elections in February, 2001. Members of Likud, some settlers, and their supporters in the United States were saying, in effect, We told you so. Read the school books they give to their children. The Palestinians are still unwilling to accept the very existence of Israel. Norman Podhoretz wrote in *Commentary* that a "fundamental truth" had been forgotten. "They (the Palestinians) just want us out of the Middle East." Daniel Pipes argued that Israeli concessions were perceived by the Arabs as signs of weakness and so provoked further demands. The Israelis, in implementing the Oslo agreement, did not require reciprocal peace-oriented measures by the Palestinians. Pipes has advocated more aggressive deterrence in order to convince the Palestinians that their only hope is to accept a cease-fire and eventually recognize the legitimacy of Israel.

Other commentators offered a variety of explanations. Tom Friedman claimed that Arafat had turned to a "war strategy," encouraging young Palestinians to place themselves in the line of

fire, to create casualties, to provoke strong Israeli retaliation. The
Israeli retaliation would incense the Arab world and international
opinion, which could force Israel to give in to all Palestinian demands. U.S. Middle East envoy Dennis Ross concluded that Arafat
had not prepared his people for peace.

Still others argued that the Israelis had not fully realized the
depth of the frustration of the average Palestinian. Despite proposed agreements and partial pull-backs, Palestinian lives had not
improved. They still needed Israeli permission to go from town to
town. Some Palestinian homes were being demolished not for security reasons but for the purpose of joining Israeli neighborhoods,
thus containing the Palestinian neighborhoods into crowded areas. Israeli "Rabbis for Human Rights," led by Arik Ascherman,
have been protesting this policy. Tel Aviv University Professor Avivi
Yavin held that the mutual trust which had begun to develop
under Rabin and Peres had evaporated under Netanyahu. During
Barak's administrations, settlements continued to be expanded and
Palestinian property confiscated. In such a climate Barak proposed
ideas whose time had not yet come.

However, the "peace camp" was not united. Many of its members came to believed that Arafat could never be trusted as a part-
ner. Some had assumed all along that if Israel offered generous
compromises consistent with Israel's security and those compromises were rejected, then the Palestinians would be exposed as not
being ready for a real peace. Ironically, it was Barak's concessions
that exposed Arafat as being neither willing nor able to agree to a
peace that would assure Israel's security.

To those who, with 20-20 hindsight vision declared the land-
for-peace formula to have been a colossal blunder, supporters of
the peace process responded: There were many indications that
the Palestinians would accept the reality of a Jewish state once
their own state was established. These indications ranged from the

PNC's belated acceptance in 1988 of the 1947 partition resolution to such suggested solutions as that of Israeli Mark Heller of the Jaffa Center for Strategic Studies and Palestinian nationalist professor Sari Nusseibeh in their collaboration, *No Trumpets, No Drums.* Their compromise did not envision a significant number of refugees returning to their homesteads in Israel. The Palestinians had to be tested in order to discover if they would agree to such moderate positions. Shimon Peres put it simply: "We had to try."

In December, 1999, President Clinton made one last desperate attempt to revive the peace talks and reach an agreement. He proposed that Israel give up sovereignty over the Temple Mount above ground but maintain sovereignty over the Western Wall and over the ground beneath the Temple Mount, where the ruins of the ancient Temples are believed buried. In return, the Palestinians would give up the right to return. This would have meant the Palestinians' relinquishing their most fundamental article of faith: that Israel bears sole responsibility for the refugees. Arafat's refusal to accept the Clinton compromise forced both sides to confront the moral issue of the refugees.

The Israeli position on the refugees is based on the assumption that Israel does have a right to exist as a Jewish state, as legitimized by the Partition Resolution of 1947, and by the acceptance of Israel in the United Nations in 1949. If one recognizes Israel's right to exist, then the attacks by the Arabs on the Jews of Palestine leading to the War for Independence were acts of aggression. Because the Arabs were the aggressors and because the consequence of that War was the refugee problem, it is, therefore, the Arabs who bear primary responsibility for the plight of the refugees. True, some Israeli actions (at Deir Yassin and between Lod and Ramle) accelerated the flight; however, had the Arabs accepted the partition principle, there would have been no flight at all. The usual Palestinian response has been that, indeed, Israel has no right to exist; therefore, it was the Palestinian Jews (later the Israelis) who were the aggressors by defending their "illegitimate" state. But in 1988 at Algiers, the Palestinian National Council did accept the partition resolution of 1947, which called for both a Jewish and a Palestinian state. The more recent refusal of the Palestinians to relinquish the right of return to homes within Israel undermined the credibility of the PNC.

As Israelis entered the year 2001, they had to choose as their prime minister either Ehud Barak or Ariel Sharon. Barak stated that to reach a peace agreement, "we will be forced to concede most of the territories, over 90% of the West Bank." A "special authority" would govern the Old City of Jerusalem. However, the Western Wall, the Jewish Quarter and the Mount of Olives would remain under Israeli sovereignty "forever." Sharon stated"Jerusalem (will be) the united capital of the state of Israel forever, and the Jordan Valley (will be) an essential buffer between the Hashemite kingdom . . ." He would try not for a final settlement but for an interim agreement which would accept a Palestinian state, put a freeze on new settlements but not dismantle existing settlements. He would allow for the natural growth of existing settlements. Finally, he would suspend further territorial concessions, beyond the 42% already granted.

The election of February 6th took place in an atmosphere of fear, anger and confusion. Of the more than 300 fatalities due to the Intifada, most were Arabs; however, every week some Israelis were killed, and many Israelis blamed Barak for not protecting them. After the Al-Aqsa Intifada and the Palestinians' uncompromising demand for the right of return of the refugees, most Israelis did not believe that Arafat and the Palestinians would accept a peace that would give Israel security. Many also believed that Sharon would be better able than Barak to quell Palestinian violence. Ariel Sharon won a landslide victory and became the new prime minister. He formed a broad coalition, ranging from the dovish Shimon

Peres as foreign minister to the hawkish Public Security Minister, Uzi Landau. In his concession speech, Barak acknowledged that he may have been "ahead of his time" and that "the Palestinian side is not yet sufficiently mature to take decisions and confront their painful reality."

During the first year of this Intifada, 728 Palestinians and 186 Israelis would be killed. To stop the violence and reach an interim agreement with the Palestinians became the enormous challenge of Prime Minister Sharon. He received advice from all sides. Some of the proposals are presented for your response in the Topics for Discussion.

AMERICAN JEWS AND ISRAEL

There have been times during the more than half century of Israel's existence when some American Jews strongly disagreed with Israeli government policy. When the issue pertained to religious pluralism in Israel, specifically with the right of non-Orthodox forms of Judaism to be given the same status as Orthodoxy, then non-Orthodox American Jewish leaders have not hesitated to voice their views. However, when the issue pertained to what Israel should be doing to protect her own security, then some Israeli and American Jews have insisted: "When American Jews publicly denounce Israeli government policy, they are giving aid and comfort to the enemies of Israel. We American Jews do not have our lives on the line. It is the Israelis who will suffer death and destruction if their policies are mistaken. Surely, it should be the Israelis who alone must determine how best to defend themselves and protect their nation." Virtually all American Jews agree that yes, the Israelis must make the ultimate choices affecting their own fate. However, if American Jews feel that they and the Israeli Jews are part of one internationally extended family, perhaps they should ask themselves: "If I believe a member of my family is headed in a self-destructive direction, what is my responsibility? To remain silent? To voice my views? To do what I can, in order to pressure my family member to change direction?" What do you believe is the responsibility of those American Jews who believe that the Israeli government's policy is harmful to Israel ?

A frequently asked challenge posed to American Jews is, "What would you as an American Jew do if U.S. interests are in conflict with Israeli interests? How do you respond to the charge of dual loyalty? For Judaism, this should be an easy question. A Jew's primary loyalty is not to any political entity, but to God. Should there be a clash between Israeli and American policies, Judaism would have us ask, which policy comes closer to realizing the prophetic values of justice and peace?

Israel does face internal problems that affect American Jews. The refusal or inability of the Israeli government to give equal rights to non-Orthodox forms of Judaism is deeply disturbing to many American Jewish supporters of Israel. They become particularly disturbed when the "religious" parties demand that all conversions to Judaism be done under Orthodox supervision. Perhaps when peace does come (and it must), most of the immigrants from the former Soviet Union will add their voice to the majority of Israelis who wish to curb the power of the Orthodox religious establishment. Meanwhile, Reform, Conservative and Reconstructionist Jews in America need to support their embryonic movements in Israel. May the time not be distant when strife among Jews will cease and when Israelis and Palestinians will be able to sit under their vines and fig trees and none shall make them afraid (Micah 4:4).

TOPICS FOR DISCUSSION

1. Why do so many Arabs believe that Israel has no moral right to exist as a predominantly Jewish state?

2. How do Israelis justify their right to exist? What is your opinion about Israel's right to exist as a Jewish state?

3. Do you believe a permanent peace will ever be achieved between Israelis and Palestinians? If your answer is yes, what is the best path to peace? If the answer is no, what does this imply for the future of immigration to and from Israel?

4. How might Prime Minister Sharon put an end to the violence? a) By engaging in more aggressive deterrence? b) By using force to compel the Palestinians to accept an interim agreement? c) By dismantling some settlements in order to create a climate for peace? d) By relaxing restrictions against the Palestinians?

5. Assuming that Israel has the right to preserve itself as a Jewish homeland, which, if any, Israeli actions would be contrary to Jewish moral values?

6. Do you believe there is or could be a conflict between American Jews' loyalty to the United States and their commitment to Israel? If so, how would you resolve that conflict?

7. What do you believe that American Jews should say or do, if they feel strongly that a particular policy of the Israeli government that affects Israel's security is either misguided or unethical?

6. How would you respond to an Israeli Zionist who said, "If you want to be fully Jewish, you will come to live in Israel?"

7. What effect do you believe the almost one million Russian Jews now living in Israel will have on its foreign policy, and on the role of religion in Israeli society?

8. What do you think would be the fairest way of resolving the Palestinian refugee problem?

RESOURCES

Alpher, Joseph. "Camp David and the Intifada," *Issue Briefs*. Americans for Peace Now, November 28, 2000.

Eban, Abba. *Personal Witness: Israel through My Eyes*. New York, Putnam's Sons, 1992.

Elon, Amos. *Jerusalem: City of Mirrors*. Boston, Little, Brown & Co., 1989.

Elon, Amos. *The Israelis*. New York, Holt, Rinehart & Winston, 1971.

Elon, Amos. *Herzl*. New York, Holt, Rinehart & Winston, 1975.

Ezrahi, Yaron. *Rubber Bullets: Power and Conscience in Modern Israel*. New York, Farrar, Straus & Giroux, 1997.

Friedman. Tom. *From Beirut to Jerusalem*. New York, Farrar, 1989.

Haberman, Clyde. "Dennis Ross's Exit Interview," in *The New York Times Magazine,* March 25, 2001.

Halevi, Yossi Klein. "Jewish Unappeal," *The New Republic,* Feb. 5, 2001.

Hazony, Yoram. *The Jewish State: The Struggle for Israel's Soul.* New York, Basic Books, 2000.

Heller, Mark A. and Sari Nusseibeh. *No Trumpets, No Drums: A Two-State Settlement of the Israeli-Palestinian Conflict.* New York, Hill and Wang, 1991.

Hertzberg, Arthur (ed.). *The Zionist Idea.* New York, Atheneum, 1976.

Mendes-Flohr, Paul (ed.). *A Land of Two Peoples: Martin Buber on Jews and Arabs.* Oxford, Oxford University Press, 1983.

Morris, Benny. *Righteous Victims: A History of the Zionist-Arab Conflict, 1881-1999.* New York, Alfred Knopf, 1999.

Podhoretz, Norman, Daniel Pipes, Hillel Halkin and Efraim Karsh. "Intifada II, *Commentary*, December, 2000.

Sachar, Howard. *A History of Israel.* New York, Alfred Knopf, 1976.

Samuel, Maurice. *Light on Israel.* New York, Alfred Knopf, 1968.

Sykes, Christopher. *Crossroads to Israel: Palestine from Balfour to Bevin.* London, Nel Mentor, 1967.

Film: *Wall in Jerusalem.* Alden Films, 7820 20th Ave., Brooklyn, NY, 11214.

PART SIX:

WHAT'S SPECIAL?

21.

CHOOSING JUDAISM: THEN AND NOW

In 1978, when Rabbi Alexander Schindler was president of the Union of American Hebrew Congregations, he launched the occasionally misunderstood Outreach Program. Its purpose was and still is to reach out to mixed-married couples and give them the opportunity to gain an understanding of what Judaism can mean to mature men and women and their children. Outreach is not an effort to persuade non-Jews who find meaning in their own faith to convert to Judaism. However, observers of religion in America have long noted the growth of a totally secular lifestyle. Many who were born Jewish or born Christian have drifted from their respective religious roots and some are looking for a spiritual perspective that makes sense to their minds and appeals to their hearts. In 1994, I carried out a survey of interfaith families with the help of the Jewish Outreach Institute, led by sociologist Egon Mayer and affiliated with the City University of New York's Graduate Center for Jewish Studies. My survey involved forty-six interfaith couples who had expressed the intention of giving their children a Jewish education. Only 22% of those raised as Christians held to the belief that God came to earth in the form of Jesus who was the messiah. The Outreach Program is based on the assumptions that Judaism does have something to offer those who are still searching and, in the words of UAHC Outreach Director, Dru Greenwood, "it is a mitzvah to draw near those who are far."

Some have considered the UAHC's Outreach Program to be a reversal of the traditional Jewish attitude toward proselytizing. The conventional view is that Judaism has historically been disinterested if not opposed to converting non-Jews to Judaism. That this is very far from the truth has been documented by Rabbi Joseph Rosenbloom in his study, *Conversion to Judaism, From the Biblical Period to the Present*. Much of what follows in this section is based on this fine scholarly work.

During the Biblical period thousands of non-Israelites joined the Covenant People who believed they had made a contract with God at Sinai. Jacob's sons, Judah and Simeon, married Canaanites; Joseph's Egyptian wife was the daughter of the priest of On (but their children were Israelites). Moses married the Midianite, Zipporah. King Solomon married wives from Egypt, Moab, Ammon, Edom, and Sidon. Intermarriage among the leaders was reflected in the general population. True, the prophets warned against the influence of pagan religion, but for centuries intermarriage brought thousands into the covenant community.

In the Bible we read how the *nakhri* (alien) became a *ger* (proselyte). In earliest times there was no ritual, just a simple affirmation. Ruth said to Naomi, "Thy people shall be my people; thy God, my God." After the Persian King Cyrus allowed Jews to return from exile to Judea, the second Temple was built and a simple conversion ceremony was introduced: the *ger* brought to the Temple two doves as an offering God (Rosenbloom suggests, this was to end the state of uncleanness). Male proselytes were circumcised. Ezra, when he returned from exile, forced Israelite husbands to divorce their foreign wives, not because they were foreign but because they had not become part of the Jewish people and faith. Because the Jews were a small minority in Judea, Ezra feared that without conversion, intermarriage would pose a danger to Jewish continuity. Still, the dominant Biblical attitude was acceptance of all who joined the covenant-people. When the Moabite Ruth is

portrayed as an ancestor of David, the author is elevating the status of the *ger/giyoret* (Hebrew terms for those men and women, not
born Jewish, who have chosen Judaism); without Ruth there would
be no united kingdom under David . . . no messiah.

During the rabbinic period, conversion became more formal-
ized. Immersion in the *mikveh* (ritual bath) was required of men
and women. Perhaps the water was originally intended to symbolize a spiritual cleansing from the pagan state. It became a means of
entering the covenant. Before the Macabbees (165 BCE), historian Salo Baron estimates that there were in Judea about 200,000
Jews. After Judea was established as an independent state under
Simon, there was a ten-fold increase in the Jewish population.
Surely many of those two million were converts. After Judea was
conquered by Rome, conversion activity continued. (In *Matthew*,
Jesus is quoted as saying that the Pharisees would travel by land
and sea for a convert). By about 300 CE, there were eight million
Jews in the Roman Empire, many thousands of them converts, all
this during the most creative period of Rabbinic Judaism.

Why such intense conversion activity? The rabbis did not have
the motive of Pauline Christianity: that the only way to save one's
soul from damnation was to accept a particular creed. However,
the rabbis did believe that their religion was true, and they looked
forward to the messianic age when all people would turn to the
worship of the one God. Of course, a larger population would
assure Jewish survival. Perhaps there were commercial advantages
in having Jews strategically located throughout the Empire. Also,
such proselytizing may have been a competitive reaction against
Christians' attempts to proselytize Jews.

A minority of rabbis feared that converts would dilute the
Jewish religion. They argued that a non-Jew whose reason for converting was his/her love for a Jew should not be accepted. However, a majority of rabbis disagreed. Rav said that such non-Jews
should be warmly welcomed because their motives may be pure.
Some rabbis made the connection between God and *gerim*: God
dispersed the Israelites so that they might gain proselytes. It was

said that the *ger/giyoret* is dearer to God than born Israelites because he/she came into the covenant not as a result of the miracle at Sinai but because of his/her own free will. (Even the Biblical prohibition against the Amorites becoming *gerim* was abrogated, because after the Assyrian King Sennacherib, there were no pure races.)

Given this universalist thrust of Biblical and Rabbinic Judaism, how did so many ever come to believe that traditional Judaism is provincial, parochial, and not welcoming to converts? This tribalist tendency was triggered not by the rabbis but by the Emperor Constantine who in the early-fourth century made Christianity the official religion of the Roman Empire. In 315, Constantine promulgated the law that any Jew who converted a non-Jew would be put to death. This law was reformulated (in 409 and again in 438) in language that branded Judaism as a "nefarious sect" and the synagogue as a "brothel." During the Middle Ages the *non-Jew* who converted could be executed. In 1222, a Deacon of Oxford who converted and married a Jewess was publicly burned at the stake. Understandably such penalties put a damper on Jewish conversion activity.

Yet surprisingly, even in the Middle Ages, there were some converts to Judaism. In the fourteenth and fifteenth centuries, anti-conversion laws were not enforced in France and Germany, and 25 responsa dealing with converts have been discovered. Probably many more such responsa exist but have not been found. In eleventh-century Italy, a Christian cleric became a Jew named Obadiah, and the Jewish mystic, Abulafia tried to convert Pope Martin IV, but without success. In Moslem countries there was also conversion activity; many slaves owned by Jews accepted Judaism. There were group conversions, the largest being that of the Khazars in Southern Russia.

These were exceptions. Because in most times and places, the medieval Church made conversion activity a capital offense, *gerim* were rather rare. It may well have been the case that many rabbis made a virtue of necessity and began righteously preaching, "Who needs converts? Without them we will remain more distinctively Jewish." The practice of dissuading a prospective convert three times became another protection against what some rabbis considered impure influences.

One might think that after Europe's Jews were gradually emancipated from the ghetto, they would have returned to the pre-medieval practice of active proselytizing, but this did not happen. Why not? Although there were no longer legal prohibitions against Jews converting Gentiles, some of the strictly Orthodox had become convinced that non-Jews would dilute authentic Judaism. Others did welcome converts who would accept the authority of *halakhah*; however, because the obligations involved in becoming truly Orthodox appeared quite demanding to most non-Jews, the number of conversions to Orthodox Judaism was relatively small. Among the more integrated Jews, there was fear that proselytizing, especially if it appeared too assertive, would stir up anti-Semitism. In the eighteenth century, the Swiss cleric, Lavater, challenged the rationalist Jewish philosopher Moses Mendelssohn either to convert to Christianity or if he believed Judaism was more reasonable, to try to persuade Lavater to become Jewish. Mendelssohn replied in a famous letter. In essence he wrote. both of our religions provide foundations for moral behavior. Why should I try to undermine your foundation? From the time of Mendelssohn, many a modern rabbi has said, in effect, that it is enough if Christians practice the ethics of Jesus. Unlike fundamentalist Christians, Jews do not believe one must accept our religion in order to be "saved." Just be a *mensch.* So, for a variety of reasons in eighteenth and nineteenth century Europe, rabbis, from the Orthodox to the Reform, were disinterested in proselytizing.

When Judaism came to America, the seeds of today's Outreach program were planted. While rabbis did not actively proselytize, as intermarriage increased, there was greater openness to and acceptance of converts. Classical Reform Rabbi, David Einhorn, included a conversion service in the first widely used American Reform prayer book. Einhorn was concerned lest non-

Jews be put off by the more tribal aspects of Judaism. For him the essence of Judaism was the Jewish people's commitment to one God, the law of love, and Israel's mission which was to bring justice and peace to the world. Einhorn proposed calling the Jewish religion, Yahvism, after the original name of the Hebrew God ("Judaism" was too tribal) While this proposal was not taken seriously, Reform leaders Isaac Mayer Wise and Kaufmann Kohler, in 1890, agreed that circumcision would not be required of male converts and *mikveh* and *bet din* were discontinued.

In the twentieth century Reform Jewish efforts to explain Judaism to non-Jews (e.g., through the Jewish Chatautqua Society) were motivated by a desire to decrease anti-Semitism and increase acceptance of Jews, certainly not to suggest that non-Jews might convert to Judaism. After World War II, as Jewish survival became a critical issue and the world had shown its capacity to allow the barbarity of the Holocaust, Leo Baeck argued that humanity is hungry for a religion like Judaism. We should expand for humanity's sake and our own. Rabbi Allen Maller, an advocate of outreach before Outreach, asked rhetorically: Why prefer an assimilated Jew to an interested gentile unless one is racist?

In the late 1970's, as the rate of mixed marriage soared, Rabbi Alexander Schindler proposed and the UAHC adopted the Outreach program. Its purpose is to reach out to all those who are searching for a religion that can meet the spiritual and moral needs of human beings today. This is definitely not an effort to persuade Christians or other non-Jews to give up their religion and accept Judaism. As suggested earlier, Outreach does recognize that there are large numbers of non-Jews who do not accept traditional Christian beliefs. Some have married Jews who may not fully appreciate their Jewish heritage. Outreach is a way of enabling people, whatever their background, to discover what Judaism can mean to a searching, inquisitive mind; a heart that appreciates the warmth and symbolism of tradition; and a spirit that seeks the support of a community that shares humane values.

Today, the Jewish community, especially the non-Orthodox,

HENRY COHEN

is more open than it has been in centuries to accepting and welcoming non-Jews who would become part of our faith and people. Such "outreach" is not a rejection of traditional Judaism but a return to the more universalist spirit of Biblical and Classical Rabbinic Judaism! Among the programs established by Reform Jewish Outreach are, "A Taste of Judaism: Are You Curious?" (for beginners, a three-session introduction to Jewish spiritual, ethical and community values); "Times and Seasons" groups for interfaith couples; and "Introduction to Judaism" classes offered by 80% of UAHC congregations. There is even an alternative religious school program ("Stepping Stones"), for children whose interfaith parents have not made a decision regarding the children's religious identity. Also, many Reform synagogues have Outreach Fellows, lay leaders trained to support the conversion process for the increasing numbers of people choosing Judaism.

The process of reaching out beyond the Jewish community has led many Jews to feel greater pride in their heritage. When Jews begin to see Judaism through the eyes of non-Jews on a spiritual search, then they may more deeply appreciate values of their heritage that they perhaps had taken for granted. As has often been the case, outreach has often led to "in-reach," to adult Jews re-discovering or discovering for the first time what their heritage can mean to mature minds and open hearts.

All movements within Judaism require that the potential convert go through a period of study, usually at least several months. This may be accomplished privately with an individual rabbi or with a class. There should always be an opportunity for one interested in conversion to share with a teacher or mentor his/her feelings about developing a sense of Jewish identity. Often a potential convert may say or silently feel, I can accept the beliefs and values of Judaism, and I enjoy the traditions, but I just cannot feel myself to be part of the Jewish people. According to traditional Judaism, when one converts, one is accepting the essence of the people and is, therefore, considered just as much a part of the people as one who was born Jewish. His/her spiritual ancestors were slaves in Egypt! Of course, being considered part of the people does not mean that one "feels Jewish." To become really one with the faith and fellowship of Israel requires more than intellectual or even emotional assent. To feel Jewish requires experience: of study, *tikkun olam*, prayer, socializing, and participating in Shabbat, festivals and holidays. So as fully to participate in worship services, the Jew by choice should be able to read Hebrew and understand the prayers. True, many Jews are "Hebraicly" challenged, but that is a condition they can correct. Reform Jewish Outreach sponsors support groups to facilitate the conversion process and to provide a warm welcome into the congregational community.

There are differences between Reform, Reconstructionist and Conservative rabbis as to exactly what is required for an authentic conversion. (See Chapter 17.) In addition to a period of study, there is usually a ceremony in the synagogue, during which the convert is welcomed into the faith and fellowship and given a Hebrew name. The rabbi may hand the Jew by choice a Torah scroll and he/she may repeat the *Shema*. Often the convert expresses the meanings he or she has found in Judaism.

Interfaith couples may find guidance by contacting Ms. Dru Greenwood, Director of Outreach, at the UAHC in New York. (See Resources.) An agency that provides information on the conversion process of all branches of Judaism is the Jewish Outreach Institute, founded by Dr. Egon Mayer in 1987. The Institute conducts research on the effect of mixed marriage on the Jewish community and has set up a national directory of outreach programs on the web. (See Resources.)

TOPICS FOR DISCUSSION

1. Why do many non-Jewish spouses who do not accept the basic beliefs of Christianity or any other faith choose not to convert to Judaism?

2. What do you believe are the most appealing aspects of Judaism to non-Jews?

3. How would you respond to potential converts who fear they will never be really accepted as Jews by synagogue members?

4. Do you believe that rabbis should use the media or other means of presenting Judaism to Americans who have no religious commitment? Why or why not?

RESOURCES

Diamant, Anita. *Choosing a Jewish Life.* New York, Schocken, 1997.

Epstein, Lawrence. *Conversion to Judaism.* Northvale, N.J., Jason Aronson, 1994.

Kertzer, Morris, revised by Lawrence Hoffman. *What Is a Jew?* New York, Touchstone(Simon and Schuster), 1993.

Kukoff, Lydia. *Choosing Judaism.* New York, UAHC Press, 1981.

Mayer, Egon. *Love and Tradition: When Jews and Christians Marry.* New York, Plenum, 1987.

Rosenbloom, Jospeh. *Conversion to Judaism, from the Biblical Pe-*

riod to the Present. Cincinnati, Hebrew Union College Press, 1978.

Contacts: UAHC Outreach Dept., 633 Third Ave. New York, NY, 10017-6778. It may be found on the Web at http://uahc.org. Phone: 212-650-4230.

Jewish Outreach Institute, 1270 Broadway, Suite 609, New York, NY, 10001. Its National Directory of Outreach Programs may be found on the Web at www.joi.org. Phone: 212-760-1440.

22.

WHAT'S SPECIAL ABOUT JUDAISM?—

THE JEWISH GESTALT

Many have been the reasons given for Jewish continuity. We are the chosen people, elected by God to be witnesses to God's Oneness and to be "a light unto the nations" by following the commandments of love, justice and peace (Chapter 3). We have heard the 614th commandment: "You shall not (by assimilating) give Hitler a posthumous victory"(Chapter 19). We value the Jewish emphasis on social justice: "My concern for justice, for peace, for enlightenment, all stem from my heritage"(Justice Arthur Goldberg). A potential convert was impressed by "the absence of dogma, the humanity of it all." Remember Mordecai Kaplan's response: A civilization whose idea of God does not conflict with reason and whose values are humane does not need a rationale to survive. It simply will.(Chapter 18).

One could contend: Every individual idea within Judaism can be found in other religions or ethnic groups. Today's studious Asian-Americans have been called "the new Jews." Jews often have close families, but so do Italians. Judaism is not the only religion with different paths to or conceptions of God; Hindus have four paths to God who may be conceived of as personal or impersonal. However, in my opinion, there is no other religion or civilization that contains the same *combination* of beliefs, values, and traditions. What is special about Judaism I have called "the Jewish gestalt." Not only is the constellation of concepts, communal life and customs unique but the whole of Judaism is somehow greater than the sum of its parts; hence, a Jewish gestalt. I would emphasize 10 parts that I have considered special, in the sense of meaningful characteristics of Judaism, understood as the diverse religious expressions of the Jewish people.

1) The dual roots of Jewish values. As explained in Chapter 2, the historic experience of the Jewish people has encouraged many Jews to find special meaning in the pursuit of justice for the oppressed of the world; the warmth of family life; the almost continual emphasis on study and learning; a "holy skepticism" that questions the platitudes and prejudices of every generation. Of course, one can find Jews who mis-use their historic experience by becoming more provincial. That is why the second root—the various forms of the Jewish religion with its faith in one God, the commandment to love the stranger because we were strangers, and its law, lore and traditions that embody the values—is so very important. Faith and history can be a powerful force for the good. This relation between faith and history can be expressed in the concept of the chosen people, the choosing people, or both.

2) The wide variety of beliefs about God, all of which find in God the source and motivation for our moral values and that affirm the reality of a Power that will help us move toward love and peace. In the *Avot* prayer the text reads, "God of Abraham, God of Isaac, God of Jacob." The rabbis asked why the phrase "God of" was repeated. Why not simply "God of Abraham, Isaac and Jacob?" They answered their own question by stating that "God of" is repeated three times to show that each of the patriarchs believed in and experienced God in his own unique way. So should we.

Each Jew is free to draw on the insights of different and contrasting beliefs in order to arrive at his or her own personal faith. Indeed, this I have done over the years. Like Spinoza, my intuition tells me that behind all is an underlying Oneness, that despite apparently random events, the Unity and the order are more fundamental than the diversity and disorder. Like Buber, I believe that when we achieve an inner oneness within ourselves, this harmony enables us to achieve empathy and intimacy with others. From this I-Thou relation there flow the *mitzvot,* the commandments to pursue justice and peace. As Buber wrote, "love is responsibility in action." Like Kaplan, I believe that within each of us is a Power that makes for mental and emotional growth, for the capacity to have moral responsibility, and for a sense of joy in being alive. This Power that I did not create is deeper than my intellect and will. When I am feeling "down," I find strength in the faith that God has provided a Power that can lift me up. When I pray, I call upon this Power. At times, God responds, and if there is no response, I still find hope in the faith that God is potentially present. Like the Psalmist, I believe that prayer is more than a cry for help. Prayer is also the feeling of wonder and gratitude for life and love. Like Heschel, I believe that "the most amazing fact is that there are facts." Like Steinberg, I recognize that even God is in some sense limited. Perhaps it is in the nature of reality that if there is to be a universe at all, there will be suffering that is tragic and not at all fair. Still, whatever God's limits, I thank God that life, with all its inequity, is infinitely better than no life at all. I thank God for laws that can help us understand and improve life. Most of all, I thank God for the Power each of us has to become one within ourselves and with others and for the capacity to grow in mind, heart, and spirit.

I share my personal belief not to convince or persuade but to invite others to explore the different paths to God within Judaism and, after traveling those paths and searching one's own soul, to arrive at a faith that gives meaning to one's life.

3) No belief or creed is essential for achieving "salvation," however one defines the term. There is an ancient midrash in which God says, "Would that My children would deny Me, if only they would keep My commandments." Of course, the rabbis believed that faith in one God provides the foundation for morality and that atonement is achieved through repentance, prayer, and right action. Still, they were realistic enough to recognize that many an *epikoros* (rabbinic term for non-believer) has lived a more ethical life than some who attend services every Shabbat.

4) Humans are not born in a state of sin but with a potential for both good and evil. The Torah tells us: "I have put before you life and death, blessing and curse. Choose life, that you and your descendants may live."(Deuteronomy 30:19) There is a Hasidic story in which a student told his rabbi that he was angry at God. "Why?" asked the rabbi.

"Because God has created a world so full of misery and suffering."

The rabbi replied sharply, "And you think you could make a better world?"

"Yes," said the student, "I do think I could make a better world."

The rabbi boomed, "Then begin!"

5) Within Judaism are various views about immortality. In some sense, the spirit lives on beyond the grave. Judaism puts the emphasis on this life, and our rabbis do not threaten us with eter-

nal damnation. Our mourning customs are aimed at enabling us to express our grief and then move step by step back to life.

6) Judaism is a well-balanced religion. There is room for both the rationalist and the mystic, for Kaplan and Heschel. We may find a balance between reason and faith, between self-respect and concern for others, between the well-being of the Jewish people and of all humanity, between individual freedom and communal standards, and between human effort and the support of a Divine Power.

7) Judaism provides a treasure house of traditions that give us strength and hope at every stage of life, from birth to Bar/Bat Mitzvah to marriage to death; traditions that throughout the year celebrate and teach the ideals of freedom and justice and an awareness of the wonder of life; and traditions that bring us together with our own families, with the family of the Jewish people, and with the larger human family.

8) Judaism acknowledges that there are very different ways of being Jewish. I agree with Ellis Rivkin's thesis that Judaism from age to age and from stage to stage has allowed for maximum diversity while at the same time retaining the link to the Jewish people and to a God who is the Oneness that subsumes all diversity. Judaism has shown the capacity to change to meet new historic conditions but at the same time to link those changes to the past.

This diversity, along with a link to the past, has been one important reason for Jewish survival.

9) We find in the Hebrew Bible the foundation of our faith and in the writings of rabbis, Hasidim and philosophers we find moral and spiritual insights. While the *Halakhah* is an evolving system of law viewed differently by the movements within Judaism, all recognize the need for standards that can guide our way in

a world where relativism too often leads to the justification for self-indulgence.

10.) Judaism believes in the *bringing* of the messianic age of peace. "Seek peace and pursue it" was considered by some rabbis to be the greatest commandment. According to a Talmudic legend, the messiah told Joshua ben Levi that he would come today. Elijah explained to Rabbi Joshua, "He meant today if you would but hearken to My voice."

What is special about Judaism, in the sense of its uniqueness, is not necessarily a single aspect but the combination of the ten characteristics cited above. However, there is something more, the whole that is greater than the sum of even these parts. This whole we may experience as a blend of thought and feeling, a deeply rooted sense of Jewish identity. In the postscript to *I and Thou,* Buber maintains that when we see a tree as a whole, we see more than a combination of roots, trunk, branches and leaves. When we focus on "the unity and wholeness" of the tree, "something lights up and approaches us from the course of being (or Being, itself)." This suggests to me an analogy. When we experience Judaism as a whole, we experience more than a collection of characteristics. "Something lights up and approaches us from Being, itself." Could we be linked by the Being that some call God?

On a more personal level, I am reminded of Abraham Cronbach's cryptic comment, "We are Jews, because we want to be Jews." My wanting to be a Jew has to do with a stubborn refusal to deny that which I feel to be very much a part of me. My wanting has to do with the ease I feel with people who will not let the world forget the Holocaust and will not turn their backs on Israel. My wanting has to do with the radical freedom I prize when my mind searches for the meaning of God and the values that best serve humanity. I cherish the thought that almost wherever my mind roams, I can find within the Jewish community someone to join me in my dissent.

My wanting to be a Jew has to do with feeling at home with a heritage that even in the midst of despair has held out hope for the human family. My wanting has to do with the conviction that the experiences of the Jewish people have in some way influenced my own feelings about family, learning, justice and peace, an influence that has, on balance, been for the good. My wanting has to do with a moral chip on my shoulder that was put there by my forebears and that makes me skeptical of every establishment. My wanting has to do with a year full of celebrations that say yes to life and symbols that evoke memories I refuse to forget.

More important than my wanting is yours. It is my hope that this volume has provided you with sufficient understanding and stimulation so that you may discover your own answer to the question: What, for you, is special about Judaism?

TOPICS FOR DISCUSSION:

1. Which of the 10 characteristics of Judaism presented above has the most meaning for you? Which has the least?

2. Of all the Jewish thinkers discussed in this book, to whom do you feel the closest affinity?

3. If you were to create your own "movement" within Jewish life and thought, what beliefs, values, and traditions would it include?

4. What, for you, is special about Judaism?

RESOURCES

Belin, David. *Why Choose Judaism?* New York, UAHC Press, 1985.

Silver, Abbat Hillel. *Where Judaism Differed.* Philadelphia, Jewish Publication Society, 1957.

Wolpe, David. *Why Be Jewish?* New York, Henry Holt & Co., 1995.

APPENDIX

THE JEWISH CALENDAR

You may hear Jews say, "The holidays are early this year," or "I don't remember Yom Kippur ever being so late." As a child, I was mystified and could not understand why the Jewish holidays seemed to jump around our "regular" (i.e., Gregorian) calendar. I developed my own system of determining whether the holidays were early, late or on time: When Yom Kippur fell after the World Series, the holidays were late; when Yom Kippur fell before the World Series, the holidays were early; when Yom Kippur fell during the World Series, they were on time.

The actual answer is more complicated. The Gregorian calendar is based on the earth's movement around the sun, which takes 365 1/4 days; hence, our months of 30 or 31 days (except for February which has 28 except once every four years when it has 29). In contrast, the Jewish calendar is lunisolar. The months are reckoned according to the moon (from the time the moon is directly between the earth and the sun until the next time it is between earth and sun). A lunar year, with months of 29 or 30 days, would be 354 days, i.e., about 11 days shorter than a solar year. Some adjustment was necessary, because if the Jewish calendar were strictly lunar, then Passover could come in the Fall, or even the Winter. This could not be, because Passover, Shavuot, and Sukkot are tied to specific harvests during the year.

So the rabbis figured that over 19 years, the solar calendar would exceed the lunar calendar by about 209 days, or approximately seven months. In order to adjust the lunar to the solar calendar, one would have to add a "leap month" in seven of nineteen years. This was accomplished by adding a second Adar (or Adar Sheni) of 29 days after the Adar that began in February or March. Even this mathematical manipulation did not make everything come out exactly even, so the months Heshvan and Kislev were allowed to vary between 29 and 30 days. If this explanation does not satisfy you, read the article on "calendar" in the *Encyclopedia Judaica*, vol. 5.

For our purposes, it is enough to know that a full month (*malay*) was 30 days and a "lacking" month (*haser*) was 29. The Jewish calendar in Biblical times began with Nisan. The months with their holidays and fast days (according to *halakhah*) are as follows:

Nisan (30): 15th, first day of Passover; 27th, Holocaust Memorial Day*

Iyar (29): 5th, Israel Independence Day*; 18th, Lag Ba-omer(weddings allowed)

Sivan (30): 6th, first day of Shavuot

Tammuz (29): 17th, fast day: Babylonians enter Jerusalem

Av (30): 9th, fast day: fall of Jerusalem

Elul (29): Selichot (penitential prayers) recited from Elul 1st (Sephardic) or from Sunday before Rosh Hashanah

* Date set by Israeli Knesset

Tishri (30): 1st, first day of Rosh Hashanah; 3rd, fast of Gedaliah (murder of last Judean governor under Babylonians); 10th, Yom Kippur; 15th, first day of Sukkot; 23rd, Sh'mini Atzeret; 24th, Simchat Torah.

Heshvan (29 or 30)

Kislev (29 or 30): 25th, first day of Hanukkah

Tevet (29): 10th, fast, beginning of siege of Jerusalem

Shevat (30): 15th: Tu B'Shevat

Adar I (29 or 30): 14th, Purim(except when there is Adar II)

Adar II(29): 14th, Purim(Adar 13, a fast day unless it falls on Sunday; then it is the previous Thursday. (only in a leap year)